Y0-BZE-301

Existentialism and Alienation
in American Literature

BY THE SAME AUTHOR

Composer and Nation
Realism in Art
How Music Expresses Ideas
Jazz: A People's Music
Art and Society

EXISTENTIALISM
and ALIENATION
in AMERICAN
LITERATURE

by Sidney Finkelstein

INTERNATIONAL PUBLISHERS
New York

© copyright 1965, by INTERNATIONAL PUBLISHERS CO., INC.

Second Printing, 1967

ACKNOWLEDGMENTS

The author wishes to express his appreciation to the following publishers for permission to quote from books published by them:

To The Dial Press, Inc., for James Baldwin's *Another Country*, Copyright © 1962 by James Baldwin, and *The Fire Next Time*, Copyright © 1963 by James Baldwin; to Farrar, Straus & Giroux, Inc., for James Purdy's *Malcolm*; To Grove Press, Inc., for Henry Miller's *Tropic of Cancer*; to Harcourt, Brace & World, Inc., for Robert Lowell's *Lord Weary's Castle*, T. S. Eliot's *Complete Poems and Plays* and *Selected Essays*; to Houghton Mifflin Co. for John Dos Passos' *U.S.A.*; to Alfred A. Knopf, Inc., for John Updike's *Run Rabbit* and *The Centaur*, and Thomas Mann's *The Coming Victory of Democracy*; to Random House, Inc., for the *Collected Stories of William Faulkner* and William Styron's *Set This House on Fire*; to Charles Scribner's Sons for *The Stories of F. Scott Fitzgerald* and F. Scott Fitzgerald's *The Great Gatsby*; to The Viking Press Inc., for John Steinbeck's *The Grapes of Wrath* and *Travels With Charley in Search of America*; and to Mr. John Dos Passos for his *Manhattan Transfer*.

Picture on cover: Goya's etching, "The sleep of reason begets monsters," from the Caprichos.

Library of Congress Catalog Card Number: 65-16394

Manufactured in the United States of America

CONTENTS

1

INTRODUCTION: *Art and Philosophy*

This is a study of existentialism, first in its rise as a philosophy in Europe and then in its influence on literature, particularly that of the United States today. The aim is to show that the philosophical development and the literary expression make up one continuous history, behind which lies a succession of social crises that have reached their highest intensity now in the mid-20th century.

Since this study embraces both philosophy and art, some discussion is required of how they are viewed here, along with their similarities and differences. The philosopher, whatever the experiences he draws upon—his own, those of his contemporaries and those of the history of society—generalizes at the point where the particularities of individual and temporal life drop away. His concepts, put in abstract form, are brought together into a more or less coherent system, or way of thinking about life, offered as applicable to all conditions and people.

The artist, on the other hand, however philosophically he may have thought about life and arrived at broad generalizations, projects them as images of life. These are not necessarily replicas or "imitations" of what we see in the world about us, and even when they seem to be so, as in a novel, play or painting, their quality as art does not rest on their being recognizable replicas. It rests on their power to evoke in the audience a complex of emotional responses adding up to a distinctly shaped "psychology," a recognizable reaction to the outer world, a recognizable state of life. We can call these states of life "human portraits," in the broadest sense, and it is with such "portraits" that the artist builds his work of art.

Philosophy and art, then, differ not in the depth and general quality of their thinking about life, but in the form taken by the working out of this thinking. A work of philosophy offers itself in terms abstracted from the concrete life and the social and historical conditions that gave birth to it. A work of art offers itself as the very life it is discussing. And so, when we approach philosophy and art, we must recognize not only the crucially important differences in form, but also the crucially important matter of their common ground; the real world which the philosopher and artist share with everybody.

We can, of course, approach a philosophy strictly on its own terms: namely, discuss its use of logic, whatever errors may be found in it, the consistency or lack of consistency of the system, and so on. So, with a work of art, we can limit ourselves to its craftsmanship or its particular tools of expression. But this is only of peripheral service to the public, for philosophers and artists have far greater tasks to carry out.

To take the further step of discussing how "intriguing" a philosopher's ideas are, or how delightful or touching an experience a work of art provides, would not be enough, for it relegates philosophy and art to the category of entertainments, even "time killers." Much more is involved, for to understand a philosophy, granted familiarity with the methods and traditions of philosophy itself, we must first ask whether it is possible to live by its "world picture" or "system," its assumptions and conclusions. We must also put it back into the living social context from which it sprang, among the real, historically evolved and pressing questions which it was designed to answer. We can often learn more that is valuable to us from the philosopher's process of search than from his findings. Similarly, to understand a work of art, granted familiarity with the sensitivities and ways of apprehending reality that are unique to art, we must see it as not merely a replica of life and not merely an "experience," but as a way of thinking about life. Only thus can we ascertain to what extent, no matter what the artist seems to be talking about, he is also talking about us.

And so we approach both philosophy and art through different channels, but conclude with the same question: to what extent does it open our eyes and mind to reality? By reality we mean both that which we live in today and the historical development of the outer world and the human mind which brought this reality into being. Of both the philosopher, who presents his abstractions as eternal truths, and the artist, who presents his conclusions in terms that seem to be life itself, we ask, again: how broad is the context of not merely individual but also social experience that he has drawn upon? How involved has he been in the movement of society itself? We thus see philosophy and art as social-historical statements. The philosopher may scorn the test of whether society can live by his philosophy, but this is a tacit admission that philosophy to him is merely an intellectual pastime, with no relevance to the real problems people face. The artist may disclaim any other end in his work than that of giving vent to his own feelings, but he must then face the question of why anyone else should have concern for his work. The interest an artist's "self" has for others lies in the extent to which that "self" has embraced the lives of others. Or, put in another way, the interest any artistic portrait or self-portrait has lies in its typicality; its revelation of a response to a challenge raised by life which can be found in others because they share the same world.

The first part of this book will take up the existentialist philosophical tradition, focussing on those philosophers whom the existentialist movement has brought into the cur-

rents of American intellectual life today. It will examine the
origin of their ideas and discuss their relevance to the problems of today. The second part will take up the psychological
phenomenon of alienation, discuss its social roots and literary
expression, and show it as a connecting link between existentialist philosophy and its American literary currency. In this
context, it will take up the American "disillusionment" literature that followed the First World War, tracing in it an
earlier stage of the kind of thought that would become existentialist, and then go on to the literary "rebellion" of the
1950's. The intention is not to offer a definitive appraisal of
each writer's life work, but only to trace a developing pattern
of thought among writers, show its organic tie to the style,
form, content and esthetics of their works, relate what this
tells us to the life of the country, and so throw, it is hoped,
some light on the problems we face.

2

THE ENLIGHTENMENT: *Doubts*
and Concepts of Progress

Existentialism entered American cultural life soon after the
Second World War, largely through the poetic and imaginative power of the works of two French authors, Jean-Paul
Sartre and Albert Camus. To their striking literary gifts was
added the distinction of their having fought fascism as members of the French Resistance. Its appeal soon broadened
until, working back in time, it encompassed the entire existentialist philosophical tradition.

Among those whose works were translated, published and
studied were Edmond Husserl, Karl Jaspers and Martin Heidegger, three 20th century German philosophers who had
hardly been known before in the United States. Søren Kierkegaard, who had previously been rated a minor figure in 19th
century theology, a mystic and a rebel against the Danish
Lutheran Church, was elevated to a major prophet. Friedrich
Nietzsche, too, was brought into the new pantheon, having
been cleansed somewhat of the fascist dust on his portrait.
He had been a strong influence on American writers in the
first two decades of the 20th century, but as an apparent
apostle of irrationality and breeder of anti-Semitism, his stock
had fallen in the America of the 1930's.

The extent to which existentialism has become a force in
American thought is indicated in this comment by the
theologian, Paul Tillich:

It is now common knowledge in this country that existentialism in the Western intellectual world starts with Pascal in the 17th century, has an underground history in the 18th century, a revolutionary history in the 19th century and an astonishing victory in the 20th century. Existentialism has become the style of our period in all realms of life. Even the analytic philosophers pay tribute to it by withdrawing into formal problems and leaving the field of material problems to the existentialists in art and literature.[1]

Although the term "victory" is an exaggeration, and there is much about the popularity of existentialism that is faddist, there is no question that it offered a view of life and reality to which a number of gifted and sensitive writers quickly responded. If it seemed at first to be an "importation," it soon established itself as a universally applicable way of thought, as suited to American conditions as the 18th century European "enlightenment" that had assisted the birth of American independence and democracy. And the problem we face can be seen in the difference between the new "enlightenment" and the old. The old had been revolutionary in the new vistas it opened of human progress. Existentialism, however, is a rebellion against the old "enlightenment," expressing disillusion with progress, rejecting the very concept that human beings can add to their knowledge and improve their life by extending their collective mastery over nature and society.

The phrase "disillusion with progress" is not used here in a necessarily condemnatory sense. While the concept of progress is dear to people, it could be an illusion, and if so, it were better to know it. Furthermore, even an attitude of disillusion with progress can have value for progress if it provokes a search for the truth of life, in the course of which dogmatically and blindly accepted traditions and beliefs are held up to question. Insights can emerge which may be carried beyond the limitations of the questioner. But in an appraisal of existentialism, it is necessary to know that it represents a challenge to the view that there is a hopeful future for humanity.

And so a question that must be answered is whether the realities of the world justify such a challenge; and, if not, what are the conditions that make it appear to so many to be "truth."

The challenge is no less potent because it is indirect rather than direct. Existentialism does not see itself as a philosophy primarily devoted to a study of history and society, or as a body of thought with a specific social and historical origin. Like the metaphysical philosophies that preceded it, it offers itself as eternal truth, but differs from them in not being a "closed" system. Its distinction lies in the question which it raises, seeing this as fundamental and claiming that it alone has raised this boldly, directly and in depth. This is the question of how to answer the absurdity of man's "existence," resulting from his awareness that his "essence"—his consciousness of his "being"—is surrounded by "nothingness" and will dissolve into death. It asserts that the whole of one's life is shaped by the way one confronts this central question, which takes precedence over all others. In the course of this argument it challenges the knowability of the world, which is the foundation stone of any valid concept of human progress.

Of course, there is no unanimity among existentialist writers and thinkers. For example, Gabriel Marcel, a French Catholic existentialist, repudiates the "atheism" of existentialist Jean-Paul Sartre. Neither Kierkegaard nor Nietzsche used the term "existentialism," nor for that matter did Dostoievsky, who today is considered by the existentialists to be "one of theirs." The term originated in the 20th century with Jaspers's "Existence Philosophy." Sartre and other writers applied it not only to their philosophy, but to that of Kierkegaard and Nietzsche. Heidegger, however, whose thought influenced Sartre, and is accepted today as a central figure in existentialist thought, disclaims the term.

Yet for all this diversity, all existentialist philosophies share certain concepts aside from their insistence on "existence" or "essence" as the central question, and their accompanying death-hauntedness. They all regard the material or outside world as "absurd" or impervious to "reason," are contemptuous of natural science, or at best dismiss it as irrelevant to the "real" or "important" problems, and take a similar attitude toward history, economics and politics, asserting that nothing real or basic can be learned from them. All posit their concept of freedom on the separation of the individual from society. This is true even of writers like Camus, who proclaim the artist's obligation to speak for the plight of others in the world, but see this as a purely individual "decision" with no consequent social responsibilities or ties. In general, existentialism has no faith in democracy, but tends to be "elitist"; that is, it regards the mass of people as hopelessly blind to the real problems of life, of which only a select few, an aristocracy of the mind, are aware.

While existentialism is not a 20th century creation, its influence has been strengthened by the catastrophes of recent times. Thus Gabriel Marcel (b. 1889) speaks in his An Essay in Autobiography of the growing war tensions preceding 1914, and then of the war itself. "We tried hard to believe that humanity in the West could withstand the assault of the forces that were driving it towards catastrophe. I think that not one of us could suspect the fragility, the precariousness, of the civilization which enveloped us like a tegument; a civilization on which the wealth of centuries seemed to have conferred a solidity we would have thought it madness to question." Accordingly, Marcel suspects reason, and its product, science. "Whatever its ultimate meaning, the universe into which we have been thrown cannot satisfy our reason, let us have the courage to admit it once and for all." The individual thinker, he says, must find his way outside of society. "The imperishable glory of a Kierkegaard or a Nietzsche consists perhaps mainly in this, that they have proved, not

only by their arguments but by their trials and by their whole
life, that a philosopher worthy of the name cannot be a man
of congresses, and that he deviates from his path every time
that he allows himself to be torn from the solitude which is
his calling."[2]

Let us contrast this typically existentialist view to the opening statements of the Declaration of Independence:

When in the course of human events, it becomes necessary for
one people to dissolve the political bonds, which have connected
them with another, and to assume among the powers of the earth,
the separate and equal station to which the Laws of Nature and
of Nature's God entitle them, a decent respect to the opinions of
mankind requires that they should declare the causes which impel
them to the separation. We hold these truths to be self-evident,
that all men are created equal, that they are endowed by their
Creator with certain inalienable rights, that among these are Life,
Liberty and the pursuit of Happiness. That to secure these rights,
Governments are instituted among Men, deriving their just powers
from the consent of the governed. That whenever any Form of
Government becomes destructive of these ends, it is the Right of
the People to alter or to abolish it, and to institute new Government, laying its foundation on such principles and organizing its
powers in such form, as to them shall seem most likely to affect
their Safety and Happiness.

Implicit here is the conviction that individual growth,
progress, happiness, must be achieved socially, by the
"people," together. There is no antagonism between individual and society. Implicit, too, is the confidence in science,
the "laws of nature." To respect them, and operate by them,
is to make progress, win liberty. The God of the Declaration
is not the God of miracles, for if God endowed human beings
with inalienable rights, they must still win the enjoyment of
these rights for themselves. He is not the God of the after-
life, for love of whom one must renounce the material world,
but the God who operates through the laws of nature. Human
society, it is affirmed, can and does progress. It can even over-

haul its most imposing institution, its government, when this stands in the way of further progress, and set up a new one. These views were not uniquely "American." They were products of the "Age of Reason," and appeared in the French Revolution and its Declaration of the Rights of Man, and in the subsequent democratic revolutions. But today, not only in America but in the other lands where these views were held, we have a spreading despair. Is this despair "truth"? Were the high hopes of one and two centuries ago "illusions"? To begin to answer these questions, we must glance back to the conditions under which the existentialist questions of progress first arose. Let us begin with the 17th century when, as Tillich says, existentialism "starts with Pascal."

In this period the forces unleashed a century before, with the rise of independent nations, the discovery of the Americas, the flood of gold pouring into the economic arteries of Europe, the overhauling of medieval dogma by Renaissance humanism and Reformation Protestantism, rapidly transformed European economic, political, social and intellectual life. The middle class of merchants and manufacturers, supported by the peasant bitterness against the feudal aristocracy, strengthened its place in the state and its grasp on the new opportunities for trade and colonization. Sometimes it allied itself with a mercantile-minded wing of the aristocracy. In England a king was beheaded and the way laid open for parliamentary government. Holland won its independence from Spain. In France, out of civil war, an absolute monarchy emerged with the burgeoning middle class playing an increasing role in economic life. With this came revolutionary developments of science, opening broad avenues for the study of the real world.

Typical of the great thinkers who gave the age its forward-looking ideas was Francis Bacon (1561-1626), who, early in the century, helped fashion the scientific world view. Asserting that knowledge could come only from the study of nature, Bacon helped break the grip of medieval dogma. In *Novum Organum* he wrote, "Man, being the servant and interpreter of nature, can do and understand so much and so much only as he has observed in fact or in thought of the course of nature: beyond this he neither knows anything nor can do anything." Ignorance of the laws of nature made people helpless before their operation. Discovery and understanding of these laws enabled society to use them as tools, to master the forces behind them. "Nature," he wrote, "to be commanded, must be obeyed." To Bacon, one formidable barrier to truth was the "reason" of the medieval Scholastics who ignored the actual world, and maintained a colossal structure of argumentation and abstract logic on dogmatic premises which they held to be revelation. "It cannot be that axioms established by argumentation should avail for the discovery of new works; since the subtlety of nature is greater many times over than the subtlety of argument. But axioms duly and orderly formed from particulars easily discover the way to new particulars, and thus render sciences active."

Progress in that age had its contradictions; the slave trade and the near depopulation of Africa, the massacre of the native populations in the colonies and other evils. In Europe rising mercantile wealth was accompanied by spreading misery of the dislocated and exploited working people. The mercantile-minded nations were engaged in trade wars with one another. Science could throw no light on the upheavals taking place in social life and in the "human condition." Its great achievements were in such realms as astronomy, mechanics, optics, other branches of physics, and physiology. What emerged from this science was an overall picture of a mechanistic, "clockwork" universe in which conflict, change, transformation, evolutionary development and the problems of the "human heart" had no place.

Against this background, Blaise Pascal (1623-1662) raised the question: Is this progress? He did not pose the question in the interest of the underprivileged, the impoverished, the suffering, nor did he indict the bourgeoisie for using the opportunities opened up for the mastery of nature to exploit both people and resources, and to engage in ruthless competition. He reflects however a *malaise* or unhappiness of the "privileged"; a feeling that all is not well, that the best-appearing plans can lead to apparently inexplicable disasters. Whether he can be called an existentialist is open to question. But what appears to put him in this tradition is that he raises this question of whether progress is progress, not trying to solve its contradictions but seeing the "vanity" of its hopes, and raising against this the spectre of death.

Pascal was a brilliant, creative mathematician and physicist. In his *Pensées*, he wrote, "all our dignity, then, consists in thought." But the importance of thought to him was not that it could help the further penetration of the secrets of the universe and add to human powers. Rather, it was that through thought, man became aware of his own death, discovering "that our pleasures are only vanity; that our evils are infinite; and, lastly, that death, which threatens us at every moment, must infallibly place us within a few years under the dreadful necessity of being for ever annihilated or unhappy. . . . There is nothing more real than this, nothing more terrible."

Pascal's answer to this anguish is that the thought of death must lead man to faith in God. "Faith is a gift of God; do not believe that we said it was a gift of reasoning. Other religions do not say this of their faith. They only give reasoning in order to arrive at it, yet it does not bring them to it." The new science and the political-economic wars carried on in religious guise had given heavy blows to the old Christian dogma. Pascal finds a new form for his faith. The medieval scholastics had taken Heaven and the after-life, with its hierarchies, its beatitudes and punishments, its rewards and torture dungeons, as objective reality, more real than life on earth. They had elaborated its laws into remarkable structures of logic and "reasoning." To Pascal, however, the "other world" is not objective reality. It is outside the operations of reason. He has no use for theological rationalizations. Belief and faith are subjective, "inner" entities, matters of the "heart" and of its own dissatisfactions with life. "The heart has its reasons, which reason does not know. . . . I say that the heart naturally loves the Universal Being, and also itself naturally, according as it gives itself to them; and it hardens itself against one or the other at its will. You have rejected the one, and kept the other. Is it by reason that you love yourself?"

To say that the "heart has its reasons" is to rebuke the mechanistic world picture, which, in the name of science, leaves no room for human hopes, desires, freedom, growth. But its weakness lies in posing unsolved problems as a "higher truth," and ignoring the solutions already achieved of real problems. If Pascal does not mention specifically the greed and self-aggrandizement that masked the progress his age was making, they seem nevertheless to be in the back of his mind. Rejecting the love of oneself implicit in them, he sees no alternative to this other than to love God.

If we can see in Pascal an expression of disillusion as an aftermath of the first revolutionary upheavals out of the feudal world, we can see what Tillich meant when he said that in the subsequent "Enlightenment," existentialism had an "underground history." For this "Age of Reason," which began before and was prolonged beyond the 18th century, was devoted to the concept of progress. Spurred by the achievements in science, thinkers ranged over human relations, society, politics, government, the state, and the question of human freedom. Leading thinkers, like Locke, Voltaire, Holbach, Rousseau, Montesquieu and Diderot, put the institutions of court, aristocracy, and Church to the test of "reason." They attacked the entire heritage of superstitions, meaningless rituals, hypocrisies, intolerance and fanaticism, and tested ideas by their relevance to human welfare. "Heart" and "mind" were reunited. Not one of these figures was a political revolutionary, yet each was regarded at one time or another as a danger to the established order, and their ideas shaped the American Declaration of Independence and the French Declaration of the Rights of Man.

Characteristic of most of these thinkers was their trend toward philosophical materialism. This has nothing to do with what is often described and denounced as "materialism"; an approach to life typified by selfishness, sensuality, greed and the reduction of human values to cash and profit. Philosophical materialism starts with the real world of nature, people and society. It regards this world as knowable, operating through laws that can be discovered and put to human use. It regards progress, as seen in the products of both head and hand, to be made possible only through man's efforts to master this world, labor in it, discover its secrets and remold it. It stands firmly on science and the scientific view, and so its picture of the world and the possibilities of change expands with each fresh discovery.

These 18th century materialists were not necessarily or even primarily atheists. They accepted the concept of a Deity or Creator much in the sense that the Declaration of Independence speaks of the "Laws of Nature" and "Nature's God." Central, however, is the affirmation that "life, liberty, the pursuit of happiness" rest on human efforts to know, labor in and master the real world. Thus philosophical materialism is opposed to philosophical idealism, which is not to be confused with "idealism," in the sense of dedication to noble and unselfish principles. America's Thomas Paine, a thoroughgoing materialist, devoted his life to his fellow human beings. Philosophical idealism sees God, spirit, mind or the "idea" as prerequisite to the material world and decisive in its movement. Consequently the answers to human strivings and questions must be sought in that unfathomable area, impenetrable to science and knowable only through intuition and revelation.

The greatest idealist philosophers of the time, however, whose all-embracing system still asserted the primacy of "mind," reflected and embraced the spirit of the Enlightenment. This was notably true of Immanuel Kant (1724-1804) and Georg W. F. Hegel (1770-1831). They could not see "mind" itself, or the development of consciousness and of laws and patterns of thought, as an evolutionary creation of the material world. Kant, for example, saw the laws of thought and reason as *a priori*, or "built in" the mind, to be then applied to outer reality. Hegel saw outer reality, in its change and evolution, as a form taken by the "working out" of mind. Yet, in constructing their system, they eagerly welcomed and absorbed all it was then possible to know, whether in science or history, and were supremely rational and humanist minds. They are quoted here not only as exemplars of the Enlightenment, but also because they raise issues important in the discussion of existentialism; namely, the achievement of science, the criticism of dogmatism, and the organic interaction of the individual personality and the outer world.

In the preface to the second edition of *The Critique of Pure Reason*, Kant writes that Galileo's experiments on falling bodies, and Torricelli's on air pressure, were revelations to "all natural philosophers." They learned, he says, "that reason only perceives that which it produces after its own design; that it must not be content to follow, as it were, in the leading-strings of nature, but must proceed in advance with principles of judgment according to unvarying laws, and compel nature to reply to its questions." We can see here the idealistic bent of Kant's thought. Reason, to him, is an *a priori* pattern in the mind, a built-in structure instead of a way of thought developed through the actual process of working with nature, changing it, learning its make-up and laws. But he also exalts the scientific imagination which not only classifies data but, through its experiments, raises questions and compels nature to answer. So he exults in the power of human beings to master nature, and expresses his confidence in progress, or the ability of human beings in society to overcome the obstacles before them.

Reason must approach nature with the view, indeed, of receiving information from it, not, however, in the character of a pupil, who listens to all that his master chooses to tell him, but in that of a judge, who compels the witness to reply to those questions which he himself thinks fit to propose. To this single idea must the revolution be ascribed, by which, after groping in the dark for so many centuries, natural science was at length conducted into the path of certain progress.[3]

In the same treatise (Book II, Chapter III, Section V), Kant attacks dogmatism, which holds ideas to be absolute truths without examining the actual foundation, origin and real supporting data. "For the very essence of reason consists in its ability to give an account of all our conceptions, opinions, and assertions; upon objective grounds, or, when they happen to be illusory and fallacious, upon subjective grounds."

Hegel, in his *Science of Logic*, thus states the basis for an organic and fruitful relationship between the "I" and "others," or between the individual and society:

Independence having reached its quintessence in the One which is for itself, is abstract and formal, destroying itself; it is the highest and most stubborn error, which takes itself for the highest truth; appearing, more concretely, as abstract freedom, pure ego, and further, as Evil. It is freedom which goes so far astray as to place its essence in this abstraction, flattering itself that, being thus by itself, it possesses itself in its purity. Determined more closely, independence is that error which regards as negative, and maintains a negative attitude towards, that which is its own essence. It is thus a negative attitude towards itself, which, seeking to possess its own Being, destroys it; and thus its activity only manifests the vanity of its activity.[4]

In a parallel passage from *The Philosophy of Fine Art,* Hegel criticizes those who believe "that art can have no alternative but to dissever herself absolutely from all connections with this world of relative appearances." To Hegel, this is an illusive view of "ideality," which actually reveals "that the thinker's courage has failed him to come to terms with the external world in question." And so he concludes:

For such a man the only relief available is a complete withdrawal into the secret world of the emotions, a prison-house of unreality he steps out never. Here he remains in what he conceives to be the temple of wisdom gazing ecstatically at what he takes to be the stars, and naturally values at the price of a nutshell all that is found on the Earth.[5]

Thus Hegel demands that a thinker root himself solidly in real life and the affairs of society. This is put not as a moral imperative but in terms of the disastrous results of a withdrawal, to the very independence and free individual development which the individual seeks when he flees this reality. Another contribution of Hegel is interpreted and expanded by Frederick Engels in his essay, *Feuerbach*:

No philosophical proposition has earned more gratitude from narrow-minded governments and wrath from equally narrow-minded liberals than Hegel's famous statement: "All that is real is rational; and all that is rational is real." That was tangibly a sanctification of things that be, a philosophical benediction bestowed upon despotism, police government, Star Chamber proceedings and censorship. That is how Frederick William III and how his subjects understood it. . . . Now, according to Hegel, reality is, however, in no way an attribute predicable of any given state of affairs, social or political, in all circumstances and at all times. On the contrary. The Roman Republic was real, but so was the Roman Empire, which superseded it. In 1789 the French monarchy had become so unreal, that is to say, so robbed of all necessity, so irrational, that it had to be destroyed by the Great Revolution, of which Hegel always speaks with the greatest enthusiasm. In this case, therefore, the monarchy was the unreal and the revolution the real. And so, in the course of development, all that was previously real becomes unreal, loses its necessity, its right of existence, its rationality. And in the place of moribund reality comes a new, viable reality—peacefully if the old has intelligence enough to go to its death without a struggle; forcibly if it resists this necessity.[6]

Important here is the view of what is "rational." To think rationally does not mean to build an abstract structure of reason and logic upon any premise. To think rationally is to think of a problem in terms of the real processes, forces and movements involved in it, discerning what is passing and what is being born. Emerson put this in a different way when writing of nature, in *The American Scholar*. He said, "Its laws are the laws of his own mind. . . . So much of nature as he is ignorant of, so much of his own mind does he not yet possess."

The ideas of the "Enlightenment" are a permanent part of the education of humanity because, despite their errors and gaps, they were rational in this deepest sense, reflecting, clarifying, encouraging, clearing the way for a great social transformation in which stifling and oppressive institutions were swept away, along with the superstitions that fostered them and the ideologies that hailed them as eternal. The "Enlightenment" did not answer all questions. In fact, it helped bring a society into being in which a host of new questions would be raised. And it is in this new society of parliamentary democracy and triumphant capitalism that existentialism reappears, as, in Tillich's words, "revolutionary."

CAPITALISM VIEWED BY KIERKEGAARD AND MARX

A limitation of the thinkers of the "Enlightenment" was the implicit belief that if the touchstone of fact and reason could be applied to superstitions, dogmatisms, fanaticisms and illusions, these would pass away and humanity would become one happy, rational family. They had not grasped the role of economic classes in society and the battle of ideas; a role that would become evident in the revolutionary upheavals and their aftermath. During the 18th century many liberal aristocrats had been interested in the new ideas and their social criticisms. But as the crisis approached, the main weight of court and landed aristocracy was thrown against social change and against the widespread propagation of ideas that encouraged change.

The uprisings of the oppressed peasantry and city workers in France precipitated the revolution. The middle class of manufacturers and merchants inaugurated the "Reign of Terror," called on the masses of people to defend the new republic against reaction and invasion, then turned against the radical "Left" and set up the basic institutions of the new society. This class was forward moving, standing for progress in the new productive forces it unleashed, but was itself exploitive of labor, avaricious, "practical" in its willingness to abandon or corrupt the very democratic principles through which it had come to power when these stood in the way of its own advancement. And so a new world appeared much different from what the "Enlightenment" had envisaged.

This new world, that of 19th century capitalism, has been amply charted, not only in histories and tracts but in realistic novels, like Balzac's great panorama, which delineated the birth of new kinds of personalities and new ways of life. It was a fiercely competitive world in which, in the minds of those who held the reins, the noble principles of the "Enlightenment," of universal human rights and freedom, dwindled to "free trade" and the sacredness of private property. All human creations including those of the mind were reduced to market-place terms, tolerated only as profitable commodities. In the competitive war, with each producer trying to outproduce or undersell the other, production periodically glutted the market, and the wheels of industry came to a halt, bringing unemployment, bankruptcies and starvation. The politics of parliamentary democracy declined to a battle of rival economic interests, with legislators and politicians open to be bought and sold or themselves representing greedy interests, while the land's resources were devoured. It was in this period that, as Tillich says, existentialism became "revolutionary." The question, however, is "revolutionary" against what, and for what?

Søren Kierkegaard (1813-1855), hailed today as the germinal existentialist thinker in the 19th century, was a Dane who, in his middle twenties, went through a drastic change in his religious beliefs that altered his entire attitude toward life, including such matters as family, marriage and career. His first major book, Either/Or (1843), is notable for its brilliance, wit and charm. Despite its verbosity, it belongs with the lasting works of 19th century literature. Issued under a pen name, it further purports to be written by three different people, the author explaining that it is made up of papers he found in an old desk drawer. The first volume,

Either, consists of essays presumably written by a young esthete—such as Kierkegaard himself might have been in his younger days—on how to see life "esthetically" and get the most enjoyment out of it. The stress is on the erotic, with analyses of love-making and a seduction. It draws on musical examples, as in a lengthy discussion of Mozart's opera *Don Giovanni*. Its closing section is a masterfully written *Diary of The Seducer*, which indicates how accomplished a novelist Kierkegaard might have become.

For all its tone of the author "acting a part," it is a side of himself that Kierkegaard presents. A hint of his own discarded youthful ideas is expressed in the summing up of Mozart's Don: "the lust for enjoyment sounds through the primitive seething which is his life."[1] The intimation is that this is less than a happy life, and perhaps even a desperate one.

Just as Kierkegaard's contemporary, Robert Schumann, frequently signed his music and his critical writings "Florestan" and "Eusebius" to indicate that they were different sides of his personality, so Kierkegaard assumes another personality for most of the second volume—*Or*. He is now an older man, a friend of the young esthete, writing serious yet sympathetic letters to him, trying gently to convince him of the greater joys of the "ethical" life, of married love, of actions guided by conscience and "duty." Although this second personality seems at first to be a little stodgy and pedantic, he too deepens. There is a sharp commentary on the hypocrisy of the times:

In our own time they have sought also in other ways to enervate the ethical view of life. For although they find that the business of being a good man is a pretty poor career in life, they nevertheless retain a certain respect for it and are disquieted when they see its claim asserted. . . . It is quite natural, therefore, that in the modern drama the bad is always represented by the most shining talents; the good, the upright, by a grocer's clerk. The spectators find this a matter of course and learn from the play what they knew beforehand, that it is far beneath their dignity to be put in the same class with a grocer's clerk.[2]

And then Kierkegaard's basic theme enters: the "despair" that infuses all of life. The man "who lives esthetically" knows this despair, for he is terrified at the "annihilation" of his own personality by death. And the "ethical" man also feels despair. "The ethicist simply carries through the despair which the higher estheticist began but arbitrarily broke off."[3] There is but one solution to the problem; to unite oneself with the "universal human," which is to love God and abase oneself before God. This is the answer to death and "despair." It involves something quite different from expressions of religious belief and attendance at church. It is a way of life which abandons all pretenses to knowledge or to the exaltation of human powers over the world. And the closing section of the second volume is an eloquent sermon written by a third figure, an anonymous pastor, on the theme, "Against God we are always in the wrong." Only by knowing this can there be true faith. With other people whom we want to love, we sometimes find that they injure us, that they are therefore wrong and we right, and this conflicts with our desire to love them. With God, however, since we know we are "always in the wrong," our love is complete. And there is no need to search for any other kind of knowledge or truth. This truth brings salvation from despair. "Only the truth which edifies is truth for you."[4]

It is like a return to the Middle Ages, but on a different plane. The medieval theologians taught that life was a "vale of tears," that it was sinful to enjoy it or try to improve one's lot, that one must fix his eyes on the next world, with faith in God. Then, however, faith was bolstered with terrifying pictures of the torments of hellfire, described as if hell were an objective reality more real than the real world itself. But the "Enlightenment" having destroyed Hell, in the 19th century

Hell becomes "internal." It is not punishment in the next life that to Kierkegaard threatens people, but "despair" in this life.

From this point on, Kierkegaard fought a two-sided battle. On the one hand, he attacked the Danish Lutheran Church for what he saw as its worldliness, its practical-minded conformity to a corrupt society, its abandonment of what he saw as true Christianity, or the dedication to love of God. On the other hand, he attacked science and reason. He included philosophy, to the extent that philosophy engendered skepticism, particularly the philosophy of Hegel, which he thought far too worldly. Hegel's view of God, as the "idea" evolving through the history, achievements and discoveries of mankind in society, was to Kierkegaard insidiously disguised materialism. It eliminated any personal relation between man and God. And in *Fear and Trembling* (1843), he complains bitterly that rational philosophy deprives people of their faith. "I do not however mean in any sense to say that faith is something lowly, but on the contrary that it is the highest thing, and that it is dishonest of philosophy to give something else instead of it and to make light of faith."[5] He wrote in his *Journal*, in 1846: "In the end all corruption will come about as a result of the natural sciences."[6]

The book *Fear and Trembling* is a long, impassioned sermon, on the need to accept life as "absurd," taking for its text the Biblical story of Abraham and Isaac. Like the existentialist thinkers who followed him, Kierkegaard has no interest in the real history of humanity, nor does he have any awareness that the problem he faces is itself historically evolved, the creation of a certain social situation. If there is reference to an actual crisis, it is only in the sense that this serves to awaken the mind to fundamental, glossed-over, eternal truths. Yet we can glimpse in the book that what is afflicting Kierkegaard's mind is the commercialism of bourgeois society. The very first words of the Preface are a witty commentary on the marketplace, which has also become a marketplace of ideas: "Not merely in the realm of commerce but in the world of ideas as well our age is organizing a regular clearance sale. Everything is to be had at such a bargain that it is questionable whether in the end there is anybody who will want to bid."[7]

Philosophy itself, Kierkegaard says, has become such a commodity—skepticism. "Every speculative price-fixer who conscientiously directs attention to the significant march of modern philosophy, every Privatdocent, tutor, and student, every crofter and cottar in philosophy, is not content with doubting everything but goes further." He himself, he says, is not a philosopher. He has no "system." He is only an "amateur." He writes because he has to, knowing that he is against the direction of the times and no one will listen to him. There is a touch of self-pity. He feels lonely and persecuted, saying of himself: "He can easily foresee his fate in an age when passion has been obliterated in favor of learning, in an age when an author who wants to have readers must take care to write in such a way that the book can be easily perused during the afternoon nap. . . . He foresees his fate—that he will be entirely ignored."[8]

Kierkegaard then goes on to recount the story of Abraham, when he is told by God to take his beloved son Isaac, the son of his old age, whom he had waited for, and murder him. The word "murder" is Kierkegaard's. Since Abraham sets about obediently to do this, he is, to Kierkegaard, the greatest of all heroes, for he expected not the "possible," not the "eternal," but the "impossible." "He who expected the impossible became greater than all. . . . Abraham was greater than all, great by reason of his power whose strength is impotence, great by reason of his wisdom whose secret is foolishness, great by reason of his hope whose form is madness, great by reason of the love which is hatred of oneself."[9]

The very fact, Kierkegaard says, that Abraham "believed the preposterous" makes him "the guiding star which saves the anguished." Abraham accepted and lived by the absurd. "The whole earthly form he exhibits is a new creation by virtue of the absurd. He resigned everything infinitely, and then he grasped everything again by virtue of the absurd." He "grasped the whole of existence by virtue of the absurd."[10]

Kierkegaard can see no connection between heart and mind, between the emotions and the intellect, between rationality and passion. He cannot realize that to discover some aspect of reality which opens up possibilities for the transformation of the conditions of life, to replace darkness with light, to discover one's own humanity and that of others in common action with others, engenders the most profound emotions, because rationality is here tied to human freedom. To Kierkegaard, "faith begins precisely there where thinking leaves off." One must forego real achievements and possibilities, and look for miracles. One must forego thought, intellect, knowledge, so that one can experience passion. "Faith is a miracle, and yet no man is excluded from it; for that in which all human life is unified is passion, and faith is a passion. . . . Faith is the highest passion in a man."[11]

If the tone Kierkegaard adopted in his writings was that of an impassioned lay preacher, this was not unique to him, but a characteristic expression of the revulsion of many minds of the time against rampant greed and marketplace "materialism." We can find this happening in the United States. And it is worth dwelling on this, both for the parallels to Kierkegaard, and for the highly significant differences.

Emerson, for one, took up the essay and the lecture platform as a form of sermonizing, after abjuring all specific dogmas. Thoreau wrote in a similar tone in *Walden*. Hawthorne's stories are parable-sermons, and the climax of *The House of Seven Gables* is the author's sermon over the dead body of Judge Pyncheon, lamenting the futility of a life devoted to amassing his "real estate in town and country, his railroad, bank and insurance shares, his United States stocks." Melville early in *Moby Dick* gives the reader Father Mapple's sermon, then sardonically pictures the miserly, haggling Bible-quoting Quaker owners of the whaling vessel to whom "a man's religion is one thing, and this practical world quite another." Again and again, Melville puts his own sermons into the novel.

In the young American republic, that prided itself on showing the way to freedom, the contrast between noble promise and scurvy fulfillment took an especially gruesome form; the mushrooming of slavery and the slave market, which even monarchic Europe frowned upon. The mental and moral corruption this engendered extended even to organized religion, with most sects sanctifying slavery. Slavery was justified on Biblical grounds, as well as racist grounds of alleged African inferiority, and the "practical" ground that even if it could not be morally condoned, slaves were "private property" and to violate "private property" was to wrench out the central pillar of civilization.

The attitude of the American rebels and questioners, however, was anything but disillusioned. What they sought was the regeneration of a democracy in which, as they saw it, capitalistic greed was an alien and diseased growth. In this their thinking differs from Kierkegaard's existentialism, which questioned and attacked as "worldly" the very concept that human beings could improve their conditions of life in the real world, and saw in the attempts to chart the material world only a path to destruction. Hawthorne, for a while, joined an experimental socialistic community. Emerson expressed optimism and hope for the future, and told his readers to "study nature." Thoreau showed that he could live for two years at Walden Pond by his own hands, to prove that money was not so important that a person had to waste his life for it. But as he himself said, this deliberate assertion of his own independence, his ability to live outside of the treadmill, was as "experiment." He never really withdrew from society, nor did he ever want to. Even when living at Walden Pond, he would stroll over to town to chat with friends. He attacked slavery, defended John Brown, condemned the war against Mexico. Melville's *Whitejacket* helped abolish flogging in the American navy. If they saw materialism in its corrupted face of selfish utilitarianism, and so sought in the realm of the "spirit" for more genuine values of life, what they were fundamentally interested in were the values of life on earth. They remained social minds, and did not suffer from the intense fears which Kierkegaard's loneliness, generalized into a doctrinal war against all society, bred in him.

Kierkegaard would have regarded Emerson, for example, as little a "true Christian" as Thoreau or Tom Paine. To live as a social-minded or a misguided humanist only substituted temporal pleasures for eternal happiness. He wrote in *Concluding Unscientific Postscript* (1846), "Now if for any individual an eternal happiness is his highest good, this will mean that all finite satisfactions are volitionally relegated to the status of what may have to be renounced in favor of an eternal happiness."[12] This doctrine seems to have a medieval, ascetic ring, but its modern "existentialist" character lies in the fact that he does not withdraw to a monastery or cave, but carries his personal despair, or "existential predicament," wherever he goes, and must exhort others to see life similarly.

He does not flee from society but is engaged in society as a self-proclaimed "outsider." As he says in the Introduction to *Concluding Unscientific Postscript*, most Christians would regard the very question he raises of true Christianity, or "eternal happiness," as a kind of "insolence," and he admits that it could be a "special kind of madness." The implication is that if what the rest of the world does is "sane," then he, renouncing worldliness, is quite willing to be "mad." For he has found "truth." It is that Hell is within him, and must be accordingly lurking within everyone. He wrote in his *Journal* of May 12, 1839, "The whole of existence frightens me . . . the most inexplicable thing of all is my own existence."[13] The world is to him something implacably hostile, instead of a place where he can stretch his wings and grow. He fears such enticements. He attacks all attempts to make the world more livable or understandable, through science or social reform, for these only nurture and intensify "worldliness." By his logic, they accordingly only make for greater despair. Like an evangelist, he cries to his readers to be "saved," by recognizing that the world is "absurd" and must be countered by a faith itself "absurd."

The spectre of despair is raised most frighteningly in another impassioned book-sermon, *Sickness Unto Death* (1849). Again Kierkegaard first attacks "worldliness."

What is called worldliness is made up of just such men who (if one may use this expression) pawn themselves to the world. They use their talents, accumulate money, carry on worldly affairs, calculate shrewdly, etc., etc., are perhaps mentioned in history, but themselves they are not; spiritually understood, they have no self, no self for whose sake they could venture everything, no self before God—however selfish they may be for all that.[14]

Within this there is a valid question, especially sharp in a bourgeois world which has abandoned the heaven and hell of the next world, and turned to the exploration of life on earth. The question is, what are the values of life? Has the world itself been lost by turning its genuine riches into commodities, and thus shriveling up the possibilities of rounded, expansive, truly human life? Thoreau raises such a question in *Walden*. "Rise free from care before the dawn, and seek adventures. . . . Let not to get a living be thy trade, but thy

sport. Enjoy the land, but own it not. Through want of enterprise and faith, men are where they are, buying and selling,
and spending their lives like serfs." And so when he says, "the
mass of men lead lives of quiet desperation," he means this
as a challenge, to open one's eyes to the real possibilities of
the world. But Kierkegaard attacks all "worldly affairs"; not
only greedy profit-seekers but those whose "talents" run to
other ways, to science, to art, to the expansion of the boundaries of knowledge, to the liberation of people from oppression, misery and poverty. Worldliness means attention to this
world. It is what everyone is guilty of who does not abandon
his life to love of God. And the penalty for worldliness is
"despair," which is the "sickness unto death." The world
is hell. Everyone who is not a Christian suffers despair, and
most who are Christians are also in despair, for they are
worldly Christians, not true Christians.

One might say perhaps that there lives not one single man who
after all is not to some extent in despair. . . . At any rate there
has lived no one and there lives no one outside of Christendom
who is not in despair, and no one in Christendom, unless he be
a true Christian, and if he is not quite that, he is somewhat in
despair after all. . . . It is not a rare exception that one is in despair;
no, the rare, the very rare exception is that one is not in despair
. . . the fact that the man in despair is unaware that his condition
is despair, has nothing to do with the case, he is in despair all the
same.[15]

There can be little doubt, from the passion with which
Kierkegaard writes, that he himself felt this despair. Whether
he also arrived at the beatitude of faith he argues for, or
whether he is really arguing with himself, is an open question.
For what he projects as an alternative to accepting the world
—which by his own definition is worldliness and therefore
despair—is a state of mind, not a way of life. And yet he must
live in this world, which constantly erodes this state of mind.

Thoreau again offers in *Walden* a significant contrast. He, too, like Kierkegaard, derided those who play at philosophy. But he raised a much more significant question: whether they live as they think. "There are nowadays professors of philosophy, but not philosophers. . . . To be a philosopher is not merely to have subtle thoughts, nor even to found a school, but so to love wisdom as to live according to its dictates, a life of simplicity, independence, magnanimity, and trust. It is to solve some of the problems of life, not only theoretically but practically."

That Thoreau, in his short life, amply carried out this thinking is seen in his "experiment" in living at Walden, his aiding of Negro slaves to escape, and his refusal, for which he went to jail, to pay poll taxes to a government that supported slavery and instigated the war with Mexico. According to Kierkegaard's logic, Thoreau should especially have felt despair. For, to Kierkegaard, despair is not dependent on any satisfactions or lack of them that life offers. It rises out of the knowledge that however one lives, one must inevitably die. And Thoreau knew at the age of 43 that he had not much longer to live. It turned out to be two years. Yet in none of his writings, in which he speaks so openly, freely and intimately, is there a hint of despair. When a minister, Channing, asked him near the end what he thought of the after-life, his answer was, "one world at a time."

Kierkegaard hits home when he exposes the fears, dissatisfactions and unhappiness among people living under the most comfortable circumstances, and questions the values people live by. But when he comes to make his own affirmation, to assert his "cure" for the sickness, he resorts to the philosophic tradition he despises. He turns to metaphysical argument and abstraction, even to Hegelian dialectic, in order to give the argument a seemingly objective weight, a logical structure. In the tract, *Concluding Unscientific Postscript,* he takes up the crucial question of truth:

When the question of truth is raised in an objective manner, reflection is directed objectively to the truth, as an object to which the knower is related. Reflection is not focussed on the relationship, however, but upon the question of whether it is the truth to which the knower is related. If only the object to which he is related is the truth, the subject is accounted to be in the truth. When the question of truth is raised subjectively, reflection is directed subjectively to the nature of the individual's relationship; if only the mode of this relationship is in the truth, the individual is in the truth even if he should happen to be thus related to what is not true.[16]

Thus to Kierkegaard, whatever a person passionately believes to be true, is true, even though objectively, as a phenomenon of the physical world, it is not true. He is not saying anything so unsubtle as that if a person passionately wishes something to come to pass, it comes to pass. What he is saying is that the physical existence of things in the actual world has only an accidental relation to the individual who views them. They are not involved in the impassioned question of what he is as an existing being. What is deeply involved with this existence is the "infinite," or Eternity and God. And so, to believe in God passionately is truth, even though God cannot be seen, felt, heard, like something in the actual world. It is a higher truth, or, as he says, a "necessity." He sums up: "An objective uncertainty held fast in an appropriation-process of the most passionate inwardness is the truth, the highest truth attainable for an existing individual. . . . Subjectivity is the truth."[17]

Despair like Kierkegaard's does not come from the awareness that at some time or another one must die. It comes when life as one lives it offers no satisfactions, or only illusory ones. The medieval peasants had taken "subjectivity" as "truth" to the extent that they accepted the promise of an after-life as an answer to their very real miseries in this life. But this was no mere promise of beatitude; rather, a "Day of Judgment" when their tormentors, including kings and noblemen, would be judged and dragged off to Hell. This is illustrated in anonymous church sculptures, and in the Flemish fantasy paintings of Hieronymus Bosch. Kierkegaard's mentality is that of the anguished petty bourgeois, afflicted by the competitive war he himself engenders. He has, unlike the peasant who hates the feudal lord, no "tormentor," for he himself creates, lives by and fosters the marketplace battle or dog-eat-dog life which threatens to bankrupt him. To hate his class is to hate himself. And so he transfers this hatred to all of society, with which he confuses his class. Thus Kierkegaard's castigation strikes at democracy; not at its perversions, but its essence. He attacks the "mob," ignoring the repeated struggles of the common people throughout history to break through the ignorance, fear and confusion in which they were kept, struggles which brought all society to a higher, more humane level; the peasant revolts of the Middle Ages, the American War of Independence, the tearing down of the Bastille doors. He writes, in the posthumously published *That Individual*:

The crowd is untruth. Therefore was Christ crucified, because, although he addressed himself to all, He would have no dealings with the crowd, because He would not permit the crowd to aid him in any way, because in this regard He repelled people absolutely, would not found a party, did not permit balloting, but would be what he is, the Truth, which relates itself to the individual. And hence every one who truly would serve the truth is *eo ipso*, in one way or another, a martyr. . . . No witness for the truth (Ah! and that is what every man should be, including you and me)—no witness for the truth dare become engaged with the crowd.[18]

Thus Kierkegaard, seeing himself in that light, a martyr to democracy, attacks social progress, and shuns the actual plight and misery of people in the world. The kind of "love" he preaches is withdrawal from social concerns, convinced that few will follow, that he is one of the select handful concerned with "truth." Reality, in the face of death, is "absurd," and to encompass it one must believe in the impossible, the preposterous, in miracles. This is "freedom"; the denial and renunciation—in mind—of anything that has the face of "necessity," of any obligations the world may lay upon the individual. Even knowledge of the make-up of the world must be scorned as an unwelcome necessity, for by its very nature it influences one's actions and therefore infringes on "freedom." This denial of any "necessity"—in mind alone, of course, for it cannot be done in actual living—is the "freedom" of existentialism. By accepting despair, wallowing in it, exalting it as the essence of life, it turns into its opposite, faith and happiness. If this faith is "absurd," what other answer can there be when reality is "absurd"? Subjectivity is truth.

In the 1830's and 1840's, when Kierkegaard's writings were appearing, the first writings were also appearing of Karl Marx (1818-1883) and Frederick Engels (1820-1895). They analyzed capitalist society from the standpoint of dialectical and historical materialism. It was dialectical in that it saw the world in terms of movement, change and transformation, and historical in that it bent itself to chart the laws of this change and development in society and its history. The historic *Communist Manifesto*, published in 1848, makes an implied criticism of the "Enlightenment." The sweeping away of the irrationalities, the outmoded institutions and beliefs, of feudal society, in the name of freedom and the "rights of man," had not created a society in which human beings can live in free and cooperative relationships. "The modern bourgeois society that has sprouted from the ruins of feudal society has not done away with class antagonisms. It has but established new classes, new conditions of oppression, new forms of struggle in the place of old ones."

Far more sharply than Kierkegaard, the *Manifesto* reveals the "marketplace" mentality of the new society.

The bourgeoisie, wherever it has got the upper hand, has put an end to all feudal, patriarchal, idyllic relations. It has pitilessly torn asunder the motley feudal ties that bound man to his "natural superiors," and has left remaining no other nexus between man and man than naked self-interest, than callous "cash payment." It has drowned the most heavenly ecstasies of religious fervour, of chivalrous enthusiasm, of philistine sentimentalism, in the icy waters of egotistical calculation. It has resolved personal worth into exchange value, and in place of the numberless indefeasible chartered freedoms, has set up that single, unconscionable freedom—Free Trade. In one word, for exploitation veiled by religious and political illusions, it has substituted naked, shameless, direct, brutal exploitation.

There is no hint here, however, of a backward look, of nostalgia for a lost peace of mind, of "disillusion" with progress. Marx and Engels have critically looked at, absorbed, made their own, and carried further, the lights turned on the world by the viewpoint of science and its discoveries, by the French materialist philosophers, by the dialectic of Hegel, and by the English classical economists who brought science into the realm of human and social relations. There is no lament for the passing away of feudal darkness, misery, poverty and backwardness. A genuine forward leap has taken place.

The bourgeoisie has disclosed how it came to pass that the brutal display of vigor in the Middle Ages, which Reactionists so much admire, found its fitting complement in the most slothful indolence. It has been the first to show what man's activity can bring about. It has accomplished wonders far surpassing Egyptian pyramids, Roman aqueducts, and Gothic cathedrals; it has conducted expeditions that put in the shade all former Exoduses of nations and crusades.

It is not in the great expansion of production, however, that this leap is primarily seen, for this is accompanied by crises, degradation and poverty. The most important forward step is that human beings can now begin to solve their problems realistically, with knowledge of what they actually are.

Constant revolutionizing of production, uninterrupted disturbance of all social conditions, everlasting uncertainty and agitation distinguish the bourgeois epoch from all earlier ones. All fixed, fast-frozen relations, with their train of ancient and venerable prejudices and opinions, are swept away, all new-formed ones become antiquated before they can ossify. All that is solid melts into air, all that is holy is profaned, and man is at last compelled to face with sober senses, his real conditions of life, and his relations with his kind.[19]

Thus, at about the middle of the 19th century, two opposite critiques of capitalist society take shape. In one its evils and unredeemed promises lead only to disillusion with the concept of progress itself. The other bases progress on science, which moves into the discovery of the laws of society. To both Kierkegaard's existentialism and to Marxism, human freedom is the primary concern. To both, freedom and truth are organically linked. To Kierkegaard, however, truth is a subjective, irrational response to an "absurd" real world. To Marxism, truth is objective, consisting of the discovered laws of the real world which, once known, become powers in human hands, enabling them to change the conditions of their life. Truth is never absolute, its discovery never complete. Each farther step raises new questions but also makes possible a new stage in the growth and development of human powers or of freedom.

In his *Anti-Dühring*, Engels takes up Hegel's insight that freedom is the appreciation of necessity, and that "necessity is blind only so far as it is not understood." Here are two "opposites"; the human being with potentialities for growth, action, movement, the enrichment of powers and perceptions and, on the other hand, the realities of nature and the external world, with their laws that exist regardless of what human beings want them to be. To the metaphysical, non-dialectical or existentialist thinker these opposites are irreconcilable.

Engels observes:

Freedom does not consist in the dream of independence from natural laws, but in the knowledge of these laws, and in the possibility this gives of systematically making them work towards definite ends. . . . Freedom of the will therefore means nothing but the capacity to make decisions with knowledge of the subject. Therefore the *freer* a man's judgment is in relation to a definite question, the greater is the *necessity* with which the content of this judgment will be determined; while the uncertainty, founded on ignorance, which seems to make an arbitrary choice among many and conflicting possible decisions, shows precisely by this that it is not free, that it is controlled by the very object it should itself control. . . . Freedom therefore consists in the control over ourselves and over external nature, a control founded on knowledge of natural necessity; it is therefore necessarily a product of historical development. The first men who separated themselves from the animal kingdom were in all essentials as unfree as the animals themselves, but each step forward in the field of culture was a step towards freedom.[20]

This, an expression of dialectical materialism, offers a quite different view of reality from the mechanistic materialism of the 17th century, with its "clockwork" universe. And it enables us to understand the frame of mind which shapes Kierkegaard's statement that "subjectivity is the truth." For we can be moved by Kierkegaard, especially in those passages where he foregoes theological argumentation, his attempt to build a rational structure on unreal or irrational premises, and where, instead, his self-portrait emerges as a frustrated and tormented human being, finding no satisfaction in the world around him. It is blindness to say that subjectivity is truth, ignoring the reality of the objective, material world of nature and society, and refusing to distinguish what is real from what is fantasy. But real, too, is the subjective life of the human being, what goes on in his mind, his response to the world, his yearning for freedom, and his conflicts with the outer world. To turn this into viable truth, however, we have to see it in the context of the real-life conditions that engendered it. In other words, we cannot say with Kierkegaard that "subjectivity is the truth," but we can say that within his subjectivity, his anguished disillusion with progress, his attack on "worldliness," there is a kernel of reality which becomes truth when put into a clearer picture of Kierkegaard's own world. Kierkegaard is a mind controlled by the very forces it should itself control.

This is not, of course, the approach of the present-day existentialists to Kierkegaard. They take his anguish as an external truth of the mind or soul, as the basic character of "being." It is as if we were to take Macbeth's:

> . . . *a tale*
> *Told by an idiot, full of sound and fury,*
> *Signifying nothing*

as a great philosophical truth about life. In this very "existentialist" statement Macbeth goes on to an affirmation of defiance very much like one of Camus's or Sartre's existentialist characters. He fights to the end.

> *Blow, wind! come, wrack!*
> *At least we'll die with harness on our back.*

But Shakespeare shows this as the despair of a man who has murdered to become a king, and has found himself forced to murder again, and still again, spreading death wherever he moves. Alienated from the forces in the real world making for life, he has destroyed his own humanity. He is now friendless, hated, feared, and discovers that in each step he took toward what he saw as his own freedom, he roused new forces that would destroy him. In the end, he finds his own life joyless, meaningless, "absurd." He has been, for all his intelligence, the "idiot." To Shakespeare, a great rational mind, there is psychological truth in the subjective state of a human being, but subjectivity is not truth. His great personages are always active in a society, and their subjective life of inner conflict is always significantly connected to the conflicts and problems of the outer world they confront. Truth lies not in the subjective decisions alone, but in the conditions to which they are a response and in the way these decisions, when made, begin to operate in the real world, which develops them according to its own reality.

4

DOSTOIEVSKY: *Realist and Anti-Realist*

Whether Feodor Dostoievsky can properly be called an existentialist is debatable. But he is frequently claimed by existentialists. Because of this, and because the problems raised in his books overlap those of existentialism, he demands discussion here.

Walter Kaufmann, in his anthology, *Existentialism: From Dostoievsky to Sartre,* includes, as an existentialist statement, Part I of Dostoievsky's short and early two-part novel, *Letters from the Underworld* (1864).[1] A kind of "confession" to the reader by the "I" of the story, it strikes a new tone in the novel. In it the writer admits his depravity, asserts his indifference to the anticipated contempt of the readers, declares himself at odds with the world about him, yet furiously attacks it and the values by which his readers will judge him. It starts, "I am ill; I am full of spleen and repellent." The "I" describes himself as one who has held a minor civil-service post for 40 years, and can now retire on a small inheritance. He hates the milieu in which he has moved, for from it he has gotten nothing but blows and insults. He has no illusions about his own nobility of conduct. "If there lies within me any nobility of soul, such nobility has never been able to do anything for me beyond torment me with a consciousness of the utter uselessness of possessing it." He compares himself to a mouse, "a very sensitive mouse," and cries that even such a mouse, despised by the wealthy, strong and powerful, has human feelings.

It will have collected about itself a fatal quagmire, a stinking morass of misunderstandings, emotions, and lastly, spittle discharged at it by the independent persons, judges and dictators who are solemnly standing around it in a ring, and saluting the little animal with full-throated laughter. Naturally, nothing will be left for the mouse to do but to make a disdainful gesture with its little paw, indulge in a smile of deprecatory contempt wherein even the smiler itself will have no belief, and retire shamefacedly into its hole. There, in its dirty, stinking underworld, our poor insulted mouse will soon have immersed itself in a state of cold, malignant, perpetual rancor.

Like this mouse, the "I" of the story has "buried himself" in an "underworld." For 40 years he has hidden his lacerated humanity from the contemptuous eyes of "official society," while dreaming of "revenge"; an outburst which he knows will not hurt his enemies but will only bring down their wrath upon him. And yet he finds a "strange delight" in this secret life, as an "outsider" aware of realities to which they are blind. In his reveries he spits at this official society.

When Dostoievsky wrote this Russia was ruled by an autocratic imperial court, supported by a landed aristocracy, and church hierarchy, living on the backs of an illiterate, poverty-stricken, oppressed peasantry. A belated growth of capitalism was taking place, without any democratization of the governmental structure but generating changes in economic life. The new capitalist class profited from the emancipation of the serfs in 1861, which merely turned peasants into share-croppers and drove great numbers of them to the city slums, to starve or slave in sweat shops. Many landowners' sons, needing ready money to keep up their "position," impoverished themselves by mortgaging or selling their land to the new merchant class. As the ideas of the "Enlightenment" entered Russian intellectual life they were contaminated for many by their connection with what seemed to be their 19th century products in both Russia and Western Europe: greed, money obsession, self-aggrandizement and corruption.

The "official society" in which the "I" mingles is made up of the gentry in the army and civil bureaucracy. He detests particularly the "liberals" among them who are playing with "advanced ideas," and also hates the practical-minded merchant class profiting from these ideas. He attacks science, the extension of knowledge, the "Enlightenment," as raising a "stone wall" of "necessity," which he himself rejects.

What stone wall, do you say? Why, the stone wall constituted of the laws of nature, of the deductions of learning, and of the science of mathematics. When, for instance, people of this kind seek to prove to you that you are descended from an ape, it is of no use to you to frown; you must just accept what they say. . . . "Pardon us," so these people bawl, "but you simply *cannot* refute what we tell you. Twice two makes four; Nature does not ask your leave for that; she has nothing to do with your wishes on the subject, no matter whether you approve of her laws or not. You must take her just as she is, and with her, her results. A wall still remains a wall,"—and so forth, and so forth. Good Lord! What have I to do with these laws of Nature, or with arithmetic, when all the time those laws that twice two make four do not meet with my acceptance? Of course, I am not going to beat my head against a wall if I have not the requisite strength to do so; yet I am not going to *accept* that wall merely because I have run up against it, and have no means to knock it down.

The parallels with Kierkegaard are obvious. The existentialist rejection of the world as it is, is here expressed in a passionate attack upon the practical, contented, well-to-do, and on the concept of progress through science. The attacker sees himself as an outsider, one of the persecuted and insulted. Dostoievsky himself, like the "I" in the novel, came from the impoverished gentry. But there is also a profound difference from Kierkegaard, which helps explain Dostoievsky's greatness as an artist. For if Dostoievsky attacks the values of his milieu, there is no rejection of society itself. Rather, there is the most perceptive documentation of it. If his narrator's ideas are shared by Dostoievsky, he is nevertheless self-critical, and puts the confessing "I" in a clear social setting, describing him in the introduction to the novel as "a personality due to the *milieu* which all of us share in Russia." In other words, the confession is presented not as a revelation of truth for all time, but as an expression of a definite social psychology, created by outer realities.

With vivid detail he depicts this seedy member of the gentry, who has held a petty government post. He has a threadbare coat but it boasts a fur collar. His apartment may be mean, but he has a man-servant. He works and mixes with people who, by their very freedom with money, and their indulgence in the purchasable comforts and pleasures of life, make him feel his own insignificance. And then, in Part II of the novel, Dostoievsky discloses that if he himself has rejected his class and been rebuffed by it, he is not stewing in his own subjective sense of injury. His eyes, heart and mind are open to the humanity and the right to live of the mass of the suffering people, the "insulted and injured" of Russia, the poor, the "nobodies" of society.

In Part II the narrator describes a private dinner party held by three young gentry, colleagues of his who barely tolerate him in the office. To their disgust, he practically forces himself on the party, borrowing the money to do so. Admitting everything, he reveals his own divided feelings. He despises these gamblers, drunkards, skirt-chasers and braggarts, yet yearns to be accepted by them. His behavior seems to them that of a madman, at one moment abasing himself before them and at another hurling violent insults at them. Then he goes, half-drunk, to a brothel and wakes up, some hours later, with a peasant-girl prostitute. His talk with her is gentle and sympathetic. He learns from her the bleak family conditions that had driven her to prostitution, and her hopes to leave it. He promises to be her friend but back at home, he curses himself for having befriended her, worried that she will actually come to see him. She does come, some days later. But to his surprise and shame, she is not put out by the fact that he is obviously not a "great gentleman" and shows sympathy for the miserable circumstances of his life.

And so, if Part I of this novel sounds "existentialist," Part II gives it an entirely different character. Delineated here are the two opposed classes of Russian society in Dostoievsky's time; the parasitical aristocracy, and the oppressed peasantry, part of which has moved from the misery of village life to the misery of city slums, its daughters forced into prostitution. And if both are degraded, one by its self-indulgence and the other by want, it is not the exploiters but the exploited who are on a higher level of humanity and decency, who show a capacity for love and tenderness toward others.

This conviction in the basic decency of the common people is central in Dostoievsky's thought as a novelist, in contrast to the elitism of existentialism, with its contempt for the "mob." There is no rejection of society in Dostoievsky; throughout his career he showed an awareness of social problems. He continued and intensified his diatribes against science, social reform, liberalism, the socialism propagated in his time, and the theories of material progress, but his presentation was marked by social realism and historical truth reaching beyond any specific answers he could find.

His answer was a religious one, but one separated from religious institutions. It rested on faith in a God who bade men to live with love for all people. If one expressed this love, he believed others would respond to it, as he shows them responding to the saintly Alyosha, in The Brothers Karamazov[2] (1879-1880). And this novel shows us, on the broadest scale, the conflict between Dostoievsky's "existentialism" and his grasp of social reality.

The Brothers Karamazov resembles the earlier book in its self-revelation, almost like a confession. For if, unlike the Letters from the Underworld, the story is not told in the first person, what is nevertheless evident is that Dostoievsky has drawn upon himself for his characters, and the depths of conflict they reveal are his own. The psychological links up to the social. The novel almost trembles with the awareness running through it that the country is in a state of crisis, and the central question is, where is Russia bound?

The breadth of the social picture is seen in the varied characters of the Karamazov family. The father, Fyodor, is a seedy landowner who, abandoning the "old order" for the new, has become an avaricious moneylender who glories in the power his money gives him to buy everything, even simulated love. His oldest son, Dmitri, is a typical son of the gentry, a handsome army officer careless with money which he squanders on gambling, mistresses and uniforms. He is self-centered, impulsive, sometimes cruel, yet capable of generous acts and abject contrition. When his father is murdered, the evidence points to Dmitri, who is tried and found guilty although he is innocent. The ordeal he goes through brings him back to faith in God. Ivan, the second brother, is a rationalist and convinced atheist, whom Dostoievsky presents as a cold, intellectual advocate of progress, devoid of human sympathies. Yet he too, after the ordeal of the murder, is afflicted by doubts, and becomes fearful that his atheistic rationalism is the devil's work—therefore there is a God. He also holds himself guilty of his father's murder, for it was he who infected the actual murderer, his illegitimate half-brother, Smerdyakov, with the amoral rationalism which he thinks inspired the murder.

Alyosha is attracted to monastic life and becomes a disciple of a venerated "elder," Father Zossima, on whose death he conceives it to be his mission to quit the monastery and go out into the world to spread the gospel. There he must judge nobody, condemn nobody, but show love for everyone, while

disabusing them of any ideas they might have of false progress, such as science or socialism. Yet, though Dostoievsky
calls Alyosha the "hero" of the novel, he is the least substan-
tial of the major figures in the book, for he has no conflicts
and no passions. He has oversimplified life.

The pervading thought that here connects Dostoievsky with
existentialism is that science, reason, the "Enlightenment,"
are identical with selfish, amoral money-grubbing. The loathsome, money-hungry old Karamazov cries out in the monastery: "You cursed me with bell and book, you spread stories
about me all over the place. Enough, fathers! This is the age
of Liberalism, the age of steamers and railways." Ivan, the
rationalist intellectual, says, "Our papa was a pig, but his
ideas were right enough." The saintly elder, Father Zossima,
says, "They have science; but in science there is nothing
but what is the object of sense. The spiritual world, the
higher part of man's being, is rejected altogether, dismissed
with a sort of triumph, even with hatred. The world has
proclaimed the reign of freedom, especially of late, but what
do we see in this freedom of theirs? Nothing but slavery and
self-destruction!"

Yet, this is but one aspect of the novel. Accompanying it is
the awareness of a real world of human exploitation, and that
this must be changed. Never far from Dostoievsky's mind is
the suffering of the peasant masses, "the Russian peasant,
worn out by grief and toil, and still more by the everlasting
injustice and everlasting sin, his own and the world's." He
speaks of the "hard lot of the peasant women," who go back
to "exhausting toil too soon after hard, abnormal and un-
assisted labor in childbirth," who suffer from "hopeless
misery, and beatings." And it is not pity that Dostoievsky is
asking for. His insight is deeper, even prophetic. The Russian
peasant, he says, is moving toward an upheaval.

There is a remarkable picture by the painter Kramskoy, called "Contemplation." There is a forest in winter, and on a roadway through the forest, in absolute solitude, stands a peasant in a torn kaftan and bark shoes. He stands, as it were, lost in thought. Yet he is not thinking; he is "contemplating" . . . if he were asked what he had been thinking about, he would remember nothing. Yet probably he has hidden within himself the impressions which had dominated him during the period of contemplation. He may suddenly, after hoarding impressions for many years, abandon everything and go off to Jerusalem on a pilgrimage for his soul's salvation, or perhaps he will suddenly set fire to his native village, and perhaps do both. There are a good many "contemplatives" among the peasantry.

The dominating preachment in the book is that to abandon faith in God is to abandon all basis for morality. People are freed to do anything evil. Father Zossima says, "If it were not for the Church of Christ there would be nothing to restrain the criminal from evildoing." But the real "crime" haunting Dostoievsky's mind is not robbery, rape or murder. It is the fear that the disinherited and impoverished will rise against their oppressors. It is the attraction of socialism. With keen insight, he points out that the very science and rationalism with which the bourgeoisie had destroyed feudalism, could be used against them. Father Zossima says:

It is different with the upper classes. They, following reason, want to base justice on reason alone, but not with Christ, as before, and they have already proclaimed that there is no crime, that there is no sin. And that's consistent, for if you have no God what is the meaning of crime? In Europe the people are already rising up against the rich with violence, and the leaders of the people are everywhere leading them to bloodshed, and teaching them that wrath is righteous. But their "wrath is accursed, for it is cruel." But God will save Russia as He has saved her many times. Salvation will come from the people, from their faith and meekness.

And so Dostoievsky, who might have had the Paris Commune uprising of 1871 in mind, is not, like Kierkegaard, preaching faith in God as an answer to the "absurdity" of a world in which death overwhelms everything. He is preaching faith in God as an answer to socialism, and demanding that those with faith give the people—in real life, not the next world—what socialism promises. When he introduces Alyosha to the reader, he says, "If he had decided that God and immortality did not exist, he would at once have become an atheist and a socialist." Dostoievsky is always conscious of the power of the people. Father Zossima says, "The salvation of Russia comes from the people. And the Russian monk has always been on the side of the people." Dostoievsky here is really pleading that religion take the side of the people. In *The Brothers Karamazov*, he is sounding the alarm, pointing out what a seething cauldron Russia really is, and on how flimsy a base the pillars of authority stand.

Thus we can find existentialism in the complex genius of Dostoievsky. When the "I" of *Letters from the Underworld* rejects the "compulsion" of laws of nature and all outer "necessity," he is both paralleling Kierkegaard's attack on science and stating what would later be Camus's central argument against the assertion that there are laws of history. And Dostoievsky has also furnished an arsenal of weapons against liberals, social scientists, reformers and socialists. This appears not only in the diatribes he has put in the mouth of his characters, but also in his characterizations. Every scientific-minded critic of society is drawn as a cold-hearted rationalist, hypocrite, murderer or suicide. Central in Dostoievsky's political and social thinking is his impassioned insistence that such theorists cannot and do not ever really "love the people," nor can they feel any kinship with them. From Dostoievsky comes that perennial pious excuse for inaction, "To eliminate

evil from the world, it is first necessary to remove evil from
the human heart."

A quite different lesson, however, can be drawn from Dostoievsky, not asserted but latent in his art; the truth that the
greatness of an artist's mind, and therefore his art, lies in
the breadth of living social reality that he can make his own,
absorb and express in his art. He cannot encompass more
reality than his ideology permits; but this reality can become
part of a historical truth outreaching his limited ideology.
And so, his grasp of historical actualities provides the basis
for a critique of his own "existentialism." Typical of such
combination of insight and blindness is the character of Ivan
Karamazov. In this skeptic deliberately trying to destroy his
own human sympathies, Dostoievsky thought he was creating
a social reformer, an apostle of revolution. What he actually
created was a quite different personage who would move into
history, a sort of Nietzsche; the atheist existentialist who
retorts to the religious existentialist, "God is dead!"

There is a passage in *The Brothers Karamazov* where Ivan
is suffering from the hallucination that he is conversing with
the Devil, although he is actually debating his own skeptical
ideas. The Devil says, "Conscience! What is conscience? I
make it up for myself. Why am I tormented by it? From
habit. From the universal habit of mankind for the seven
thousand years. So let us give it up, and we shall be gods."
And it is Nietzsche's thesis that man has to be liberated from
"conscience," from Christian morality, which he terms "slave
morality," and that this liberation will be carried on by a new
breed of leaders, or "supermen."

5

NIETZSCHE: *The Myth and the Unconscious*

Nietzsche can be quoted for quite opposite attitudes; as one who gave a fresh ideological impetus to anti-Semitism, and as a critic of anti-Semites; as a German nationalist, jingo, and proto-fascist, and as a critic of jingos; as one who exalted aristocracy, and one who scorned the Junkers and aristocrats in the German government of his time; as an atheist, who proclaimed in *Thus Spake Zarathustra* "God is dead," and as a religious thinker who upheld "myth" against science. Nor is this confusion a simple matter of misreading him. So ardent a disciple of Nietzsche as the modern German existentialist philosopher, Karl Jaspers, writes of him in *Reason and Existenz*: "His effect in Germany was like that of no other philosopher. But it seems as though every world-view, every conviction, claims him as authority. It might be that none of us really knows what this thought includes and does."[1]

But Nietzsche is not quite so baffling when put into his social and historical context. There, what seems so contradictory when read as eternal truth or pure inspiration, takes on the contours of an understandable response to a real dilemma or conflict. Nietzsche influenced so many rebellious artistic minds of the late 19th and early 20th centuries because he spoke in the tone of a revolutionist. He appeared to be gleefully and derisively exploding all the outmoded conventions and moral hypocrisies of official society, and calling for an ecstatic "welcome to life." And yet, in a polemic which took all society and history in its scope, he wrote without any

grasp of the real history of society, of the way people worked
and lived in the Germany of his time, of the actual forces
operating the German state. It is this revolutionizing "in the
air" that makes him sound like an inspired prophet whose
words, however, can be used for the most dire, reactionary
ends.

Not only in Germany, but in many other countries, such
figures began to appear at the time; sensitive, original, perceptive minds, highly cultured in certain fields, capable of
keen psychological insights, yet in social, scientific and political matters, including the very forces shaping the world
they judged so sweepingly, approaching what the classic
Greeks, or the philosophers of the "Enlightenment," would
have called "idiots." An American contemporary who could
be cited is the gifted and dedicated novelist, Henry James.
But James was an exception. More characteristic of the period
were the veteran Mark Twain, and others like Garland,
Howells, Crane, Norris and Dreiser, who were embarking on
the keenest critical study of what was doing in America, and
creating the first great body of American literary critical
and social realism.

In Germany, the atmosphere was different. There had been
a German tradition of the "Enlightenment," in which Kant,
Lessing, Schiller, Goethe, Hegel had belonged. Beethoven
read the "forbidden" books of Voltaire. But with the defeat
of Napoleon, the autocratic state of Prussia took increasing
leadership in Germany, continuing serfdom, reviving anti-
Semitism, stifling the ideas of the "Age of Reason." If Marx
and Engels carried on the spirit of the "Enlightenment,"
giving it a new rational development in terms of capitalist
society, they were soon forced into exile. Arthur Schopenhauer
(1788-1860) provided in *The World as Will and Idea* (1818)
what would soon become a highly influential philosophical
attack on reason, exalting the blind and unconscious "Will"

over knowledge, and proclaiming the "futility" of life. Despising science, his own temperament leaned towards spiritualism and magic. There had been a democratic revolutionary movement in Germany in 1848-49, in which Marx and Engels played an active and heroic role, but it had been crushed due to the weakness of the middle class. And so Germany became a unified nation without an anti-feudal revolution, Prussia creating a German state run by an autocratic emperor, the feudal-minded Junker military caste, the bankers and the Krupp armament works. In 1870 the "new Germany" defeated France, which had been corrupted by the Second Empire of Louis Napoleon. Then the German army joined with the French reactionaries to crush the Paris Commune, which had sought to set up a genuine democratic republic.

In the new German Empire, with the Junkers running the army and the great steel and armament combines running the economy, the course was being set for a challenge to the earlier arrived nations, like England and France, for their colonies, spheres of investment, markets and sources of raw materials. Intellectual life and philosophy tended toward a tacit surrender to militarism, a surrender taking the form of a professed concentration exclusively on things "of the spirit." It rejected "materialism," ignored the real problems of the people as not worthy of an intellectual's consideration, and agreed that politics had best be left to the politicians.

To the tradition of "disillusion with the concept of progress," Nietzsche adds something new, which was born out of the defeat of the democratic revolts in 1848-49, and the formation of the German state under reactionary auspices. It is a furious disillusion with the common people, the masses of humanity. The attitude is that of a person who, viewing himself as a revolutionist in spirit, feels "let down" by the masses. Consequently, his attitude toward the "Enlightenment" differs from Kierkegaard's, to whom it appeared as an evil rationalism that had destroyed "faith." To Nietzsche, the "Enlightenment" was a high-minded but illusory view of life, deluding itself by not realizing the hopeless baseness of most mankind. Thus he wrote in *Beyond Good and Evil* (1885), commenting on Beethoven, "There is spread over his music the twilight of eternal loss and extravagant hope—this same light in which Europe was bathed when it dreamed with Rousseau, when it danced around the Tree of Liberty of the Revolution, and finally almost fell down in adoration before Napoleon."[2]

This is not quite what happened in history. The French people in 1789-93 demolished a store of useless feudal furniture. If they didn't create Utopia, to Nietzsche's disappointment, they did create, in 1793, the most enlightened constitution that had appeared up to that time. The middle class, frightened by its democratic provisions, turned against its allies, the working class and the "left," and so weakened the republic that Napoleon was able to take over. And it was the aristocracy of Europe, after Napoleon beat them, more than the masses, that fell down in homage before him. Napoleon's triumphant career was first turned back in Spain by the popular uprising of national liberation against his invading armies and it was the guerrilla war in Russia that broke his powers. After his downfall, the "Holy Alliance" tried to turn back the clock of European history, but through the 19th century, nevertheless, the people swept three French monarchs off their thrones.

It suits Nietzsche's anger and frustration, however, to see himself as a lonely rebel among a mass of human sheep. Disdaining to examine what really happened in history, he relies on his own intuition, or in effect generalizes out of his own disillusion. Subjectivism becomes "truth." In this spirit he creates for himself the pattern of the "individual as revolutionist." As he proclaimed in *Thus Spake Zarathustra* (1883-

92), "Not to the people is Zarathustra to speak, but to companions! Zarathustra shall not be the herd's herdsman and hound. . . . Not any more will I discourse unto the people!" This prophetlike self-exaltation is the counterpart to the sweeping generalization of history.

In Nietzsche's first major work, *The Birth of Tragedy from the Spirit of Music* (1872), he already projected such an all-embracing view of human history. It is a "psychological" interpretation of history which not only expressed Nietzsche's own existentialism, or "tragic view of life," but was to provide hints to Freud and Jung for their theory of the all-powerful "unconscious."

That book purports to be a study of the Greek tragic drama of the fifth century B.C. But even this examination proceeds subjectively, for the aim of the book is really to harness these classics to the chariot of Nietzsche's cultural hero, Richard Wagner, whose opera-dramas drew upon German "myth." Great advances had been made in the knowledge of ancient Greek life, society and art, but Nietzsche arrogantly dismisses them as the pedantry of scholars, by whom "the ragged tatters of ancient tradition are sewn together in various combinations and torn apart again."[3] There is no hint, in Nietzsche's tract, of what life was like in Athens, of the conditions under which drama grew, of the remarkable revolutionary achievement in creating the world's first democratic institutions, of the notable Greek leaps in scientific inquiry; let alone the effect all these must have had on the exaltation of human powers which Greek art so movingly expresses. Nietzsche even has little to say about the dramas he claims to be discussing. The lineaments of Aeschylus and Sophocles remain cloudy, and as for the realistic-minded Euripides who was skeptical of myth, he fits the Wagner image so badly that Nietzsche castigates him as a politician and betrayer of true tragedy.

Nietzsche's thesis is that there are two forces in the human mind, or two kinds of mentality, the Dionysian and the Apollonian. The Dionysian is closely responsive to nature, instinctive, irrational, passionate, primitive and tragic. It is "folk-wisdom." It expresses itself in and creates "myth." It creates music and lyric poetry, which are instinctive forms of art. The Apollonian is a reflection of life through thought, transforming life into a dream of lucid, harmonious form and beauty. It is the "art-impulse" and creates the pantheon of gods on Olympus, as well as the structured art of drama and sculpture. The Dionysian is fundamental truth, ever-present in the mind, but not as conscious thought, for it is instinctive; man "as nature." The Apollonian illusion, however, is necessary so that man can continue to live in the face of the tragic truth of life, which is suffering and death.

The Greek knew and felt the terror and horror of existence. That he might endure this terror at all, he had to interpose between himself and life the radiant dream-birth of the Olympians. That overwhelming dismay in the face of the titanic powers of nature, the Moira enthroned inexorably over all knowledge, the vulture of the great lover of mankind, Prometheus . . . all this was again and again overcome by the Greeks with the aid of the Olympian *middle world* of art; or at any rate it was veiled and withdrawn from sight. It was out of the direst necessity to live that the Greeks created these gods.[4]

Tragedy, Nietzsche says, while a creation of the Apollonian impulse, achieves greatness and truth because it also embraces the Dionysian.

In the collective effort of tragedy, the Dionysian once again dominates. And the Apollonian illusion thereby reveals itself as what it really is—the assiduous veiling during the performance of the tragedy of the intrinsically Dionysian effect; which, however, is so powerful, that it ends by forcing the Apollonian drama itself into a sphere where it begins to talk with Dionysian wisdom, and even denies itself and its Apollonian consciousness. Dionysius speaks the language of Apollo; Apollo, however, finally speaks the language of Dionysius; and so the highest goal of tragedy and of art in general is attained.[5]

Nietzsche's view of "no progress," in which myth is "truth" and which fixes man in the cave age, is the diametric opposite of the view of Marx and Engels, who find that human beings started as little different from the rest of the animal kingdom, but that each step in the mastery of the laws of nature, of society and of the human mind, each step in knowledge, was a step to freedom. To Nietzsche, such steps, like science which fosters the mastery of nature, and the increasingly rational organization of society, like democracy, only cut man off from his natural and instinctive roots. They censor and repress the instinctive, Dionysian impulses.

Nietzsche castigates realism and democracy in his treatment of Euripides' plays. Through Euripides, Nietzsche says, "the average man forced his way from the spectators' benches on to the stage itself; the mirror in which formerly only grand and bold traits were represented now showed the painful fidelity that conscientiously reproduces even the abortive outlines of nature." Euripides gave tragedy over to the "commonplace."

Civil mediocrity, on which Euripides built all his political hopes, was now given a voice, while heretofore the demigod in tragedy and the drunken satyr, or demiman, in comedy, had determined the character of the language. And so the Aristophanean Euripides prides himself on having portrayed the common, familiar, everyday life and activities of the people, about which all are qualified to pass judgment. If now the entire population philosophizes, manages land and goods and conducts lawsuits with unheard-of circumspection, the glory is all his, together with the wisdom with which he has inoculated the rabble.[6]

Science, which attempts "to make existence seem intelligible, and therefore justified," Nietzsche says, only suffers from a powerful illusion which "hastens irresistibly to its limits, on which its optimism, hidden in the essence of its logic, is wrecked." The scientist runs up against the "unfathomable." And so, "When to his dismay he here sees how logic coils round itself at these limits and finally bites its own tail— then the new form of perception rises to view, namely *tragic perception*, which, in order even to be endured, requires art as protection and remedy."[7]

Nietzsche misses one of the most valuable lessons to be drawn from Greek classic art, one confirmed by the Renaissance and by the arts in Europe from the 17th century through the 19th, that of the close ties between science and art. It is not that art becomes "scientific," or science becomes "artistic." It is that an advance in the scientific exploration of the outer world and natural law, studying the world in its own terms, is accompanied by an advance in the artistic exploration of the human being, his personality, mind and social relations, in their own terms. Each reflects, in its own way, a stage in human freedom. If science opens up a "brave new world," art reflects it in new-born human personalities. And if art raises unsolved problems, so does science. Neither art nor science presents a "closed" view of reality. If science presents real tools for reshaping the world, art reveals the human repercussions of the use of these tools.

But to Nietzsche, science is the purely rational, the optimistic, the illusory. Art is fundamentally tied to the irrational, tragic, Dionysian reality. From the realistic historical view, one of the achievements of the Greeks, inspired by both their science and their bold reshaping of their society, was their great stride out of the ignorance and fears of primitive myth, recasting their legends and gods to take on the lineaments of real people in real social situations; in other words, the rationality which makes their art "classic." But to Nietzsche, primitivism is "truth."

Before leaving the poetically written tract, it is worth noticing how much it prefigures Freud and Jung. Freud, seeking some overall psychological scheme into which to fit and make "eternal" his keen observations of the aberrations and inhibitions of love relations in bourgeois society, posited, very much like Nietzsche's "Dionysian mind," an all-powerful "unconscious," the home of the "instincts," the mind close to nature, almost nature itself. It is the center of the life forces, of sexuality, of, in Freud's term, the "id." The Apollonian "dream" of a harmonious world, the impulse to ordered creation, can be translated into Freud's "sublimation." The Nietzschean tragic sense of life becomes the "death wish." Just as to Nietzsche, science, rationality, knowledge, all the products of civilization and the developing mastery of the world, social relations and democracy, were dangerous to the Dionysian instinctive life, so to Freud, these are society's "censorships" and "repressions," creating the "Superego," or the guilty conscience. While Freud was more directly influenced by Schopenhauer than by Nietzsche, Jung abandoned Freud's sexual patterns of the "unconscious," and presented a purer Nietzschean doctrine. To him, the ancient myths and primitive beliefs represented the archetypal forms of the mind, eternally present in the "collective unconscious" of human beings, hidden sometimes by rationality, civilization, science, but always fundamental, untouchable, and therefore "truth." Let us consider this passage from Jung's essay, *Psychology and Literature*:

It is not alone the creator of this kind of art who is in touch with the night-side of life, but the seers, prophets, leaders and enlighteners also. However dark this nocturnal world may be, it is not wholly unfamiliar. Man has known of it from time immemorial—here, there and everywhere; for primitive man it is an unquestionable part of his picture of the cosmos. It is only we who have repudiated it because of our fear of superstition and metaphysics, and because we strive to construct a conscious world that is safe and manageable in that natural law holds in it the place of statute law in a commonwealth. Yet, even in our midst, the poet now and then catches sight of the figures that people the night-world—the spirits, demons and gods. . . . In short, he sees something of that psychic world that strikes terror into the savage and the barbarian.[8]

To Jung, at each time of crisis in the world, this "collective unconscious" breaks through the veneer laid over it by science, reason and civilization. "The World War was such an inruption which showed, as nothing else could, how thin are the walls which separate a well-ordered world from lurking chaos. But it is at the same time with every single human being and his reasonably ordered world. His reason has done violence to natural forces which seek their revenge and only await the moment when the partition falls to overwhelm the conscious life with destruction."[9]

Now here is Nietzsche, speaking of the "German character." What he gave, not only to Jung but to fascist propaganda, is obvious.

All our hopes stretch longingly towards the perception that beneath this restlessly palpitating civilized life and educational convulsion there is concealed a glorious, intrinsically healthy, primitive power, which, to be sure, stirs vigorously only at intervals in stupendous moments, and then continues to dream of future awakening. It is from this abyss that the German Reformation came forth: in the choral-hymn of which the future melody of German music first resounded. So deep, courageous, and spiritual, so exuberantly good and tender did this chorale of Luther sound—as the first Dionysian luring call breaking forth from dense thickets at the approach of spring. To it responded with emulative echo the solemnly wanton procession of Dionysian revelers, to whom we are indebted for German music—and to whom we shall be indebted for *the rebirth of the German myth.*[10]

Like Nietzsche, Freud and Jung ignored or discarded the available knowledge of social life, economics, history, and all the real forces at work in the world. The quarrel raised here

is not with their purely psychological data, recording the conflicts and problems in bourgeois society in crisis, but with the
world view they erected on these problems, taking them as
patterns of the mind fixed for all time. Similarly behind
Nietzsche's sweeping generalizations, it is not hard to find
the lineaments of the bourgeois world he hated.

The real insight, the core of truth in Nietzsche, is his perception that underlying the bourgeois pretensions to morality,
to rational behavior, to concern for social and human welfare,
is the ruthless, greedy, competitive war for profit. Marx had
put it this way, discussing the operation of economic laws in
capitalism: "The only wheels which political economy sets in
motion are avarice and the war amongst the avaricious—competition."[11] Nietzsche, however, generalizes the practical
amorality of the master class—familiar in America as the mentality of the "robber barons"—into an eternal law of the
human heart and mind. It is "the Will to Power." His "revolutionary" solution is to separate this from avarice. He writes
in *Beyond Good and Evil*: "A living thing seeks above all to
discharge its strength—life itself is Will to Power. . . . The
world seen from within, the world defined and designated
according to its "intelligible character"—it would simply be
"Will to Power," and nothing else."[12]

Nietzsche's thinking then moves as follows. Since the "Will
to Power" is the secret of life, it cannot be denied. Some feel
it and follow it, others don't. The few who do are the masters,
the true aristocrats; the rest are slaves. Morality, conscience,
Christianity, democracy, are all inventions of the "slaves";
attempts to crush the life-giving force in the masters. To
Nietzsche modern history is the slow, evil, steady encroach-
ment of the "slave masses," with their shallow optimism,
their belief in cooperation and in alleviating each other's
poverty and misery, their faith in social progress, their appeals
to "conscience" and to the morality of care for another human

being, against the true aristocrats. The aristocrats are the born masters, who feel and express the "Will to Power," who stand for and welcome life, who alone have the capacity for real "suffering" since theirs is the underlying tragic awareness of life.

This fantasy-history was not meant by Nietzsche to serve the aggrandizement and power of Bismarck, or the Hohenzollerns, or the Junker landowners, or the Krupps and German bankers, who were not considered by him "true aristocrats." Nietzsche considers himself a revolutionist. The people, he thinks, have failed him by being weak, sheeplike, afraid. It is the individual who will have to carry through the reorganization of society. He envisions a "superman" or "overman" hero, a true aristocrat, a combination of artist, prophet, philosopher and commander. In his writings, as he says in *Beyond Good and Evil*, he, Nietzsche, will inspire "the rearing of a new ruling caste for Europe."[13] As for the qualifications of this new ruler, he must be a kind of barbarian-artist. That is, he possesses, recognizes and acts by the "Will to Power." However, he does not do this for his own enrichment. His mission is to be a leader in the world he will liberate. Science is not for him. In fact, as Nietzsche writes in *Beyond Good and Evil*, one of the virtues of such an "aristocrat" is his ignorance, since knowledge interferes with the "creative" impulse.

The gulf between knowledge and capacity is perhaps greater, and also more mysterious than one thinks: the capable man in the grand style, the creator, will possibly have to be an ignorant person;—while on the other hand, for scientific discoveries like those of Darwin, a certain narrowness, aridity, and industrious carefulness (in short, something English) may not be unfavorable for arriving at them.[14]

That Nietzsche sees himself, the unappreciated, unrecognized prophet, as one of the true "aristocrats," is evident in his late, autobiographical book, *Ecce Homo*, the very title of which links him to the persecuted Jesus Christ. The book is full of the most astonishing self-praise, like "Why do I know more than other people?" or "Some day men will declare of Heine and myself that we were by far the greatest of all artists in the German language," or "my works bespeak a psychologist who has not his peer." Nietzsche apologizes to the reader for having made Wagner the hero of *The Birth of Tragedy*. It was really himself whom he should have praised. "Speaking psychologically, all the significant traits of my own character are presented as belonging to Wagner—the juxtaposition of the most lucid and fateful forces, a Will to Power such as no man has yet possessed, reckless spiritual courage, an unlimited capacity to learn without any corresponding diminution of capacity for action."[15]

Being thus, in his own eyes, the true revolutionist and rebel, Nietzsche in *Beyond Good and Evil* must wield his thunderbolts against all the false—to him—theories of progress, democracy, social welfare, that rest their hopes on the common people. "Where the populace eat and drink, and even where they reverence, it is accustomed to stink."

Christianity to him is "the sacrifice of all freedom, all pride, all self-confidence of spirit; it is at the same time subjection, self-derision, and self-mutilation." But he advises the true masters, those who are strong and independent, destined and trained to command, in whom the judgment and skill of a ruling race is incorporated, to use religion to keep the people in subjection. "Religion itself may be used as a means for obtaining peace from the noise and trouble of managing grosser affairs, and for securing immunity from the unavoidable filth of all political agitation." He attacks democracy as an outgrowth of Christianity, both being examples of the "herding-animal morality" now being found in "peacefully industrious democrats and Revolution-ideologues," as well as in "the awkward philosophasters and fraternity-visionaries who call themselves Socialists and want a 'free society.'" The only society these people plan, he says, is that of the "autonomous herd."

We, who regard the democratic movement, not only as a degenerating form of political organization, but as equivalent to a degenerating, a waning type of man, as involving his mediocrising and depreciation: where have we to fix our hopes? In new philosophers—there is no other alternative: in minds strong and original enough to initiate opposite estimates of value . . . in forerunners, in men of the future, who in the present shall fix the constraints and fasten the knots which will compel milleniums to take new paths.[16]

In describing the philosophy and views of life that will imbue these "new philosophers," the "supermen" of the future, Nietzsche ridicules the Marxist view that people can cooperate, that the working class will eliminate all exploitation of one class by another:

Life itself is essentially appropriation, injury, conquest of the strange and weak, suppression, severity, obtrusion of peculiar forms, incorporation, and at the least, putting it mildly, exploitation;—but why should one forever use precisely those words on which for ages a disparaging purpose has been stamped? . . . people now rave everywhere, even under the guise of science, about coming conditions of society in which "the exploiting character" is to be absent: —that sounds to my ears as if they promised to invent a mode of life which should refrain from all organic functions. "Exploitation" does not belong to a depraved, or imperfect and primitive society: it belongs to the nature of the living being as a primary organic function; it is a consequence of the intrinsic Will to Power, which is precisely the Will to Life.[17]

In *The Genealogy of Morals* (1887), Nietzsche implemented these thoughts with an invented history of Europe, and in the process, provided a virulent new ideology for anti-Semitism. The basis for his peculiar chauvinism had been laid

in *The Birth of Tragedy*, where he had invented a "pure"
German "character" or "spirit" based on German "myth."
Whether he meant by this something so crazy as that the
German people of his time represented a pure-blooded race
in direct descent from the early Germanic tribes, it is impossible to say, for Nietzsche here, as always, ignores historical
data. However, he insists on this purity. "So highly do we
rate the pure and vigorous kernel of the German character
that from it alone may we venture to expect this elimination
of forcibly ingrafted elements."[18] In this earlier book, where
Nietzsche gloried in the victory over France, the "foreign"
element referred to was the "Romanic," or in other words,
French (racially as mixed as the Germans). Now, in *The
Genealogy of Morals*, it is the Jews. He gives a new twist to
medieval anti-Semitism which, ignoring the fact that the early
Christians had considered Christ and themselves to be Jews,
indicts the Jews as the killers of Christ. To Nietzsche now,
the Jews conspired to invent Christianity out of hatred for the
Gentiles. To revenge themselves, they decided to transmute
all values and invented a slave-morality.

It was the Jews who, in opposition to the aristocratic equation
(good equals aristocratic equals beautiful equals happy equals
loved by the gods) dared with a terrifying logic to suggest the contrary equation . . . namely, "the wretched alone are the good; the
poor, the weak, the lowly, are alone the good; the suffering, the
needy, the sick, the loathesome, are the only ones who are pious,
the only ones who are blessed, for them alone is salvation—but
you, on the other hand, you aristocrats, you men of power, you are
to all eternity the evil, the horrible, the covetous, the insatiate, the
godless."[19]

Then, Nietzsche goes on, the Jews killed Christ to pretend
that he was their adversary, and so to entrap the Gentiles into
following Christ's teachings. "Is it not due to the black magic
of a really great policy of revenge, of a far-seeing, burrowing

revenge, both acting and calculating with slowness, that Israel himself must repudiate before all the world the actual instrument of his own revenge and nail it to the cross, so that all the world—that is, all the enemies of Israel—could nibble without suspicion at this very bait?"

The truth which these Jewish-Christian teachings tried to obscure, Nietzsche says, is that the "Will to Power" is the guiding principle of history, as it is of the organization of society. "I used the word 'State'; my meaning is self-evident, namely a herd of blond beasts of prey, a race of conquerors and masters, which with all its war-like organization and all its organizing power pounces with its terrible claws on a population, in numbers possibly tremendously superior, but as yet formless, as yet nomad. Such is the origin of the 'State.' That fantastic theory that makes it begin with a contract is, I think, disposed of."

In the last words, Nietzsche is referring to Rousseau's theory of the "social contract" as the foundation of the state; a theory which, historically, is no more factual than Nietzsche's, but the importance of which lay in the affirmation that the justification of all government rests on the agreement of the governed. To Nietzsche, the organization of society will always be a dictatorship of the blond beasts, except that he proceeds to transform them into the supermen, the artists-philosophers-commanders of the future. "They are ignorant of the meaning of guilt, responsibility, consideration, are these born organizers; in them predominates that terrible artist-egoism, that gleams like brass, and that knows itself justified to all eternity, in its work, even, as a mother in her child."[20]

Ironically, Nietzsche's visionary "revolution" provided exactly the ideology needed to carry through the fake "revolution" of German fascism. It was no revolution since the same great steel, armament and chemical trusts and combines, and the same banks, that had dominated the German economy before the coming of fascism, also dominated it under fascism. There was the same contempt for democracy as a form of "decadence," the glorification of the born "commanders," the scorn for humanitarianism, for any concern over the plight of the poor and exploited, and for socialism. All were attacked as manifestations of "sentimentality," "slave morality," or "herd philosophy." There was the same glorification of the "Will to Power," which became a justification of ruthless violence. There was the same exaltation of a mystical racial "character," the turn to tribal myths as "truths" of the German spirit. There was anti-Semitism, which gloatingly proposed the extirpation of the Jews as alien, destructive intruders.

For the decade or more of the Third Reich's ascendancy, it seemed to many, in Germany and elsewhere, that Nietzsche had spoken "truth." This "truth" was however resoundingly refuted by the debacle of fascism. The forces of democracy, of socialism, of people with conscience and humanity, proved to have more strength than the strutting master race, the "supermen," the born "commanders" of the "herd." But today, in the wave of existentialist writing and philosophizing, a rehabilitation of Nietzsche as thinker, prophet and "liberator" is being undertaken.

Some of this rehabilitation is done on a very low level, exploiting "cold war" prejudices and characterizing socialism in terms lifted out of fascist propaganda manuals. Thus Jean T. Wilde and William Kimmel, editors of an existentialist anthology, *The Search for Being*, claim that Nietzsche offers freedom from "those historico-eschatological prejudices which place mendacious limits and duties on man and divest him of the power of free choice, and which lead him into dishonesty, irresponsibility, sluggishness and cowardly submission before any Molochlike futuristic idol—be it of the socialistic, classless society or of the Christian, heavenly brand." At a time when the great problems facing humanity are the elimination of starvation, poverty and war—social problems which can only be dealt with socially—they invoke Nietzsche to assure people that they must "heroically" renounce any collective action with their fellow human beings and thus assert their "individual freedom." Nietzsche, they say, "stood out as a lonely champion of health and sanity."[21] Since in the very excerpt they offer from Nietzsche, he remarks that life should be "guided not by science, but by instincts and powerful illusions," and "science makes us speak of 'poisons,'" we wonder what they mean by "sanity." Furthermore, since nowhere in the book is there any mention of fascism—not even in the discussion of Heidegger, who was an open propagandist for it—we wonder what they mean by "honesty."

On a higher level are the writings of Walter Kaufmann. Kaufmann's own philosophy leans toward a Nietzschean "elitism," a disdain for democracy and for the mass of people. The following remarks from his book, *From Shakespeare to Existentialism*, are quite typical.

> Shakespeare's tragic world view is ignored not only by those critics who are much too democratic to allow for the bare possibility that our greatest poet might have felt such a profound contempt for most men. . . . Shakespeare, like the Greeks before him and Nietzsche after him, believed neither in progress nor in original sin; he believed that most men merited contempt.[22]

We might question the kind of historical sense which examines Shakespeare on political democracy before there was a glimmer of such a development in Europe. Furthermore, considering the warmhearted affection Shakespeare shows for the common people, as in the soldiers to whom King Henry V talks on the eve of the battle of Agincourt, or the sailors in the first scene of *The Tempest*; considering the tre-

mendous sweep of his interest in people from all walks of
life; considering how carefully he shows even the greatest
villains as human beings, not monsters; considering a King
Lear who discovers, when he himself is in rags, that he should
have been more aware of the miseries of the poor; it would
seem not that Shakespeare had "contempt for most men,"
but the opposite. Kaufmann appears to be hitching Shakespeare, like Nietzsche, to his own cart. But Kaufmann is an
opponent of fascism and in his discussions of Nietzsche, is
at least aware of its links with Nietzscheanism.

Kaufmann claims that Nietzsche has been widely misin-
terpreted, and ignores the fact that what he calls "misinter-
pretations" are based on the preponderant weight of what
Nietzsche himself said. In the case of a great dramatic poet
like Shakespeare, it is easy enough to misinterpret him by
taking passages out of the mouths of his characters and claiming that these are Shakespeare's own opinions. In fact, it
is precisely through such an out-of-context selection that
Kaufmann bolsters his claim that Shakespeare had "contempt
for most men." But with a philosopher writing in his own
voice, we must assume that he means to say what he says.
Kaufmann's method, however, is to "interpret" Nietzsche
into meaning something quite opposite to what he says. For
example, in his *Nietzsche*, Kaufmann discusses the concepts
of the Apollonian and the Dionysian: "In *The Birth of
Tragedy* Nietzsche did not extol one at the expense of the
other; but if he favors one of the two gods, it is Apollo."
But if we read Nietzsche's book itself, we find that he continually refers to the Apollonian as the "illusion," the "dream,"
while the Dionysian "barbarism" is "truth," "man returned
to nature," "reality," "tragic wisdom," the "true nature of
things."

We can reconcile this with Kaufmann's interpretation
only if we add that Nietzsche believes that people should

be given lies, not truth, illusions, not reality. Perhaps Kaufmann believes this too. But then, how can Kaufmann make Nietzsche into a scientist?

Nietzsche, no less than Hegel, wanted philosophy to become scientific, *wissenschaftlich*—but science did not mean the same to both thinkers. To Hegel it meant above all the rigor of a system which he opposed to the romantics' sentimental enthusiasm. . . . Nietzsche did not want philosophy to be less scientific than this but rather more so; only he had in mind the "gay science" of fearless experiment and the good will to accept new evidence and to abandon previous positions, if necessary.[23]

Now, science is not a word to be given different and arbitrary meanings. What it means is established, not by Hegel or Nietzsche, but by age-long work and achievements. It means the examination of the real world in its own terms, and the use of the scientific method, the gathering and classification of data, the experiment to disclose new data, the formation of general laws, the testing of these laws to see whether they consistently produce the expected results. This is how Hegel sees it, and this is also how Nietzsche sees it when, in *The Birth of Tragedy*, he dismisses it with contempt, as the belief which "attributes to knowledge and perception the power of a universal panacea, and in error sees evil itself."[24] The scientific method also includes, by its very nature, "fearless experiment," the eagerness to find "new evidence," and the willingness to change all previous positions. By citing these latter as Nietzsche's special contribution, apparently not found in Hegel, Kaufmann only sets up a straw man. We have noticed Nietzsche's contempt for Darwin—"a certain narrowness, aridity"—and yet Darwin showed exactly this fearlessness and willingness to change deep-rooted ideas.

Furthermore, where in Nietzsche can any "fearless experiment" be found? Where, in all his wild speculations about

history and society, with their blissful reliance on pure intuition and total disregard for historical data, is there any
acceptance of "new evidence," or any interest in "evidence"
at all?

By making philosophy "scientific," Hegel meant that however abstract its terms and formulations, philosophy had to
be based on the actualities of life and history, and that its
statements had to form as rigorous a logical structure of relations as the theoretical structures of science. It is the opposite
to Nietzsche's way of philosophy, that of pure intuition and
the transformation of subjective feelings into "eternal truths."
Reason itself, Nietzsche wrote in *Ecce Homo,* was a "dangerous, life-undermining force."[25]

If Kaufmann had acknowledged that Nietzsche disregarded
accumulated data and scientific disciplines, but claimed that
being a man of genius, he had perceptions and intuitions
worth scientific consideration, he would have a point. But
this would not make Nietzsche into a scientist or admirer of
science.

As to Nietzsche's encouragement of anti-Semitism, Kaufmann ascribes this influence to Nietzsche's sister Elizabeth,
who took over her brother's papers in the years of insanity
that preceded his death. She and her husband were rabid,
practising anti-Semites, while Nietzsche refrained from this.
But Kaufmann overlooks the fact that it was Nietzsche's own
writings that proved so useful for the purpose. Kaufmann
quotes a letter of Nietzsche, "It is a matter of honor to me
to be in relation to anti-Semitism absolutely clean and un-
equivocal, namely *opposed,* as I am in my writings." Yet
Kaufmann overlooks the point, crucial to an understanding
of Nietzsche, that Nietzsche objected not to anti-Semitic
prejudices but to anti-Semitic practices. Thus he resembled
his compatriot Wagner, who wrote diatribes against the Jews
as the defilers of German art but chose them to conduct

his music because they were better at this than anybody else.

So in *Beyond Good and Evil*, Nietzsche seems to criticize anti-Semitism. "Among present-day Germans there is alternately the anti-French folly, the anti-Semitic folly, the anti-Polish folly, the Christian romantic folly, the Wagnerian folly, the Teutonic folly, the Prussian folly."

Only a few lines later, however, Nietzsche says that while anti-Semitism should not be carried to excess, the Jews are really a despicable race and menace to Germany.

I have never yet met a German who was favorably inclined to the Jews; and however decided the repudiation of actual anti-Semitism may be on the part of all prudent and political men, this prudence and policy is not perhaps directed against the nature of the sentiment itself, but only against its dangerous excess, and especially against the distasteful and infamous expression of this excess of sentiment. That Germany has amply sufficient Jews, that the German stomach, the German blood, has difficulty (and will long have difficulty) in disposing only of this quantity of "Jew" . . . that is the unmistakeable declaration and language of a general instinct, to which one must listen and according to which one must act.[26]

What becomes clear is the real contradiction in Nietzsche's mind. It is the contradiction between his own ideas, and the revolting aspect they assumed when people began carrying them out. Thus he can voice the most virulent anti-Semitic and racist ideas, giving weapons to anti-Semitism, and yet express his loathing for the practising anti-Semites. Similarly, moved by Wagner's music, he could hail him as the great artist-egoist after the Nietzschean model, and then show revulsion against Wagner's actual life as an artist-egoist. He could derogate democracy and praise an aristocracy and "master race," and be revolted by the behavior of the actual aristocratic "commanders" of Germany. But never did this clash between his ideas and what happened when they were taken as a way of life impel him to examine his own ideas critically.

We can look upon Nietzsche as a sensitive mind at odds with his times, recoiling from his glimpses of the ruthless struggle for power underlying the pretensions to civilization, but unable to discern the real nature of the social problems and formations that troubled him. Accepting this competitive struggle as an "eternal truth" of the human mind, he linked it to his own frustrations, and expressed his subjective resentment toward this world which he abused in a gigantic Wagnerian fantasy pieced out of misapplied past philosophies and cultures. We can also be impressed by and even admire the frankness with which he laid open his own mind. But in a critical analysis, it is not the man who is "on trial." It is of the ideas that we must ask what it means to live by them. And that Nietzsche even in his own time, glimpsed something of the answer to this with horror is one of the most poignant aspects of his life, as well as a commentary on his thought. Since then, the corpses strewn all over Europe and at last over Germany itself by the Third Reich, should suggest some care in propagating Nietzsche's thinking today, and some honesty in facing its consequences.

Walter Kaufmann tries to turn Nietzsche into a great, liberating moralist, writing in a chapter entitled, "How Nietzsche Revolutionized Ethics":

The will to power is, according to Nietzsche, a universal drive, found in all men. . . . Indeed, Nietzsche thinks that all human behavior is reducible to this single basic force. He does not endorse the will to power any more than Freud endorses sexual desire; but he thinks we shall be better off if we face the facts and understand ourselves than if we condemn others hypocritically, without understanding.[27]

It is as if a thinker were to announce that fascism is deep and permanent in the human heart, that the urge to dominate others signifies strength of mind, that those who oppose it are mere sentimentalists or weak and timid characters. Following Kaufmann's logic, such a thinker would not be "for fascism." He does not "endorse" it. He only says that it is inevitable, that it is useless to oppose it, and hypocritical to condemn it. Kaufmann's argument is only for Nietzsche's sincerity. His own elitist view of humanity is too close to Nietzsche's for him to be able to examine critically whether Nietzsche speaks truth.

There is a passage in *The Birth of Tragedy* in which Nietzsche seems to foresee with joy the coming of German fascism. He is writing about the "battle" to eliminate from the German spirit "forcibly ingrafted foreign elements." This will be carried on further, he says, by a return to German "myth" and to the barbaric, primitive, irrational Dionysian mentality:

> But let him never think he can fight such battles without the household gods, without his mythical home, without a "restoration" of all things German! And if the German should be looking around timidly for a guide to lead him back to his long-lost home, whose ways and paths he hardly knows any longer—let him listen to the ecstatic luring call of the Dionysian bird, which hovers above him, and would fain point the way for him.[28]

It is quite possible that Nietzsche would not have liked Adolf Hitler or Alfred Rosenberg, would have resented their borrowings from his works, and would not have recognized them as the "new philosophers," supermen, or Dionysian myth-creators he had been speaking of. But the fact remains that he helped create the intellectual climate by which a host of artists, philosophers, thinkers, students, professors, accepted the militarism of the First World War and the coming of fascism without a murmur or finger lifted. Some quietly minded "their own business" while doing without enthusiasm what was asked of them. Others served and propagandized for war and German fascism. Their thinking in many cases was, why not conform to this movement if this was the truth of life, the "Will to Power," or the

"German myth" manifesting itself? And these were by no means stupid minds.

There was, for example, Richard Strauss, the composer, whose homage to Nietzsche was paid in the tone-poem *Thus Spake Zarathustra*, and who was not above putting anti-Semitic and chauvinistic touches in his operas. While his Jewish and non-fascist colleagues were being persecuted and driven out of Germany, he accepted honors and filled high musical posts under the Nazis. There was C. G. Jung, the connection of whose psychoanalytic theories to Nietzsche we have noticed. When the Nazis revamped the Society for Psychotherapy and the Journal of Psychotherapy, he took over the presidency of the one and editorship of the other, applauded the "political revolution" of fascism, and as a "scientist" wrote that the "unconscious mind" of the Jews was inferior to that of other peoples. There was the Norwegian novelist, Knut Hamsun, of whom Thomas Mann wrote:

For example, my great Norwegian colleague, Knut Hamsun, an already elderly man, is an ardent fascist. He gives active support to the fascist party in his own land and did not deny himself the satisfaction of openly ridiculing and insulting a world-famous victim of German fascism, the pacifist Ossietzky. However, this is not the conduct of an old man whose heart has remained particularly youthful, but of a writer of the generation of 1870, upon whom Dostoievsky and Nietzsche had a decisive literary influence. He has stuck fast in the movement of apostasy from liberalism generally characteristic of that period, without comprehending what is at stake today, and without realizing that he is hopelessly compromising his poetical genius through his political or, as I shall prefer to call it, his human behavior.[29]

And there is the philosopher Martin Heidegger, the disciple of Nietzsche, who hailed the coming to power of the Nazis.

Existentialist thought is not confined or bound to Nietzsche, and Nietzsche was not one of the actual builders of the Nazi death camps. But the kind of revival of Nietzsche in the United States today, which hides, ignores or glosses over his influence in preparing German intellectuals to accept war and fascism—unwitting as this was—would seem to be not genuine scholarship but one of the more obscurantist concomitants of the present cold war.

6

EXISTENTIALISM AND GERMAN
FASCISM: *Husserl, Heidegger and Jaspers*

Characteristic of the foremost philosophers of the "Enlightenment," as of those of ancient Greece, was that whether they were philosophical idealists or materialists, whether they embraced God in their system or found no room for God, they built their structures of thought on the basis of what was generally known about the real world in their time. Some may have been progressive in outlook and some may have been reactionary, some may have had keen insights and some may have had cloudy views, some may have stimulated fresh advances in knowledge of reality and some may have operated, through their systems, to close such doors. But it was important to them to know what was available to be known.

With Kierkegaard and Nietzsche, as we have seen, philosophy takes a drastic turn, where science and history are its main antagonists. "Knowledge" becomes "my feelings," "my heart yearnings," "my intuition," "my introspection." And this takes place precisely when knowledge in the form of scientific investigation has moved into society itself, examining its economic life that ties people together and at the same time separates them into conflicting bodies, revealing its laws of change that shape history. Thus Marxist dialectical and historical materialism directly takes up such matters as "freedom" and "morality" that idealist philosophy had re-

served as its own special realm. They are given a new understanding by being regarded in social terms. The question of
freedom becomes one of the conditions under which society,
in its collective labor, can give the individual new opportunities to develop his powers. The question of morality is
not only "should I act with love towards my fellow human
beings?" but "how can I help end the exploitation of one
class by another, so the conditions exist by which people can
live in brotherhood?" It is with a consciousness of these
trends that 20th century existentialism tries to recapture
freedom and morality as an exclusive possession of philosophy
and in the process takes them out of society.

With Karl Jaspers (*b.* 1883) and Martin Heidegger (*b.*
1899), existentialist philosophy is reformulated so that at
least in tone and style it seems to take its place in the main
tradition of philosophy itself. There is for one thing less
"poetry," more of an attempt to build a logical structure of
thought. But while these thinkers differ sharply from one
another, they are still united in their subjectivity. They base
their "systems" on introspective psychologizing, examining
the situation of the individual in a world lacking, as they see
it, in guiding lights. Philosophy is cut free from science to
pursue its own special knowledge, gained by the thinker
gazing into himself. They are acutely aware at the same time
that there is a social problem facing them, and indeed that
there is something of a crisis. Both see their work as an
"answer" to Marxism.

Before examining Jaspers and Heidegger in greater detail,
it is necessary to touch on Edmund Husserl (1859-1938)
because, while he really cannot be called an existentialist,
he was Heidegger's teacher and influenced his thinking.

Husserl, born in Moravia in 1859, taught at the universities of Halle, Göttingen and Freiburg in Germany. In 1913
his major work appeared, *Ideas: General Introduction to Pure*

Phenomenology. Husserl announces at the outset that he is entering the "most fundamental region of philosophy" and offering a "new science." He describes this "science" as a revolution in thought. It demands, he says, "that we should set aside all previous habits of thought, see through and break down the mental barriers which these habits have set along the horizons of our thinking, and in full intellectual freedom proceed to lay hold on these genuine philosophical problems still awaiting completely fresh formulation which the liberated horizons on all sides disclose to us."[1] The "liberated horizon" amounts to the conviction that "truth" must be sought not in the outer world but in patterns of thought innate in the mind.

Husserl proceeds by applying the principle of "doubt." Everything in real life that can be doubted, he says, he will place in a "bracket." He doesn't mean, he explains, that these things necessarily don't exist, but the fact that they can be doubted eliminates them from consideration. Then, having "bracketed" in this way everything pertaining to the outside world, he is left with the one thing that cannot be doubted, the consciousness of one's own being in the world and thinking about it.

Thus all sciences which relate to this natural world, though they stand never so firm to me, though they fill me with wondering admiration, though I am far from any thought of objecting to them in the least degree, *I disconnect them all, I make absolutely no use of their standards, I do not appropriate a single one of the propositions that enter into their systems, even though their evidential value is perfect, I take none of them, no one of them serves me for a foundation*—so long, that is, as it is understood, in the way these sciences themselves understand it, as a truth concerning the *realities* of this world.[2]

One might gather from Husserl's statement of "wondering admiration" for the sciences that he has learned from them,

or weighed what they had to say. But if he has, he does not
think that they have any place in philosophy. He makes no
allusion in the book to the history of humanity, social or intellectual, or to any of the insights into life that the sciences,
individually or together, have provided, or offered to provide.
Primary to them, he argues, is the thought process that creates
the sciences, the "transcendental consciousness," and so this
must be the primary study.

We are not interested in the fact-world of consciousness and the
fulfilling of its functions, but in the essential problems which
might need formulating. Consciousness, or the conscious subject
itself, *passes judgments* about reality, asks questions about it,
thinks it probable or doubts it, resolves the doubt and thereby
passes *"verdicts of the reason."* Must not the essence of this judi-
cial right and correlatively the essence of "reality"—related to all
kinds of objects, and following all the categories, formal and re-
gional—permit of being clearly understood within the system of
essential connexions of the transcendental consciousness, thus in a
purely phenomenological way?[3]

In the preface to the English edition of this book, written
in 1931, Husserl emphasizes the same point. He sees mathematics as a kind of pure logic built into the mind, *a priori*,
with all science deriving from it.

The science of fact in the strict sense, the genuinely rational
science of nature, has first become possible through the independent elaboration of a "pure" mathematics of nature. The science of
pure possibilities must everywhere precede the science of real facts,
and give it the guidance of its concrete logic.[4]

It is certainly not true in any historical sense that a "pure"
mathematics preceded the rational developments of natural
science. Rather the process of doing things with the world
concretely, and thinking about it abstractly, including the
highest abstractions of mathematics, seemed to move hand
in hand. Thus J. D. Bernal writes in *Science in History* of
Mesopotamia and Egypt:

The practise of building in brick, particularly of large religious buildings of pyramid form, gave rise not only to *geometry,* but also to the conception of *areas* and *volumes* of figures and solids reckonable in terms of their sides. . . . *Mathematics,* indeed, arose in the first place as an auxiliary method of production made possible by city life.[5]

Bernal shows in his great treatise that from then until now, doing and thinking each assisted the other. When the ancient Greeks saw the logical edifice of geometry as a higher truth, primary to the discovery of more concrete truths, this only held back the sciences and mathematics itself. Thus Bernal writes of Plato:

He embraced and extended the mystical views of Pythagoras on the cosmic importance of number and geometrical figures, and found in them examples of absolute truth independent of the senses. Plato does not seem to have contributed much to mathematics himself, but his influence undoubtedly gave it a prestige that drew many good minds to it later. Being, however, deliberately abstract and contemplative, it drew mathematics away from its origin in, and application to, practical experience and thus held back the development of algebra and dynamics.[6]

Husserl's "transcendental consciousness" with its "law and order" built into the mind, would seem to be a modern version of this Platonism. Actually, each revolutionary development in science not only aroused new problems to solve but tended to change the very ways of thinking about reality. Engels writes in the 1878 preface to *Anti-Dühring* (later transferred to the *Dialectics of Nature*):

In every epoch, and therefore also in ours, theoretical thought is a historical product, which at different times assumes very different contents. . . . The theory of the laws of thought is by no means an eternal truth established once and for all as philistine reasoning imagines to be the case with the word "logic." Formal logic itself has been the arena of violent controversy from the time of Aristotle to the present day.[7]

Husserl's limitation is not so much a lack of information, as something more fundamental and characteristic of the milieu; the absence from consciousnes of any awareness of the human labor that goes on, day in and day out, to keep the "civilization" going with the comforts he enjoys. An awareness of the presence and conditions of the working people might have given him also an understanding of the labor process in history, and its relation to knowledge and thought. There is an organic relation between "thinking" and "doing," "head" and "hand." Even the imagination which plans changes that have not yet taken place comes as a result of the fact that people have made changes in real life. The process of thinking about reality, which Husserl takes as fundamental, is inseparable from the process of doing things with reality, changing it, thus proving its existence, which he ignores. A grasp of this truth would have kept Husserl from seeking truth by "bracketing" everything thought about, away from the process of thought itself.

This also affects his language. The very glory of words, that they relate to real life and evoke the realities of life, that the most generalized terms like "love," "ethics," "justice," "truth," are concentrates of multitudinous experience, becomes inimical to his philosophy. He must use words as sheer abstractions, or give them his own abstract definitions, so that he can put them into "logical" combinations like mathematics. He becomes difficult to read, not because the thoughts are so complex but because the words themselves as he uses them do not relate to any real life. They have been "cleansed" of this, and so can be fitted together like inanimate blocks. The words themselves become "things"; something which never happens, for example, in the writings of Marx and Engels, for no matter how generalized their formulations, everything they say can be related to and tested in life.

This is Husserl on the concept of truth: "Truth is manifestly the correlate of the perfect rational character of the protodoxa, the believing certainty."[8] This seems to be Kierkegaard's proposition, that whatever one believes with certainty, or in Husserl's words, the "protodoxa," is true. What Husserl adds is that this must have a "perfectly rational" character. But this is still something purely "internal," to him.

In 1931, Husserl wrote in the introduction to the English edition of this book:

Turning inwards in pure reflection following exclusively "inner experience and empathy," to be more precise, and setting aside all the psychophysical questions which relate to man as a corporeal being, I obtain an original and pure descriptive knowledge of the psychical life as it is in itself, the most original information being obtained from myself, because here alone is perception the medium.

And what has he learned from this study of himself? The pathetic admission he makes is that he has learned nothing, although he is certain that he is on the sole right path. He describes himself as one who "has at least in his old age reached for himself the complete certainty that he should thus call himself a beginner." While he has discovered the track of true knowledge, he has not had time to find the knowledge itself. "The author sees the infinite open country of the true philosophy, the 'promised land' on which he himself will never set foot."[9] Shortly afterwards, the Nazis came to power, and he fell into disfavor. He died in 1938 in France.

Martin Heidegger, born in 1889, succeeded Husserl as Professor of Philosophy at Freiburg in 1929, and when the Nazis came to power in 1933, was appointed Rector of the University. In his inaugural address, as Walter Kaufmann writes, "he welcomed the dawn of a new era and the abolition of academic freedom. He also disassociated himself completely from Husserl, who was a Jew."[10] He later resigned from the Rectorship, but kept his Chair in Philosophy until the defeat of

Germany and the collapse of the Hitler regime, when he fell under a cloud for his Nazi connections. Soon, however, just as the cartels and industrialists that had sponsored Hitler were restored to their old roles in Adenauer's Germany, Heidegger resumed lecturing. He became the foremost influence on philosophy in the universities, with courses devoted to his work, and his pupils holding important posts.

The book that will be discussed here is Heidegger's *An Introduction to Metaphysics*, which, aside from the summary it offers of his thinking, has a special interest to those wishing to see whether the wars and wholesale murders engendered by fascism in any way changed his thought. The book includes the lectures delivered in 1935, a Hitler year, and was published by him in 1953, eight years after the debacle of the Third Reich.

Heidegger opens his book with the question, "Why are there essents rather than nothing?" He asks, in other words, why is it that we can say that certain things "are," as against there being nothing? This question, Heidegger says, of why it is that things "are," is "the most fundamental of all questions." Then he begins to play "logically" with the concept of "fundamental." Since this is the most fundamental of all questions, he says, all other questions rest upon it. "No questioning and accordingly no single scientific 'problem' can be fully intelligible if it does not include, i.e., ask, the question of all questions."

This allows him neatly to remove science from all consideration by philosophers and serious thinkers. After all, how can we properly take up secondary questions if we haven't yet answered the fundamental one? It is like telling a starving person who asks for bread that he must first answer the question of the origin and meaning of bread. Furthermore, Heidegger says, this "question of questions" is unfathomable. In other words, there can be no answer. But the real philosopher keeps on asking the question. "Really to ask the question signifies a daring attempt to fathom this unfathomable question by disclosing what it summons us to ask, to push our questioning to the very end. Where such an attempt occurs there is philosophy."

Of course—and here Heidegger shows his Nietzschean lineage—the great mass of people are below such a level of thought, "because philosophy is always the concern of the few." "The few," he says, are "the creators, who initiate profound transformations." He reiterates his belief in the uselessness of knowing science by repeating Husserl's concept of science as simply the application to factual data of the basic, undying truths of philosophy. "All scientific thought is merely a derived form of philosophical thinking, which proceeds to freeze into its scientific cast."[11]

And so he goes along, stating that since a true philosopher must occupy himself only with this question, to which there can be no answer, philosophy consists of asking the question. At the climax of the book, he writes, "The determination of the essence of man is *never* an answer but essentially a question." At the very end, he writes:

To know how to question means to know how to wait, even a whole lifetime. But an age which regards as real only what goes fast and can be clutched with both hands looks on questioning as "remote from reality" and as something that does not pay, whose benefits cannot be numbered. But the essential is not number; the essential is the right time, i.e., the right moment, and the right perseverance.[12]

It may seem as though Heidegger had started with nothing and ended with nothing, creating a hermitlike philosophy utterly withdrawn from the affairs of the world. But in the course of his argument, he develops two important lines of thought. One lays down the basis of what may be termed his existentialist philosophy (although he himself does not like

the term existentialism, drawing a distinction between "existence" and "essence"). The other takes up where Nietzsche
left off and ends with fascism.

As regards the first, Heidegger affirms that while the question of why things "are," as against "nothing," cannot be
answered, every man who is a true philosopher must continually raise this question. For through raising it, he over-
comes it, and arrives at an awareness of his own "being," or
"being in the world." An awareness of "being" is an awareness
that this is a process of appearing, emerging, living, enduring,
glowing or shedding light.

Heidegger had developed his view of "being" in contrast to
"nothingness" in a previous book, Sein und Zeit or Being and
Time (1927). The great "revelation" here is that "being"
must be seen not as something fixed and static, as when one
says that something "is," but as an activity, an engagement
with the world, involving "possibilities." This great "discovery" by Heidegger, however, is only a cloudier version of
the opening section of Hegel's Science of Logic. Here Hegel
points out the meaninglessness in relation to life, of abstract
"being" and "nothing," and links the two dialectically into
"becoming." Thus Hegel brings out that everything in life has
to be seen in terms of motion, growth, change and transformation. Hegel then proceeds to build an immense structure,
linking together every level of thinking about life, from the
most immediate response to the highest and broadest insight,
generalization and idea. Heidegger, in contrast, remains a
modern "primitive," though not as one returning to the dawn
of knowledge but as one rejecting knowledge. He holds on to
this immediate "being" as the only certainty, and rejects any
higher generalization of the make-up of the real world. It is
as if a person were to say that the only thing real is what can
be handled and touched.

To this concept of "being," Heidegger adds that what differentiates man from other animals is his awareness of the problem of "being," and that the philosophical task is to "know thyself." He may seem here to be on the track of a profound thought. For if we examine the history of society, and the developments of culture, science and the arts, we find a series of progressive leaps in the awareness of what a human being is, his increasing sensitivities and powers, and increasingly rich human interrelationships.

In *Capital*, Marx writes of the labor process, through which man appropriates "Nature's productions in a form adapted to his own wants," adding "by thus acting on the external world and changing it, he at the same time changes his own nature. He develops his slumbering powers and compels them to act in obedience to his sway." So with every stage in the mastery of nature and discovery of both its laws and its sensuous qualities, nature in turn "educates" the human being, for the discoveries and perceptions become part of his own mind and thought. The labor process is social, carried on cooperatively. Each new stage in the organization of society brings about a new development in human relationships and with this a new psychology or "inner life." The arts of each age disclose this new mentality and sensitivity.

But Heidegger's view of "know thyself" does not involve this real growth of the human being as he discovers himself and his potentiality, through his activity and his relation to others. The question which Kierkegaard had raised as a religious one—namely, "Why am I here?"—and which Nietzsche had pried away from religion by saying that "God is dead," Heidegger wants to develop as a philosophical question; not so that it can thus be answered, but so that he can draw a line between some peoples and others. To "know thyself" to Heidegger has nothing to do with society, science, labor or human relationships. It is a special personal and spiritual awareness of "being" granted to only certain races or nations that are, by that very token, destined leaders, Nietzschean supermen. Heidegger then advances the theory that this awareness of "being" is now a special German spiritual gift, and so Germany is entitled to lead the rest of the world. The only predecessors of Germany in this, he says, were the ancient Greeks. In *An Introduction to Metaphysics*, he proceeds to "prove" this by an examination of language, showing the various shades of meaning given to "being" and associated words, in ancient Greek, and in German. He reaffirms the conclusion that "along with the German the Greek language is (in regard to its possibilities for thought) at once the most powerful and most spiritual of all languages."[13]

Heidegger pursues this thought with the arrogant and egoistic disregard for the most elementary principles of scientific investigation that characterizes all Nietzscheans, including Freud and Jung, in their dealings with history, society and civilization. His method is the simple one of limiting his attention to whatever few instances fit his argument. Thus he offers no examination of other languages than the Greek and German, he pays no heed to the way in which the languages of all peoples have developed in relation to their conditions of life and work. He does not even attempt to explain why the ancient Greeks were and the modern Germans are such superior people. Does the reason lie in the "blood" or germ cells? Even a cursory knowledge of the mixture of races in both would destroy such an assumption.

Ancient Greek literature, art and philosophy are among the glories of the world. As to how they came about, some clues may be found in the historical circumstances which enabled certain strategically situated trading cities to bring together the accumulated discoveries of the Egyptians, Phoenicians and other Mediterranean peoples; in the social, comparatively unaristocratic composition of their population which enabled them to bring "head" and "hand" together and make scientific leaps of their own; in the independence they won from the land-holding aristocracy, and from the old tribal institutions; in their accompanying creation of the first known, if limited, democratic institutions; in the stimulus these achievements gave to the critical examination of inherited beliefs and superstitions, replacing them with a new concept of the powers and stature of the human being.

But such thinking is foreign to Heidegger. He finds the reason in some mystical spiritual gift, which enabled the Greeks to learn the nature of "being" in *physis*, or the power of emergence. "The Greeks did not learn what *physis* is through natural phenomena, but the other way around: it was through a fundamental poetic and intellectual experience of being that they discovered what they had to call *physis*."[14] What happened to this mysterious gift when the Greek city-states collapsed, Alexander built an empire and that collapsed, and the Roman Empire took over Greece, Heidegger does not say. It is enough for his purpose to establish the Greeks as the creators of true philosophy, the understanding of "being," and then to drop them, going on to affirm that the modern Germans are the only genuine inheritors and continuators of this philosophical spirit.

Heidegger prefaces his exaltation of German superiority by denouncing logic, following Nietzsche in the view that Greek logic represented a kind of decadence. He says, "Logic is an invention of schoolteachers, not of philosophers." It took Germans, he says, to see this. "It is no accident that the decisive efforts toward overcoming traditional logic were made by three of the greatest German thinkers, Leibniz, Kant, and Hegel."[15] And as with the Greeks, so with these great German thinkers, Heidegger utterly ignores the historical context necessary to understand them. It takes nothing away from their stature to say that all Europe contributed to the shaping of their thought; Italians like Petrarch and Galileo, Englishmen like Locke and Newton, Frenchmen like Descartes and Rousseau, Dutchmen like Erasmus and the Jew, Spinoza, and that behind them were the liberating popular movements that shattered the feudal world and were challenging monarchy and autocracy. To Heidegger, their achievement only affirms the innate German superiority whose existence he assumes. "Our nation," he says, "is the most metaphysical of nations."[16]

So, starting with his philosophy of "being," Heidegger moves to a chauvinistic assertion of innate German intellectual superiority. The next step is to affirm the German "mission" in the modern world.

It is a refurbishing of the argument advanced in Germany during the First World War: that since Germany had a superior "culture," victory for German militarism would bring to the world this great "culture." "Europe," he says, "in its ruinous blindness forever on the point of cutting its own throat, lies today in a great pincers, squeezed between Russia on one side and America on the other." The trouble with and menace of both Russia and America is that they suffer from "the same dreary technological frenzy, the same unrestricted organization of the average man." And not only is Europe in this pincers, but Germany is the greatest sufferer. "Situated in the center, our nation incurs the severest pressure. It is the nation with the most neighbors and hence the most endangered." (A neighbor to Heidegger is by definition an enemy.) And so Germany has a "vocation." It must "wrest a destiny." Germany must "move itself and thereby the history of the West beyond the center of their future 'happening' and into the primordial realm of the powers of being." The great decision regarding Europe "must be made in terms of new spiritual energies unfolding historically from out the center."[17]

It is a fantastic blindness which sees "dreary technological frenzy," namely industrialization, in America and Russia, but overlooks German industrialization with its Krupps, Thyssens and Farbens, its giant steel, armament and chemical indus-

tries. It finds both America, which was then witnessing a
growing battle for the rights of workers to join unions, and
Russia, where the people had done away with private ownership of industry, to be places of "unrestricted organization of
the average man," but ignores how Hitler had put the entire
German population into a military lockstep. This having been
written in 1935, and Heidegger having already lauded the
takeover by National Socialism, it must be German fascism
that to him represents "new spiritual energies."

Again and again Heidegger calls Germany the "center," and
preaches its mission. It is to inspire this mission, he says, that
he has raised the fundamental question of being. "That is
why we have related the question of being to the destiny of
Europe—while our own historic being-there proves to be the
center for Europe itself." He has raised his inquiry because
this is "indispensable if the peril of world darkening is to be
forestalled and if our nation in the center of the world is to
take on its historical mission." As for the nature of the
"darkening" in the world, Heidegger describes it in both
Nietzschean and fascist propaganda terms. "The essential
episodes of this darkening are: the flight of the gods, the
destruction of the earth, the standardization of man, the
pre-eminence of the mediocre."[18] Throughout the book,
Heidegger has only one reservation to make about German
fascism, which he calls a "great movement." This is that it
chooses philosophers inferior to him as its propagandists.

The works that are being peddled about nowadays as the philosophy of National Socialism but have nothing whatever to do
with the inner truth and greatness of this movement (namely the
encounter between global technology and modern man)—have all
been written by men fishing in the troubled waters of "values" and
"totalities."[19]

The Nazi wars in which German youth ultimately joined
the slaughtered, the gas chambers, the lampshades made of
human skin, the military defeat, seem not to have changed

Heidegger's thinking at all. In the preface to the German edition printed in 1953, he has no reservations to make about his praise of the Nazi movement. Perhaps the words at the close of the book, "the essential is the right time, i.e., the right moment, and the right perseverance," indicate his opinion that Hitler chose the wrong time and the wrong moment. Or it may be that his is the kind of arrogance that admits no error.

In contrast to Heidegger's fanaticism, Karl Jaspers writes with warmth, gentleness, and an awareness of world culture. Born in 1883, his first work was in psychiatry. He then turned to philosophy and became professor at Heidelberg in 1921. Where Heidegger rode the wave of German fascism, Jaspers was submerged by it. After Hitler came to power Jaspers continued to teach and publish, but in 1937 he lost his professorial post and retired to private life. The reason for his disfavor was not simply that his wife was Jewish. It was the tone of his writings. If they made no head-on attack upon the Nazi ideology, they nevertheless preserved a tradition of German humanism alien to the Nazi hysteria.

Jaspers' humanism moved between narrow limits. The questions he raised as to what were the true values of life were real, but his attempt to answer them suffered from his "elitist" view, the conviction that there were and always would be only a comparative few who were interested in the things that matter; that these few formed a lonely fraternity of true thinkers. He had no democratic convictions, felt no kinship with the working people, and feared the "masses" as an engulfing horde of barbarians. While he did not advocate withdrawal from social life, even asserting that the thinker take part in the life and responsibilities of the times, he did not feel at home in society. There is a revealing note in his essay, *On My Philosophy*, written in 1941. "In 1914 the World War caused the great breach in our European existence. The paradisiacal life before the World War, naive despite all its sublime spirituality, could never return: philosophy, with its seriousness, became more important than ever."[20] The Germany of the autocratic militaristic Empire was like "paradise" to him, imbued with a "sublime spirituality." He was not an adherent of the Kaiser and Junkers, but the movement for German democracy hardly entered his consciousness. A sensitive mind did not bother with politics.

The war and its aftermath ended this idyll. The Kaiser abdicated. There was a threat of a revolution in Germany such as had taken place in Russia. The right-wing socialists, the German Social-Democrats, desired, as William L. Shirer says, to preserve the Hohenzollern monarchy but were unable to do so; forced to take power, they joined hands with the Junker generals to drown the left-wing uprising in blood. By agreement of the Social-Democrats heading the Weimar republic, as Shirer notes, the old Prussian officer corps retained control of the army and made it a "state within a state."[21] The monopolies in control of the national economy did everything to make life miserable for the people and disillusion them with democratic government. The government did nothing to halt unemployment, curb the monopolists, and prop up the sinking standard of living.

In this atmosphere, Jaspers turned to the "serious" profession of philosophy, embracing in it an attention to social matters. A book he wrote in 1930, *Man in the Modern Age*, both gives his views on the German crisis and presents his "Existence philosophy." In a foreword written 21 years later, Jaspers says that at the time "I had scarcely any knowledge of National Socialism,"[22] although it had become a powerfully backed movement, challenging the government from the Right, but treated gently while liberals who warned of the danger were being jailed for "treason." Jaspers was, he says, "better acquainted with Fascism," meaning the Italian variety.

While Jaspers mentions fascism with abhorrence, his main attack is upon the "masses." They seem to overwhelm him, with nightmare terrors possible only to one who has never known what the people are and how they live. He understands no distinctions between forms of society. Fascism, "bolshevism," a capitalist democracy are all to him forms of "mass" rule, that destroy freedom of mind. "What the bolsheviks and the fascists respectively do in this field and what we learn of the decline of liberty in the United States, differ in respect of many points of detail—but, common to them all, is that human beings are being turned out according to standardized types."[23] The fact that people flock to low-grade amusements is not attributed to the capitalist exploitation of entertainment as a mass-produced commodity but to the consumers, as the expression of the mind and desire of the "masses." In his own Weimar republic, Jaspers disregards the dominating role of the monopolies and the army. Everything he finds obnoxious in German life is attributed to the predominance of the masses. He is aware of the complexity of modern industrial production. Marx and Engels had pointed out the contradiction of modern large-scale production, so social in its interwoven activity and involving the entire life of society, yet being run anarchistically by private individuals or groups for private profit, thus incurring periodic crises. To Jaspers, however, by an odd twist, it is the masses who run society.

It has become obligatory to fulfill a function which shall in some way be regarded as useful to the masses. . . . The masses are our masters; and for everyone who looks facts in the face his existence has become dependent on them, so that the thought of them must control his doings, his cares and his duties. . . . Even

an articulated mass always tends to become unspiritual and inhuman. It is life without existence, superstition without faith. It
may stamp all flat; it is disinclined to tolerate independence and
greatness, but prone to constrain people to become as automatic as
ants. . . . The mass-order brings into being a universal life-
apparatus, which proves destructive to the world of a truly human
life.[24]

Jaspers is aware of the economic as well as spiritual crisis
in the Weimar republic, and touches on the futility of its
"welfare state" gestures. "We have our social-welfare institutions, our systems of social insurance, savings banks, and
what not." But, as he says, this "assistance" falls "more and
more below what is regarded as the standard of a decent
existence."[25] What happened was that the government was
unwilling to wring from the monopolies the money necessary
to redeem its promises to the people, and provide employment. But to Jaspers this is only a sign of how modern industrialization creates spiritual insecurity.

He knows of Marx, and says that at one time he, like so
many others, was fascinated by the Communist Manifesto.
He briefly summarizes its position. It proposes, he says, a
classless society, without exploitation. Man will no longer be
dependent on the things he produces, but will become their
master, and will take over the conduct of his own life. But
what horrifies Jaspers is that according to it, "Man, grasping
the nature of his own being, devotes himself to the class
which will bring into existence a free, classless society—devotes himself to the proletariat." And this reactivates Jaspers'
nightmare of the "masses." What good would it do, he asks,
even if a new social system without exploitation were to provide everyone with the necessities of life? Would not the
proletariat create one great ant-colony?

And so Jaspers arrives at what, to existentialist philosophers, is the modern "predicament." He knows there is a

world crisis. He recognizes that Marxism offers a viable path
to human progress; in fact, the only viable one, in the sense
that it is based on a scientific study of economics and history.
But it revolts him, because it has the face of the "masses,"
a horrifying collectivization and standardization, the rubbing
out of his individuality. He transfers to socialism what any
intellectual and artist of sensitivity knows when he has to
"sell" his talents to a capitalist manufacturer of pseudo-art
commodities; that his mind is no longer his own. And so
Jaspers proposes an "existence philosophy"; namely to live
with the crisis, and in a corrupt, irrational, pathless world,
at least persevere and affirm his own individuality.

Existence-philosophy, Jaspers writes, "is the way of thought
by means of which man seeks to become himself." It cannot
discover any "solutions," and it "would be instantly lost if
it were once more to imply a belief that we know what man
is." It demands a certain heroism, for "to-day the hero has
to safeguard himself against the impalpable masses." This
"hero" must not challenge the masses, for they will not let
him live in the world. "He has silently to endure and to col-
laborate, unless he is willing to allow himself to be martyred
by the despotism of the masses who quietly and inconspicu-
ously destroy."

Jaspers develops this in Nietzschean terms. Relatively
few people, he says, are truly aware of how man becomes
"himself." They form a spiritual nobility. And today, "there
is beginning the last campaign against the nobility." This
comes from the "instincts of the masses." But where Nietzsche
felt that the true nobility or aristocrats would, through the
"Will to Power," whip the masses into shape, Jaspers has
no such grandiose hopes, and is content that the few who
are "aware," know each other and form a friendly fraternity.
"The best gift the contemporary world can give us is this

proximity of self-existent human beings. They are, in fact, themselves the guarantee that being exists."[26]

In three decades, Jaspers does not seem to have advanced appreciably beyond this position. He showed genuine courage in a series of lectures he delivered at the University of Groningen in Holland, in 1935, which were then published in Groningen as *Reason and Existenz*. We sense the shock that the seizure of power by German fascism must have meant to him. He has nothing to offer to counter it, and of course he does not mention it specifically, but he does not rejoice in it like a Heidegger. "Quietly, something enormous has happened in the reality of Western man: a destruction of all authority, a radical disillusionment in an overconfident reason, and a dissolution of bonds have made anything, absolutely anything, seem possible." A world that seemed to progress in rational ways has turned to chaos, and philosophy, to be authentic, "must grow out of our new reality, and there take its stand."

Like Kierkegaard, he sees the 19th century Western world not as a specific social-economic formation, and certainly not in Marxist terms as capitalism, but as the product of the "Enlightenment," of "reason." And so it is reason that has failed, and along with it, science. He hails Kierkegaard and Nietzsche as the prophets who foresaw this: "Both questioned reason from the depths of Existence. Never on such a high level of thought had there been such a thoroughgoing and radical opposition to mere reason. . . . Out of the consciousness of their truth, both suspect truth in the naive form of scientific knowledge." The truth they both disclosed is that we know nothing: "Through them we have become aware that for us there is no longer any self-evident foundation. There is no longer any secure background for our thought."[27]

What Jaspers in the end has to offer is only the consolation of philosophy. It is philosophy without a doctrine, almost the process of philosophizing rather than a philosophy, and yet with a substance of its own different from religion and science. It is not churchly religion, because it has no dogma, and does not try to influence the world. It is not atheism, which is even more worldly. It uses reason but also goes inward, where reason cannot reach, finding "existence." It provides a "freedom" for the sensitive few in a chaotic world, which cannot be changed but to which one can adjust.

Philosophy is never a sociological power like churchly belief and atheism. Powerless, the spirit of philosophy emerges out of its ever-present source in the soul only to awaken the soul and let it participate in a truth which has no "purpose" and which neither serves nor opposes any other truth. Out of its own inwardness does it lead to an experience of the presence of truth through the path of thinking out of the whole nature of man. . . . As long as man philosophizes, he knows he stands not in relation to the whole chain of "witnesses to the Truth" (in which Christ dared feel himself to be), nor to that of atheism which has always been effective in the world and spoken out; but rather he is related to the chain of private men who openly search in freedom.[28]

As it happened, fascism was not the eruption of modern man against reason that Jaspers saw it to be, and thought had been foreshadowed by Nietzsche. In the end, the Marxists, at first taken aback by its strength, diagnosed fascism accurately. It was a maneuver by the great concentrations of capital to harness the nation behind their plans for aggrandizement, profiting by the disillusion produced by the economic crisis. They shared some of the loot with a body of demagogic leaders, financed by them, who used a hysterical pseudo-revolutionary phraseology. Thus they destroyed the democratic institutions that were now a menace to them. This appraisal had a scientific quality, in that it armed people successfully to combat the manifestations of fascism elsewhere. And it was, in the last analysis, the "masses," the common people feared and despised by Jaspers, who withstood the fascist terror and, in the end, crushed it, incidentally enabling Jaspers to return to public life.

In a late book, *Way of Wisdom* (1951), Jaspers counterposes existence-philosophy to Marxism, which he concedes has been an important "scientific force" in the economic field. But Marxism, he says, infuriates him when it finds in the developing modes of production a clue to the development of ideas, and so invades the realm of philosophy and religion. It conceives itself "as the true consciousness of the classless man." This, Jaspers says, is "quasi-religious," and should not call itself science. Freedom, as a question, belongs not to science, but to philosophy, which knows what science has learned but takes for its realm the truths that cannot be scientifically investigated. "True philosophy," he says, "is the source of a truth that is inaccessible to scientifically binding knowledge. . . . Philosophical thought is inward action; it appeals to freedom; it is a summons to transcendence."[29]

In seeking through philosophy for a kind of knowledge that "transcends" science, Jaspers joins such different thinkers as Husserl and Heidegger. What they have in common as existentialists—or "essentialists"—is that they militantly take their stand on whatever "ultimate truths" science as they know it has not yet discovered, like the birth of the universe, the nature of consciousness, the guarantee of absolute human freedom and happiness.

To Heidegger, as to Kierkegaard and Nietzsche, these unsolved problems, being the only "real problems," made all science suspect or worthless. Jaspers is friendlier to science, and, in his late writings, counsels philosophers to absorb it, before going on to the "truths" beyond science.

To Marxism, which stands firmly on science, there are and always will be unsolved problems. In fact, each advance in knowledge, through the very forward stride in life that it makes possible, always raises new problems. And in seeing science as continually probing new aspects of reality, it gives philosophy a different role from what it had traditionally claimed. Philosophy has no realm of knowledge, no realm of truth that is its own sacred and special province. Engels puts it thus in *Ludwig Feuerbach and the End of Classical German Philosophy*:

With all philosophers it is precisely the "system" which is perishable; and for the simple reason that it springs from an imperishable desire of the human mind—the desire to overcome all contradictions. . . . As soon as we have once realized—and in the long run no one has helped us realize it more than Hegel himself —that the task of philosophy thus stated means nothing but the task that a single philosopher should accomplish that which can only be accomplished by the entire human race in its progressive development—as soon as we realize that, there is an end to philosophy in the hitherto accepted sense of the word. One leaves alone "absolute truth," which is unattainable along this path or by any single individual; instead one pursues attainable relative truths along the paths of the positive sciences, and the summation of their results by means of dialectical thinking.[30]

When Engels says that the "systems" are perishable, he is also recognizing the many true and valuable insights of the philosophers which live on after their system dies. But Hegel, he says, ends the era of the useful formation of "systems" themselves, which presume to answer every question of life and death, and which each subsequent stage of society finds to be more inapplicable and meaningless. In exchange, there is "real, positive knowledge of the world," never complete but sound and actual, something people can confidently live by.

The central question which Jaspers raises in his argument with Marxism is, as we have seen, whether human freedom is properly a realm that science can enter. To Marxism—dialectical and historical materialism—it is. Jaspers cannot see this. He says that since Marxism finds that the ideas of each society are a "superstructure" over the base of its mode of production, it is proclaiming that all general ideas are a disguised form of narrow self-interest. But this is "economic determinism," not Marxism. To Marxism, freedom rests on the consciousness of the growth, exercise and development of human powers, and on the repeated conquest of obstacles to this growth. The drive to freedom, in these terms, lies at the core of human history and progress. It lies behind the imagination which plans changes in the world and proceeds to carry them out. The freedom won is not absolute, not a visionary untrammeled existence. Each stage in the mastery of the laws of nature, in the knowledge of the operations of society, and in the understanding of the human mind itself— all these progressing together—makes possible a new stage in human freedom, giving it an ever-broadening content. When Marxism points out that the dominant ideologies of an age support the ruling class of that age, it is saying that these systems of ideas tend to rationalize the social relationships of the age into eternal truths of the "mind" or "heart." But it also points out that people, through their collective labor, are at the same time changing the world, discovering new potentialities in it. Thus both the old institutions and old ways of thought eventually appear as manacles, which must be broken.

To the ancient Greeks, whose civilization was based on slavery, to be "free" meant not to be a slave, and philosophers like Plato and Aristotle rationalized the practice of slavery by claiming that the slaves were an inferior kind of being. (We are not so different today when we rationalize the economic exploitation of colonies and industrially undeveloped countries by claiming that such peoples are unfit to rule themselves.) In feudal society the "freedom" of the landowning aristocracy rested on the unfreedom of the serfs and peasants, who had no rights, and whose labor left the knights "free" to fight with one another and indulge in courtly love-making. In bourgeois or capitalist society, "freedom" was free trade, the freedom to buy and sell in uncontrolled markets. A factory owner was "free" when he could bargain with his workers individually. When they formed unions and went on strike, or demanded laws restricting the work day to ten or eight hours, he regarded this as an infringement on his freedom. To the worker, however, collective action, which made the advance of one depend on the advance of all, was a necessary step in his own freedom.

In all of these stages, the freedom of the exploiting class was contaminated by the fact that it rested on the unfreedom of the exploited. On the one hand, the unfree refused to remain shackled. On the other, the "free" had continually to battle one another for their favored position. Thus the ancient slave-holding empires were afflicted by economic crises rising out of the institution of slavery, but there would have been no change in their institutions had there not been slave revolts and invasions of peoples who either refused to pay tribute or were hungry for loot. Feudal society disappeared because its institutions stifled the rising productive forces of manufacture, but it fell to pieces through the uprisings of peasants and artisans, their exploitation intensified by the wars of rivalry among the nobles for land and power. And in capitalist society, the organization of the workers rises to become a menace to the capitalist, while the awareness grows of how the "unfreedom" born of competition contaminates all society. Engels writes in an early essay:

One estate stands confronted by another, one piece of capital by another, one unit of labor power by another. In other words, because private property isolates everyone in his crude solitariness, and because, nevertheless, everyone has the same interest as his

neighbor, one landowner stands antagonistically confronted by another, one capitalist by another, one worker by another. In this
discord of identical interests resulting precisely from this identity
is consummated the immorality of mankind's condition until now;
and this consummation is competition.[31]

Engels calls this hostility of all against all, which reaches
its climax in the capitalist marketplace, the "immorality of
self-alienation." And Jaspers himself reflects this mentality
born of bourgeois life, from which he thinks that as a philosopher he is detached. Typical of such mentality is the sense
of individual isolation in a hostile world "without moor-
ings," and the fear of the masses of people as a faceless
horror, especially when they begin to find their own freedom
in cooperation with one another. Jaspers misses the true
meaning of the Marxist view of the relation of ideas to the
social-economic base. It brings about a qualitative change in
the operation of ideology in society. It serves to enable people
to analyze and discover the origins of their own ideas, the
eternal truth of which they otherwise take for granted. And
so it enables people collectively to plan change with a fuller
consciousness of what they are doing.

If the freedom won by each stage of society is contaminated, it nevertheless represents an advance over that of each
preceding stage, in scope and concept. The ancient slave-
holding societies, with their organized labor operations, like
dam building and irrigation, showed greater freedom over
primitive tribal life in their higher mastery of natural forces.
In feudal society a peasant was at least in theory granted
human status, and he was even promised equality in the next
world. In bourgeois society there was, so far as the marketplace was concerned, no privileged caste. "Money talked,"
whether its possessor had come from a family of dukes or
beggars. And bourgeois society had to come to power under

the declaration that government rested on the consent of the governed, however undermined this came to be in actual practice.

When Marxism projects another stage, the elimination of the exploitation of one class by another, it is soundly based on the kind of development that has taken place in all history. Analysis of the operations of society discloses laws that can be understood and put to work. And against the view that the "will to power" or dog-eat-dog self-interest is the dominating force in the mind, Marxism rests on the documentation of history which shows that again and again men have willingly cooperated and worked together, so that the freedom gained for each would be a freedom won for all.

Engels, in *Socialism: Utopian and Scientific*, puts the new stage this way:

Anarchy in social production is replaced by systematic, definite organization. The struggle for individual existence disappears. Then for the first time man, in a certain sense, is finally marked off from the rest of the animal kingdom, and emerges from mere animal conditions into really human ones. The whole sphere of the conditions of life which environ man, and which hitherto ruled man, now comes under the dominion and control of man, who for the first time becomes the real, conscious Lord of Nature, because he has now become master of his own social organization. . . . Only from that time will man himself, more and more consciously, make his own history—only from that time will the social causes set in movement by him have, in the main and in constantly growing measure, the results intended by him. It is the ascent of man from the kingdom of necessity to the kingdom of freedom.[32]

Each previous transformation of society and leap in the human mastery of the outer world, was preceded by a crisis in which those with eyes fixed only on the passing of the old, bewailed with deepest despair how illusory were all beliefs in progress, and lamented the futility of human hopes. And each leap was also a new phase in the growth of human individuality, attested to by fresh triumphs in the arts as they attained new realms of human sensitivity. Thus it becomes ridiculous to suppose that a still further stage, when such problems as war and starvation are solved, will end in the mindlessness of an ant colony, or a society in which everyone is a cog in a mammoth machine. This is only the expression of a mind which cannot distinguish between industrialization, with its accompanying interlocking of human labor—a tremendous potential force for human liberation—and the temporary operation of big industrial combines as privately manipulated and ruthless "profit machines." It projects to a mythical future the mechanization of labor and of the intellect which competitive private industry forces today upon those who must hire themselves to it. To blame, as Jaspers does, the "rule of the masses," for the crises and deprivations caused by the carteleers, is as shallow as calling the Egyptian pyramids the product of a "mass movement" because thousands of slaves were harnessed to drag each block of stone.

The existentialist nightmare of material progress as spiritual desolation is the outcry of the individual whose potentialities were liberated by the bourgeois democratic revolutions but who finds in the competitive life of the bourgeois world, dominated by avarice, fear and money as the symbol of security, no field for the operation of these potentialities. The world about him is the mirror of his frustrated individualism. His own drives when they appear in others, appal him by their inhumanity. The collective struggles that had liberated these powers are forgotten. Society appears as the eternal enemy of the individual, and if he cannot disengage himself from it in real life, he does so in his mind. He must attack or disparage the heritage of discovery and learning which enabled the society about him to come into being. The more the working class manifests its own individualism and the more it demands freedom of operation, the more alien it seems to him than the society which at least he has the pride of renouncing while living in it. He cannot envisage the end of his isolation because isolation has become his way of thought.

To what extent does any existing socialist country, like the Soviet Union, match the kind of future Engels envisaged? To answer this question properly one must first know that Engels was speaking of what would come about after exploitation would be a thing of the past over the entire world, for some generations. The Soviet Union furthermore faced the herculean task of building socialism in a land of frightful backwardness in industry and education, compared to any advanced capitalist country. This was done amid the active hostility of the entire capitalist world, and the land was devastated by two wars forced upon it. Yet for all the lapses, errors, human failures, the goal of the Engels picture has been steadily upheld, and strides are steadily being taken toward it. A colossal drama is being played in which a new social morality, not only preached but aimed to be practiced, is the possession of an ever-growing proportion of the population. This is tacitly recognized in the press of the West, which gleefully reports crimes that would hardly be noticed in the non-socialist world, so much are they there a part of the ordinary state of things. Its production in the arts and the participation in cultural life by a vast population have no precedent in history. The art works may bore many sincere critics, who do not find their own conflicts mirrored in them, and how many of these works will live in the future is an open question. Yet the worst depravities of the kind of cynical mass-produced "popular art," existing in the West, and blamed here on the "masses," do not exist there. And the art works reflect the presence of and urge to expand the new social morality. An example is the body of novels produced in the Soviet Union during the Second World War. Through all the portrayals of war's atrocities, there is never missing the motif of the preciousness of human life, the determination to abolish all war, the urgency for people to see each other as kin, to support each other, to sense another's woe, to preserve their own humanity. And the art works of a country tell us much of what is in the people's mind. Art cannot tell lies convincingly.

The important question for the United States is not whether to imitate the Soviet Union, but whether Marxism, an international possession, belongs in American intellectual life. As against the tacit boycott of Marxism in halls of learning, existentialist tracts flow freely. And the low level of some of these attempts to sell existentialism is exhibited by a book, *The Existentialist Revolt* (1960), by an exponent of existentialist psychoanalysis, Professor Kurt F. Reinhardt. He writes:

In individual and social life, in politics and economics, in national and international events, contemporary man is confronted with a complexity of facts and events which defies even the best-intentioned efforts of governments and administrators. . . . By losing and finding himself in his daily tasks, the tasks of the farmer, the laborer, or the artist, man attains to the mastery of the world. . . . Existentialism has risen in modern Europe because the steadily increasing pressures of collectivism and abstract idealism have forced the individual to a resolute and radical self-affirmation.[33]

So, the thesis goes, nobody knows anything about what happens in society. If one is dismayed by the rising cost of living, or the armament race, or unemployment, so are all, and it is in a bewildered way that a corporation raises the price of steel or bread, or automates its factories, or combats peace movements dangerous to its armament profits. To recognize them as social problems to be attacked socially, by people joining in common action, is the terrible menace of "collectivism." Everyone must, as people were told in the Middle Ages, devote himself to his proper task; the farmer to his farm, the artist to his art, the laborer to his labor. To assert that a man must take no active part in social life and seek no common ground with others, for by such participation he will forfeit his individuality, is called a "radical self-affirmation." Freedom is to bow one's head in perpetual ignorance of the forces that daily affect one's life.

Although, as this study has tried to show, there is a connection between existentialism and the intellectual climate that assisted the coming of fascism, Reinhardt in his tome ignores fascism, but for a casual note that Heidegger "delivered an address in which he expressed qualified approval of the National Socialist Revolution."[34] He draws no connections from this to Heidegger's philosophy, and in fact the main object of his wrath, whom he calls a "Lucifer" and apparent traitor to existentialism, is Jean-Paul Sartre, who fought fascism. It is quite a crazy situation when self-appointed mental healers can prate about "anxiety" and ignore the presence of still active fascist forces that instil real anxieties.

SOCIAL RESPONSIBILITY OF THE EXISTENTIALIST ARTIST:
Camus and Sartre

A new stage in existentialist thought, where it becomes the philosophy of the working artist, is represented by Albert Camus and Jean-Paul Sartre, both of whom had taken part in the French resistance movement against the fascist occupation. This stage was particularly potent in its influence upon American cultural life because of the social responsibility it asserted and its impressive literary qualities.

Both these French writers acknowledged their debt to the German existentialist philosophers. Both undertook a debate with Marxism, Camus always hostile but Sartre moving from hostility to friendly colloquy to partial agreement.

For both the philosophical starting point is that the world of reality is "absurd." Both discuss suicide as a serious answer to the problem, while arguing against it.

Thus Camus begins his essay, An Absurd Reasoning, printed in the book, The Myth of Sisyphus (1940): "There is but one truly serious philosophical problem, and that is suicide." And in developing the question, he cannot see reason as a guide, since reality is "absurd."

From Jaspers to Heidegger, from Kierkegaard to Schestov, from the phenomenologists to Scheler, on the logical plane and on the moral plane, a whole family of minds related by their nostalgia but opposed by their methods or their aims, have persisted in blocking the royal road to reason and in recovering the direct path of truth.[1]

In his essay interpreting the Greek myth of Sisyphus, Camus offers his own answer to the absurdity of life, which is his answer also to suicide; namely that a man can find "freedom" in scorning the world even while he lives in it. This scorn is his independence and the assertion of his own unbroken individual being. Sisyphus was condemned by the gods to endlessly roll a heavy stone up a hill, only to see it roll down again. To Camus, this futile and onerous task symbolized the absurdity of all life. But Sisyphus found freedom, he says, in his scorn for the task and those who had imposed it.

Sisyphus, proletarian of the gods, powerless and rebellious, knows the whole extent of his wretched condition: it is what he thinks of during his descent. The lucidity that was to constitute his torture at the same time crowns his victory. There is no fate that cannot be surmounted by scorn.[2]

Camus developed the thought in the first and shorter of his two novels, *The Stranger* (1939-40).[3] His are didactic novels, with situations deliberately contrived to make a point, like a fable clothed in realistic detail. Meursault, "the stranger," is an Algerian Frenchman, totally devoid of human sympathies or tenderness. He lives as in a hard shell, impervious to human touch. For three years he has rarely visited his mother, whom he has put in a home for the aged. His reasons for this neglect are that the visits would have meant giving up his Sunday and that he wants to avoid the bother of buying a bus ticket, and the tedium of a two-hour ride. Informed that his mother is dead, he attends the funeral yet feels no grief. It is simply a formality he cannot avoid. A fellow lodger, Raymond, offers his friendship, and Meursault visits with him, without any particular attachment. It is all right to have someone to eat with, sometimes. Meursault meets a girl, Marie, and has an affair with her. She asks him to marry her. "I said I didn't mind; if she was keen on it, we'd get married." She asks him if he loves her. "I replied, much as before, that her question meant nothing or next to nothing—but I suppose I didn't." His friend Raymond has maltreated an Arab girl, and is being threatened by her brother and his Arab friends. Meursault is not particularly concerned, but one day on the beach, he runs into this Arab, and on a sudden impulse, pumps five bullets into him. What impelled him to this he doesn't know. It might have been the glare of the hot sun at the moment, which dazzled him. He feels no compunction. At his trial for murder, one of the telling arguments of the prosecutor, who describes him as a monster, is that he showed no grief at his mother's funeral. The book ends with his thoughts in the death cell as the day of his execution approaches.

There are three points Camus wants to make. One is the hypocrisy of most people who self-righteously condemn Meursault for his callousness but who really feel the same selfishness, while making a show of tenderness, affection or conscience for the sake of convention. A second is the horror of capital punishment, which Camus brings out through Meursault's agony in the death cell. (There seems to be no compunction, however, in either Camus or his hero, for the Arab who was killed.) The third, and most important, is the assertion that to scorn an absurd existence like Sisyphus, is freedom. Suddenly enlightenment comes to Meursault. His own callousness is truth. The world is indifferent to human beings and he, in his indifference, has penetrated the secret of reality. He has lived within himself. This is the awareness of the truth of life. To realize this is happiness. And to consummate this, he wants to spit at the moralizing crowd which judges him.

It was as if that great rush of anger had washed me clean, emptied me of hope, and, gazing up at the dark sky spangled with its signs and stars, for the first time, the first, I laid my heart open to the benign indifference of the universe. . . . I was happy still. For all to be accomplished, for me to feel less lonely, all that remained to hope was that on the day of my execution there should be a huge crowd of spectators and that they should greet me with howls of derision.

It is a challenging book. Camus is saying to those who are shocked at his "hero's" amorality, don't respond with platitudes. Show me what in the society you live in is built on real love and tenderness for others, real conscience. You are afraid of the truth that the world is meaningless. This truth would make you free. Scorn the ties that would bind you to others and delude you into thinking there is a purpose to existence. If a God made the world, scorn him too, for he has no concern in your welfare. And the book is moving, not for any broad or deep insight into life, but because Camus himself feels so passionately that he is condemned to death, in a world where this is the only sure reality.

A similar position was advanced by Sartre, in his long tract, *Being and Nothingness* (1943): "It is absurd that we are born; it is absurd that we die."[4] The book may be described as a long essay in introspective psychology, taking a good deal from Heidegger's search for "being," although in contrast to Heidegger, there is no jingoism and more of a search for social responsibility. Starting with the individual awareness of his own existence, bounded by birth and death, Sartre tries to prove the existence of an outer world, and of others in the world. Sartre accepts natural science in that it reveals a "technical world" of "instrumental complexes." But at this stage in his thought, he cannot see science as throwing any light on society and history. Freedom becomes for him an absolute, resting on the individual's own decision as to how he will be engaged with the world.

My fear is free and manifests my freedom. I have put all my freedom into my fear, and I have chosen myself as fearful in this or that circumstance. Under other circumstances I shall exist as deliberate and courageous, and I shall have put all my freedom into my courage. In relation to freedom there is no privileged psychic phenomenon. All my "modes of being" manifest freedom equally since they are all ways of being my own nothingness.[5]

Death, or the individual personality becoming "nothing-ness," as the existentialists put it, is hardly an existentialist discovery. And certainly neither natural science nor the social sciences have been able to provide for people what some religions have at least promised, namely personal immor-tality. But by and large people have not permitted the aware-ness of individual death to interfere with their efforts to know as much as they can about real life and to improve the conditions of life themselves. Even the primitive rituals of the dead assumed that the dead became spirits which could be appealed to in order to better life on earth. In history, it has not been the view of death which affected conditions on earth so much as the other way around. At times when there was general agreement that society was moving ahead and a new stage of freedom was at hand, rendering life more pre-cious, the fact that everyone must eventually die did not seem to be so devastating as to make life itself meaningless. And it has been at times of great crisis, with misery and spreading despair, that life generally came to appear mean-ingless—that is, hostile to individual freedom—and thoughts of death multiplied, the horror of death being the objective embodiment of the emptiness of life.

For the individual personality and the individual con-sciousness are a social creation. They are shaped by both the heritage of the past achievements of society and by the fact that every step in an individual's growth is linked to those around him, not only family, but community, nation and the world. Marx wrote in his *Economic and Philosophic*

Manuscripts, "He (man) exists also in the real world as the awareness of social existence, and as a totality of human life-activity. . . . Death seems to be a harsh victory of the species over the definite individual and to contradict their unity. But the determinate individual is only a determinate species being, and as such, mortal."[6]

To expand on this, it is precisely because the individual consciousness is a product of society through all history, and in turn helps shape society or contributes to it, that individual consciousness is so precious, and at the same time the mortality of the individual does not mean the end, or meaninglessness, of society, history or mankind. The individual and society can move hand in hand. A flourishing, progressing society is one that also holds individual life precious. And there are people whose mode of life and thought intensifies awareness of the tie between their own "determinate" and mortal being, and the continued life of society, of the "species" to which they have made their contribution. The greater a person's breadth of understanding and fellow-feeling with other human beings, the richer is the content of his own individual personality. Whenever people have united against a danger that threatens them all, whether in the Athens of Pericles, the American War of Independence, or the resistance against fascism, it has fostered such a social mind; the awareness of the organic links between individual happiness and the life of the "species." In such struggles an individual needs his fellow human beings with him. To then raise the cry of "individual freedom against society" is the height of lunacy. In other words, the existentialist harping on death and "nothingness," his insistence that all people must live in the frame of mind of one in a death cell awaiting execution, would seem to be more of a "crisis" philosophy than a bold revelation of an awesome truth which the rest of humanity refuses to face.

To Kierkegaard, society was the world given over to "worldliness." To Nietzsche, it was a flock of sheep to be whipped into order by the imperious shepherd. To Sartre and Camus, society is like a woman of the streets whom a "free" man might deal with, while rejecting any obligations she may try to lay upon him. Sartre is more gentle about this. Society is also the "Others," who keep a man's memory alive after he is dead, although how they will think of him he does not know. "One who tries to grasp the meaning of his future death must discover himself as the future prey of others."[7] Camus is more furious, scorning as an infringement of his freedom the very concept that there are laws of nature and society which a man must make part of his thinking.

This scorn is the essence of Camus's attack upon Marxism, in his book on history, *The Rebel* (1954). To Marx, as to Bacon, "Nature to be commanded, must be obeyed," and so to Marx, each discovery of such "necessity," including the laws of economics and of the class forces moving history, increased man's power to change the world, thus reaching a new stage of freedom. To Camus, such recognition of "necessity" is "conformity" and an infringement of freedom. He calls Marx's view, "creative fatalism." He is shocked that Marx finds capitalism to be an advance over feudalism, and then discovers in capitalism the maturing forces that would replace it with socialism. Marx, Camus says, "justifies the order that is established in his time. The most eloquent eulogy of capitalism was made by its greatest enemy. Marx is only anti-capitalist in so far as capitalism is out of date. Another order must be established which will demand, in the name of history, a new conformity."[8]

Camus's objection to the Marxist view of laws of society is not that it is invalid, but that even if true, he wants no part of it. His "freedom" lies in the act of rebellion against "conformity," and whether this act results in any help to, progress for or liberation of others is to him irrelevant. The existentialist social theory boils down to the principle of, in a hideous world, keeping one's own hands clean. Thus Camus decides that he, personally, will not kill. "The freedom to kill, is not compatible with the sense of rebellion." One can go further, by taking up "social killing." Unearthing the laws which explain poverty, exploitation, unemployment, crises and wars, makes it possible for society to eliminate them. And certainly today, if the movement for peace is worldwide, and has promise of success, it is because people know as never before what are the social forces that have made for war. To Camus, however, "I won't kill" is immediate. To enlighten people about the social causes of war, to organize them about this, to ask people to fight in their own defense, puts its perspective in the future. And so to Camus, this thinking makes Marxism "a slave to history." Thus, he says, "it increases the domain of historic murder and at the same time leaves it without any justification, except in the future—which again demands faith."[9]

The irony is that underneath this barrage of proclamations, it is really Camus who, so far as his theories take hold, increases the domain of "historic murder." For the Marxist analysis of the economic and social forces behind fascism helped people to combat it and equipped them to recognize its reappearances. Camus, however, leaves people powerless to do anything about it. In *The Rebel*, while he expresses his distaste for fascism, he analyzes it purely in terms of its own ideology or propaganda. It is a "nihilistic revolution." The fascists were "mystics." And all one can do is to counter it with a different, or correct—that is, existentialist—theory of rebellion; an individual saying, "No!" As with Nietzsche and Heidegger, so with Camus, the generalizations of history, which treat with contempt what is really known about history, place the "free thinker" in a self-fabricated prisonhouse of primitivism and ignorance.

Camus wrote in his essay, *The Artist and His Time* (1953): "Considered as artists, we perhaps have no need to interfere in the affairs of the world. But considered as men, yes. The miner who is exploited or shot down, the slaves in the camps, those in the colonies, the legions of persecuted throughout the world—they need all those who can speak to communicate their silence and to keep in touch with them."[10] This statement, if widely accepted by artists, could appreciably raise the humanistic level of the arts today. And yet it has its limitations. It makes no promise to discover the reasons for exploitation or persecution. It is not the statement of one who feels akin to the oppressed or exploited, who shares their struggles and rejoices in their victories. It is again, the "gesture." He, the artist, will speak for the "underdog." His hands are clean.

And it is worth pointing out that, as Philip Thody writes in *Albert Camus: A Study of His Work* (1957), when, in 1956-57, the atrocities against the Algerian people inflicted by the French colonial administration reached their peak, and Sartre was making an angry attack upon the torture of prisoners, Camus refused to take part in the protest. He merely pointed out, Thody says, that he "has already made his position clear on Algeria, demanding an end of colonial practises and the setting up of a federation which would assure both Arabs and European settlers equal rights, and he is not a writer who is given to excessive repetition of his political suggestions."[11] After all, Camus can say it is not he who is killing Arabs. His hands are clean.

The test of an artist's views of life lies in his art. In this respect Camus's most widely read novel, *The Plague* (1948),[12] is illuminating. It is a symbolical and allegorical novel clothed in the most graphically realistic detail, as if it were recounting an event in history. The time is a year in the 1940's, the setting is the Algerian city of Oran. In spring, the city is disturbed by the appearance of dead rats in the streets and houses; this is followed by the outbreak of an epidemic soon recognized as the "plague" which had decimated Europe repeatedly from the Middle Ages through the 18th century, but had been considered extirpated. The city is quarantined, all travel is prohibited, no ship or train can leave. The fight against the epidemic is carried on by a handful of doctors with some aid by the city administration and volunteer sanitation squads. The death toll reaches thousands, but finally, in the course of a year, the plague runs its course and disappears.

Conspicuous throughout the novel is Camus's contempt for the great mass of people. First of all, the Africans, Arabs or Negroes do not exist for him. Only "French Algerians" figure in the story. And most of them are stunned, apathetic, selfish, each driven into his own shell.

In this extremity of solitude, none could count on any help from his neighbor; each had to bear the load of his troubles alone. If, by some chance, one of us tried to unburden himself or to say something about his feelings, the reply he got, whatever it might be, usually wounded him.

In the streetcars, people turn their backs to one another, their only thought being to avoid contagion.

The outside world gives no help at all, but for some inadequate serum and a few doctors and assistants. It seems willing to let the entire population die, so long as it can avoid contamination. The leading characters exhibit diverse personal reactions. At one extreme is the criminal Cottard, who profits from the epidemic through organized black market operations and is disappointed when the plague subsides. At the other extreme are the two existentialist "heroes," Dr. Bernard Rieux and Jean Tarrou.

Dr. Rieux is the "unconscious" existentialist. Day and night he fights the plague, not with any hope of success, but only because that is what a man has to do.

"I've never managed to get used to seeing people die . . ."
"Yes. But your victories will never be lasting; that's all."
"Yes, I know that. But it's no reason for giving up the struggle."
"No reason," I agree. "Only I now can picture what this plague means for you."
"Yes. A never-ending defeat."

Jean Tarrou is the conscious existentialist, in the sense that he has worked out his philosophy. With the anarchism organic to existentialism, he regards all government as worthless, and so organizes his own volunteer sanitary squads. They make up an "elite," the self-chosen few, who out of their innate nobility help the suffering.

"I know I have no place in the world of today; once I'd definitely refused to kill, I doomed myself to an exile that can never end. I leave it to others to make history. . . . All I maintain is that on this earth there are pestilences and there are victims, and it is up to us, so far as possible, not to join forces with the pestilences. . . . That's why I decided to take, in every predicament, the victim's side, so as to reduce the damage done."

The Plague, like *The Stranger*, is a piece of didacticism or special pleading, with everything contrived to fit Camus's argument. That the rest of the world ignores Oran in its ordeal makes the point that human beings are basically self-centered and only a few, the "elite," feel social responsibility. That the fight against the plague is hopeless, led by the relative few who do this as existentialists, demonstrates that science is a broken crutch, that history is meaningless, that nobody can really know anything about the world. Camus does say that "there are more things to admire in people than to despise." But he also says that when the plague is over, people return to pleasures as if nothing had happened. Yet the plague will strike again.

And indeed, as he listened to the cries of joy rising from the town, Rieux remembered that such joy is always imperiled. He knew what those jubilant crowds did not know but could have learned from books; that the plague bacillus never dies or disappears for good . . . and that perhaps the day would come when, for the bane and enlightening of man, it would rouse up its rats again and send them forth to die in a happy city.

Since the novel is an allegory, the "plague" can be read as many different things; a war, an invasion or the Nazi occupation of France, with the "sanitary squads" representing the Resistance. But, for all such catastrophes, the conclusion drawn is the same. People can learn nothing, for there is nothing to know.

The Plague is a fictional polemic masquerading as a social novel. This means, not that it is a "bad" novel but that a view of life imposes certain boundaries and limits for the art form. *The Plague* is unable to become a social novel because society never really enters the book. What holds it together is the eloquence of the writing, the vivid details, the powerful naturalism that actualizes the terrors and agonies of the victims, and a poetic gift that makes the oppression and then lifting of the weight so moving.

The question of whether Camus would have gone through a further development was tragically ended by his own "absurd" death in 1960, in the crash of a car driven by a friend at 90 miles an hour. Sartre, however, has gone through a considerable development. It is seen in his social activity, his defense of the Algerians against the French colonialists, his work in the movement for world peace. And it is seen in his art. Although his philosophical position started out much like that of Camus, in his art he early showed qualities that Camus lacked. One was a broad sweep of human sympathies, so that with less subjectivity than Camus, he could put in his books a wealth of keenly observed and delineated people. Another was the ability to put these individuals into a realistic social setting, so that they became both individual and typical, each revealing a different pattern of response to the conflicts and problems of a real world.

In his philosophy, even though he starts with the existentialist stress on the individual "being" or "existence" in a cloudy world, Sartre emphasizes the individual engagement with an actual situation in a way not found in Heidegger or Jaspers. Thus, in the essay, *Existentialism and Humanism* (1948), he carries further the thought of responsibility, already put forth in *Being and Nothingness*:

The first effect of existentialism is that it puts every man in possession of himself as he is, and places the entire responsibility for his existence squarely upon his own shoulders. And, when we say that man is responsible for himself, we do not mean that he is responsible only for his own individuality, but that he is responsible for all men . . . in choosing for himself, he chooses for all men.[13]

Within this brave talk about accepting responsibility, there is still the existentialist impotence. It is a keen insight for Sartre to see that an individual reflects a society, a period, a situation, an age. And his statement that what he chooses for himself, he chooses for all men, is a long step above Nietzsche's view that the "free" individual is the commander over others, the "master." But he cannot carry the thought further, and see both the society and the individual as the product of historical development. And so since the past is confusion, the future is impenetrable mystery. He cannot see that anything the "engaged" individual does can set any forces in motion, can lead to foreseeable progress.

I cannot count upon men whom I do not know, I cannot base my confidence on human goodness or upon men's interest in the

good of society, seeing that man is free and that there is no human
nature which I can take as foundational. . . . Nor can I be sure
that my comrades-in-arms will take up my work after my death
and carry it to the maximum perfection, seeing that those men
are free agents and will freely decide, tomorrow, what man is then
to be.[14]

Thus, to Sartre, the battle must be carried on without
hope and without knowledge. The terrible weakness in this
reasoning is that there is so much available knowledge and
such necessity to use it. History certainly does not tell us that
man is "good," or that he lives for the "good of society," nor
does it give us some basic, absolute and unchanging "human
nature." But what it does tell us is that, at decisive times,
human beings will generally fight for their own freedom and
will do so socially, as the only way to attain it. Men have
not especially needed to be told to fight for their freedom,
or to struggle against oppression. What they need to see
and to understand is the way to do it so that they will
actually gain freedom.

In his novel *Nausea* (1938),[15] issued during the period when
the popular front stopped the advance of fascism in France,
Sartre seems to have been far from "socially engaged." The
novel takes the form of a diary written by a historian working
on the biography of a French nobleman of the time of the
revolution of 1789 and the Napoleonic Empire. The historian, Antoine Roquentin, suddenly finds himself afflicted
by "Nausea," an overwhelming sense of the meaninglessness
of life, his own and the life outside of him. People and
nature have become utterly repulsive to him, and he finds
himself alienated even from his own body. "I see my hand
spread out on the table. It lives, it is me. . . . It is lying on its
back. It shows me its fat belly. It looks like an animal turned
upside down. My hand turns over, spreads out flat on its
stomach, offers me the sight of its back. . . . I feel my hand.

I am these two beasts struggling at the end of my arms." He has fantasies resembling surrealist paintings, in which the sex organs take on a loathsome guise, like hairy leaves crawling with insects. The sound of jazz sometimes soothes him, but it is only a temporary alleviation.

The progress of the novel is Roquentin's half-hearted struggle against the "Nausea" until he accepts it as a revelation of the essential truth of life. There is a touching scene—perhaps the best in the book—when he meets his former, now aging, mistress, in the hope that a renewal of intimacy will take him out of himself, only to find that any attachment between them is no longer possible. There is a short outburst of action, when he defends a man in a library who has been discovered making homosexual advances to a boy. But in the end,

All of a sudden, there it was, clear as day: existence had suddenly unveiled itself . . . the diversity of things, their individuality, were only an appearance, a veneer. This veneer had melted, leaving soft, monstrous masses, all in disorder—naked, in a frightful, obscene nakedness. . . . And without formulating anything clearly, I understood that I had found the key to Existence, the key to my Nausea, to my own life. In fact, all that I could grasp beyond that returns to this fundamental absurdity.

The novel can be looked upon, like Camus's *The Plague*, as an exposition of existentialist philosophy. But Sartre, within the limits of the psychological types he presents, writes more realistically than Camus, providing an authentic tie between the psychological study and an actual social setting. Thus the novel can be fitted into a social and historical reality broader than that envisaged by Sartre himself, and can be taken as a revealing analysis of an alienated human being, and part of the documentation of the inner, mental aspect of the crisis of our times.

With the trilogy of novels, *Les Chemins de la Liberte*

(*Paths to Freedom*),[16] published between 1945 and 1949, Sartre, the artist, enlarged the breadth of his social engagement. The first novel, *The Age of Reason*, depicts a group of people in the Paris of 1938, against the background of the closing stages of the war in Spain. The second novel, *The Reprieve*, takes the same characters and a number of others through the week of the Munich betrayal, in September 1938. The third, *Troubled Sleep*, carries them into the defeat of France by the German invaders in June 1940. The authenticity of the characters and situations, the intensity with which Sartre raises the question of what happened to France, and the interweaving of private life with politics, bring the trilogy close to being an outstanding social novel of modern France. It falls short because Sartre's outlook is vitiated by the existentialist theory, which abandons all search for laws and patterns of movement in society. Sartre vividly depicts the betrayers of France, who are also the betrayers of Spain, of Czechoslovakia, of peace and democracy. He portrays the defenders of France and of democracy, and those who are confused and bewildered. But what in real life originates from the clash of social classes, Sartre sees as the clash solely of individual personalities, and so, why France fell, why fascism gained its temporary domination, never emerges from the book.

The writing is marvellously skillful. The second novel is especially a remarkable *tour de force*; a dozen or more stories of individual life and political events are broken, then pieced together like a mosaic, with the characters and setting changing from paragraph to paragraph and sometimes in mid-sentence—a virtuoso climax of the structural method Sartre employs in the trilogy as a whole. This might be called the "stream of consciousness turned outward." It uses the typical material of a socially realistic novel, namely, significant characters against a background of society and politics, in the kaleidoscopic montage of an interior monologue, the scenes linked not by any line of development or dramatic conflict but by accidental parallelisms of mood or motif. Thus the style and structure are themselves embodiments of Sartre's existentialist thinking. The artist does not stew in his own subjectivism, but gets out into the world and is socially "engaged," but the social world is seen as irrational and chaotic, given meaning only by his "engagement."

In his characters, Sartre depicts the varied responses to political events. There is the wealthy financier, a homosexual, who collaborates with the fascists, accepting the "rape" of France as the welcome "rape" of himself. There is the young student, of Russian expatriate parents, who lives in defiance of all conventional moralities, but who, to hit back at the fascists, escapes from France to join the British air force. There is the Communist, whom Sartre regards as not a "free" person, being tied by party discipline, but whom Sartre describes in a friendly manner, as he tries, after the collapse of the French army, to raise morale and organize resistance among the prisoners being shipped off to Germany. The main character, Mathieu Delarue, is the medium through whom Sartre expounds his existentialism.

Delarue is a teacher of philosophy who, when we first meet him, seeks a way to be "free." He searches everywhere except in his actual kinship with people and in the social ties that would disclose the problems he shares with others. His teaching is meaningless to him, and hardly occupies his mind. His pupils mean nothing to him, but for a young girl with whom he is in love. He has a mistress whom he no longer loves, and who is pregnant. She wants to have the child but he proposes to raise money for an abortion, since marriage and family to him represent unfreedom. He feels vaguely impelled to join the Republican forces fighting in Spain, but not enough to take the step. A friend asks him to join the

Communist Party, but he refuses because he has no strong convictions. Nowhere can he find the freedom he is looking for. In typical existentialist style, he muses, "This life had been given him for nothing, he was nothing." It is part of Sartre's realistic gift that we can glimpse from the story what Sartre himself does not accept; that freedom does rise out of the recognition of necessity, that the laws of reality must be known and obeyed so that reality can be commanded, and that Delarue's avoidance of "necessity," in this sense, accounts for the futility of his search for freedom.

In the concluding novel, Delarue is one of the mass of French soldiers disorganized by the defeat, abandoned by their officers and waiting to be picked up as prisoners by the advancing German army. He runs into a platoon of soldiers who have been fighting a rearguard battle and now are determined, despite the armistice, to make a last stand, to hold a village against the entire German army until they are wiped out. They recognize that there is no reason or logic to this. It would not alter events for any of them to kill a few German soldiers and die themselves. But their pride as men demands that they refuse to acknowledge defeat, that they make this last stand in scorn for the enemy and for the whole incomprehensible and hostile world. Mathieu decides to join them. At first, as the moment of battle approaches, it occurs to him that he is about to die for nothing. "Here and now I have decided that all along death has been the secret of my life. I die in order to demonstrate the impossibility of living." Then the battle gets under way. One by one his comrades are killed. In 15 minutes Mathieu is the only survivor. These 15 minutes, he realizes with joy, were his life of freedom. As he is about to be killed, Sartre writes, "He fired; he was cleansed, he was all-powerful, he was free."

This is the existentialist revolt at the height of its social engagement. In an age of great crises and wars, of trusts and monopolies that, through fascism, threaten to destroy the very democratic institutions by which capitalism had risen out of feudalism, the range of freedom of growth that the individual can wrest for himself in this war narrows to the vanishing point. A science of society, with its promise of progress, seems to be fraud and delusion, for the mighty forces that capitalism had called "progress" are now crushing the individual. The private or love life in which he seeks refuge turns to ashes, for here, too, the alienation of human beings from one another has injected its poison. The essential core of love of life, namely the confidence in the possibilities of human development, has been blasted. He has no patience to assess the forces that history discloses, to recall how, in the past, crises have been met, and the mass of people, in their own good time, have cooperated to move forward, for these lessons are obliterated for him by the present crisis. This crisis seems to be a personal attack on him by life. He sees the vast majority of people as apathetic or deluded. Only a relative few, the "elite," have grasped the truth of the meaninglessness of life, and thus can act with "freedom." Whether his revolt is against moral conventions, science, knowledge, authority, institutions, laws, art traditions, or all of them together, the form it takes is violent because of the realization that his individual gesture is impotent to change anything. The interrelation of means and ends disappears, for the means becomes the end. Freedom lies in the act itself.

It is a psychological pattern with a long history. Shakespeare, in his eagerness to find out what goes on in every kind of mind, projected many "types" then in their infancy that developed in later periods into figures reflecting major aspects of social life. In *Macbeth* he introduces two minor characters, not even given names; the murderers whom Macbeth hires to kill Banquo. Macbeth asks are they really willing to do what he asks of them. They answer:

SECOND MURDERER

I am one, my liege,
Whom the vile blows and buffets of the world
Hath so incensed, that I am reckless what
I do to spite the world.

FIRST MURDERER

And I another,
So weary with disasters, tugg'd with fortune
That I would set my life on any chance,
To mend it, or be rid on't.

They are two different types. The first murderer, who speaks second, is "with the world," a gambler for high stakes who has lost and desperately wants to recoup. The second, who speaks first, is willing to blow up the world, and himself with it. This revenge is his freedom. Through history, this attitude will take different ideological forms, among them, the existentialist. Sartre, in a critical study, *Saint Genet*, devotes almost 300,000 words to the analysis of such a mentality.

Yet Sartre has a little more of the Shakespearean attitude than Camus. He gets out of his skin, looks objectively even at personages closest to his thinking, and is open to the currents of social life. If his social activities suggest changes in his views, he makes these changes.

In his continued debate with Marxism, Sartre has come to accept the Marxist approach to society and history. In the introduction (published here in 1963 as "Search for a Method") to a long treatise, *Critique de la raison dialectique,* the first volume of which appeared in France in 1960, he asserts that Marxism is "the philosophy of our time." Any attempts to go "beyond" Marxism, he says, "will be at

worst only a return to pre-Marxism; at best, only the redis-
covery of a thought already contained in the philosophy
which one believes he has gone beyond. . . . Existentialism
is a parasitical system living on the margin of Knowledge,
which at first it opposed but into which today it seeks to
be integrated."[17]

The integration of existentialism into Marxism, Sartre
says, is justified because Marxism "is very young, almost in
its infancy; it has scarcely begun to develop." His objection
to Marxism is that its aim, as he sees it, is to constitute itself
as "absolute Knowledge," and yet it lacks "totalization in
depth"; that is, the full penetration of psychology, of what
is going on in the individual mind. And here, he feels, existentialism can make an important contribution. He says, for
example, that when Marxism analyzes history and the movement of society in terms of the conflicts between the interests of social classes, it still cannot predict what any
individual member of a class will do, or what form his decision will take. The individual, he says, gets lost in the
"idea." It is necessary, he says, to study the "distress" of
the individual, rising from his "alienation." In a society
"founded on exploitation," he says, all individuals are "lost
since childhood." This, he says, is the province of existentialism aided by psychoanalysis.[18]

While whatever contribution Sartre will make to the
understanding of this "human dimension" rests on a study
and discussion of his completed thesis, certain things can be
said at this point.

One is that by embracing Marxist dialectical and historical materialism, Sartre has broken sharply with the existentialist tradition and trend.

Second, Marxism never claims to represent absolute or
total "knowledge," nor does it believe that human beings
will ever know "everything" about themselves and the uni-

verse. It does claim to bring into a unified picture whatever knowledge has been achieved, and to open paths for the further development of knowledge. In analyzing the relation between the material or economic realities of a society and its prevailing ideas, it points out that social classes in the aggregate act as classes, but individuals among them may act quite differently. The *Communist Manifesto* of 1848 itself pointed out how the organization of the workers "as a class" is constantly "disrupted" by competition among them, and how members of the bourgeois will go over to the working class, when they see beyond narrow class interests to "the historical movement as a whole." As Marxists see it, an individual's search for freedom will take one course when he knows the nature of the forces at work about him, and another when he is ignorant of these forces. Which way any particular person will move, they cannot say. The relation it points out between ideas and material realities does not aim at a mechanistic view of human behavior but, on the contrary, at making a contribution to freedom. It enables people to understand the origin of their ideas, to look at them critically, to make decisions with an awareness of not merely their immediate results but their continued repercussions. Sartre is really demanding of Marxism a psychological determinism it never pretended to possess; for example the ability to explain not merely the forces which led to the American independence from England, but what made George Washington a hero and Benedict Arnold a traitor.

What Sartre does put his finger on is the fact that, in the relatively short but momentous period since the publication of *Capital*, the leading Marxist thinkers have devoted themselves far more to economic and political matters than psychological ones, and so a gap exists. Nevertheless, Marxism is far from a blank so far as psychology is concerned. The works of Marx and Engels, like *Capital*, *Anti-Dühring* and

The Origin of the Family, are rich in implications concerning the inner, subjective life of the human being. And Marx's discussion of the phenomenon of alienation, in his early manuscripts, provides profound psychological insights into the mind of the individual in capitalist society, throwing light upon the problems raised by existentialism. Furthermore, Marx's thesis is that even in an exploitive society, all people are by no means "alienated" or "lost."

This study has tried to show, up to this point, that existentialist philosophy is not a discovery and expression of "eternal truths," but a product of a special, historical social situation. The successive stages of the rise of capitalism out of the feudal world brought about an immense expansion of individual sensitivity and the awareness of profound potentialities in the mind, stimulated by the new arenas opened up for human activity. But this growth was accompanied by an increasingly cutthroat competitive, internecine war raging through society, and tending to make each individual see another as his enemy, although the other was only his mirror-image. This contradiction developed with rising intensity in the 19th century and reached a climax in the 20th. Existentialism itself can be seen as one, philosophical, facet of a much broader movement; the trend in the arts of the past century to the increasing exploration of "private," inner "worlds," developing fantastic sensitivity in this direction at the expense of losing or cutting the threads which bound these internal conflicts to real and understandable conflicts in the external, social world.

What Marx's analysis of alienation does is to restore the awareness of the ties between "outer" and "inner" worlds, especially in this complex social situation. This study will try to develop Marx's concept further, in the hope of throwing light upon the appeal of existentialism to American writers of our times.

SOCIOLOGICAL AND LITERARY
DEPICTION OF ALIENATION:
Marx, Balzac and Eugene O'Neill

The concept of alienation is vividly illustrated by the title of David Riesman's sociological treatise, *The Lonely Crowd*. The "crowd" is made of people so linked together as to give it its own organic life. In the "lonely" crowd the individuals are estranged from one another, so that the links chafe like manacles, and communication and mutual understanding are replaced by estrangement and hostility. The estrangement intensifies as the bonds become tighter, just as in a crowded subway train, the more closely the riders are packed, the more violent is their elbowing and struggle for private breathing space. So it is in social life where the activity of each must link with that of others for the satisfaction of his needs, yet each looks upon the conglomerate "others" as a hostile force, stifling his freedom. The individual becomes "alienated"; that is, estranged not only from the "others" but from himself, from that part of his necessary life activity which creates and strengthens the very ties that appear so oppressive.

While only in recent years has the term "alienation" been widely used in psychological, sociological and literary discussions, Marx dealt with the phenomenon in his *Economic and Philosophical Manuscripts of 1844*, observing that alienation stemmed from private property; indeed, that it was the psychological counterpart of the economic and social domination by private property. Private property, in this sense, does not refer to the things a person uses or consumes, like food, clothing or furniture but to the private possession of the means of production by which society maintains itself. Something necessary to everybody's life, the productivity of which is socially created, like the land, natural resources, tools, machinery, becomes "private," subject to arbitrary self-interest, estranged from those whose life depends upon it. Private property, Marx showed, is not a relation of people to things, as we imply when we say that we "own" a watch or automobile, but a relation among people. The very qualities that make a thing desirable as private property are those given to it by society. To own a tract of land is meaningless as private property, unless there are people on it whose labor makes it productive, under conditions which compel them to work while the fruit of their work goes to the master. And a factory is meaningless as private property unless workers operate the machines and there is a market where the product can be sold.

The awareness of alienation differs from class antagonism, or the awareness by the exploited of how and by whom they are exploited. It is a psychological phenomenon, an internal conflict, a hostility felt toward something seemingly outside oneself which is linked to oneself, a barrier erected which is actually no defense but an impoverishment of oneself. Engendered by the distortions of life in an exploitive society, it affects both exploiters and exploited. Marx wrote of the European Middle Ages, "feudal landed property is already by its nature huckstered land—the earth which is estranged from man and hence, confronts him in the shape of a few great lords," so that the land dominates men "as an alien power."[1] The peasant expressed this alienation in his avid desire for a piece of land he could call his own, the fruit of which would also be his own. The craving for such a piece of land drove millions of peasants to America. The feudal noblemen also felt this domination of land as a power over him in the drive to acquire ever larger domains, either through marriage or war.

Just as the contradiction latent in private property rises to its peak under capitalism, with its contrasts of herculean production to glutted markets, unemployment and starvation, so under capitalism alienation reaches its peak. There is first the alienation of the worker from his product and from himself as the creator of the product. The medieval or folk artisan, however miserably he lived, could sometimes create a work of beauty, shaped by his skill and imagination. It was a piece of the outer world that he had "humanized," giving it a form through his own awakened senses, with his own life activity and growth as a craftsman crystallized in it. But the creative power of the worker in a capitalist enterprise is negated by the "machine." It is not only that he performs one specialized operation. This is not a laceration or mechanization of himself if he can combine it with mental work; that is, if he can envision the total operation of which his work is a part, appreciate the cooperation which links it to that of others, see a direct relation between his production and a better life for himself, and let his imagination work on improvements in the overall process. But under the conditions of production for someone else's private profit, the workers cannot feel any attachment to their product. The product itself is designed primarily for profit, and secondarily for use. If it is more profitable to manufacture a bad product, that is what is done. The form of the work is set not by his imagination, but by the boss. The worker gives up his life as a human being, in return for subsistence.

The more efficient a worker is, the greater is the risk of his being thrown out of work, either through a cutting down of the work force or production outrunning the market. The worker, through his work, puts himself out of work. Marx wrote:

The alienation of the worker in his product means not only that his labor becomes an object, an external existence, but that it exists outside him, independently, as something alien to him, and that it becomes a power on its own confronting him; it means that the life which he has conferred on the object confronts him as something hostile and alien.[2]

It is not only the factory worker who suffers alienation. Characteristic of recent times is the vast amount of scientific, professional and artistic talent involved in the network of industrial monopoly production, with the talented person here too alienated from his own creative skills, or from part of himself. Blame for the vacancy and dullness of most of the "popular" or "slick" fiction, music and motion pictures produced today is put on the "low taste" of the "masses." What they really reflect is the alienation of the skilled worker from his work, which no longer has the free play of his imagination and the growth of his mind, but follows a pattern set by the "sales department." Art turns into pseudo-art, mechanized and formula-ridden.

And the capitalist himself suffers alienation. He cannot live as a human being in relation to others, except in the most restricted sense. He is first of all alienated from the workers. He needs them to tend his machines, but he must treat them as machine parts, not as people. And while he benefits from them he fears them. Every step they take in an organized way, through trade unions and politics, to better their conditions menaces what he sees as his freedom. And his alienation shows itself in a very real way. The workers become "monsters" in his eyes, and especially when they assert their human strivings.

When exploitation is combined with the plunder or oppression of a national group, the alienation is expressed in chauvinistic "monster" images, found not only in common speech but in respected art works. The peoples of exploited regions are presented as sub-human, and the presentation is no less inhuman when masked in supposedly "kindly" comic caricatures. So it is with the Negroes in the United States. As long as a mass of white people conceive whatever minimal security they think they have as resting on the secondary status of the Negro, and therefore "menaced" by the struggle for equal rights, this "monster" image will emerge as a product of their own alienation. People who have essentially the same hopes, feelings and potentialities as they, who should be seen as human kin, are seen as fearsome and alien.

The alienation felt by an exploiter for the exploited can be given ideological support, like theories of the alleged inferiority of Negroes or "strangeness" of Jews. But alienation itself is psychological and self-divisive, a projection by the hater upon others of the image of the inhuman practices to which he himself feels driven. So to a racketeer everyone else has his own racket. The leaders of "civilized" nations, carrying out inhuman and barbarous practices against the "backward" peoples whose resources they have seized, accuse their victims of being barbarians.

Those in the upper brackets of ownership or management of capitalist enterprise are also alienated from their fellows. In *Capital*, Marx shows how the capitalist is a prisoner of the very operations which bring him his profits, or "freedom." He becomes, Marx says, "one of the wheels" of a social mechanism. "The development of capitalist production makes it constantly necessary to keep increasing the amount of the capital laid out in a given industrial undertaking, and the competition makes the immanent laws of capitalist production to be felt by each individual capitalist, as external, coercive laws."[3] This external coercion takes on the physiognomy of his rivals. They are his enemies. He profits from their failures. They profit from his. Whatever plans he makes clash with theirs, and so begin to operate in ways neither foresee. If competition seems to be checked by nationwide monopolization it returns with greater force on an international scale.

The very power of money capital, both in its capacity to "multiply itself" and in its position as the purchaser of all other values, makes it a force for alienation and impoverishment of life. There is, first of all, the miserliness it engenders. To spend it is to rob oneself of the "interest" or profit it can bring when invested. And also, since it can purchase everything, it becomes more precious than the things themselves. Marx points out in his early manuscripts that many new commodities do not enrich life but create artificial needs. "Each person speculates on creating a new need in the other. . . . The increase in the quantity of objects is accompanied by an extension of the realm of alien powers to which man is subjected. . . . Man becomes ever poorer as man; his need for money becomes ever greater if he wants to overpower hostile being. . . . The need for money is therefore the true need produced by the modern economic system." And so the preciousness of money inspires the "morality" of the self-denial of really human needs.

The less you eat, drink and read books; the less you go to the theatre, the dance hall, the public house; the less you think, love, theorize, sing, paint, fence, etc., the more you save—the greater becomes your treasure which neither moths nor dust will devour—your capital. The less you are, the more you have; the less you express your own life, the greater is your alienated life—the greater is the store of your estranged being. Everything which the political economist takes from you in life and in humanity, he replaces for you in wealth.[4]

But if, on the one hand, there is a puritanical self-denial, on the other there is lavish expenditure for reasons that have nothing to do with truly human enrichment. Marx writes in

Capital, "When a certain stage of development has been reached, a conventional degree of prodigality, which is also an exhibition of wealth, and consequently a source of credit, becomes a business necessity."[5] Thorstein Veblen developed this thought brilliantly and wittily in *The Theory of the Leisure Class,* with his analyses of "conspicuous consumption," "conspicuous waste," the sacrifice of the satisfaction of genuine needs for luxuries that establish social status, the craving for publicity behind philanthropic donations. And, as Marx noted in his early manuscripts, there is also the wild spending in a frustrated search for pleasure.

There is a form of inactive, extravagant wealth given over wholly to pleasure, the enjoyer of which on the one hand behaves as a mere ephemeral individual frantically spending himself to no purpose, knows the slave-labor of others (human sweat and blood) as the prey of his cupidity, and therefore knows man himself, and hence also his own self, as a sacrificed and empty being. With such wealth the contempt of man makes its appearance, partly as arrogance and as the throwing away of what can give sustenance to a hundred human lives. . . . He knows the realization of the essential powers of man only as the realization of his own excesses, his whims and capricious, bizarre notions.[6]

The precedence accorded to money (which presumably can buy all satisfactions) over human satisfactions themselves, and the valuation of things solely in terms of their profit potential, starves the senses. The enjoyment of beauty is a human response to the sensory richness of the external world. Through working with the things of the world, changing them for human use, the human being discovers not only the structure and use of these things but also their sensuous qualities. What he perceives is real, but he has had to develop the power to perceive it, and so the enjoyment of beauty is also the awareness of his own growth as a human being. The world thus "educates" the human being as he works with it. And so to recognize beauty is to respond to nature "humanized." But nature treated as a commodity becomes nature alienated.

The enjoyment of beauty is the expression of a freedom of mind which is the opposite of the obsession to "have" something, or transform it into private property. A person looking at the countryside may get a lift out of the curve of a hill or the play of trees against the sky, but a real-estate operator will see only how it can be divided into lots. If necessary he will cut down the trees or level the hill. The nearest to a dream of beauty in his mind is the vision of purchasers crowding to make down payments. Even to the art collector, rarity comes to have a greater appeal than intrinsic beauty. Marx writes: "Private property has made us so stupid and one-sided that an object is ours when we have it—when it exists for us as capital, or when it is directly possessed, eaten, drunk, worn, inhabited, etc.—in short, when it is used by us."[7]

Frederick Douglass understood this stupidity when he wrote in his *Autobiography* of his youth as a slave on the Lloyd plantation. He knew how little the fact of "property" had to do with the enjoyment of beauty. "The tops of the stately poplars were often covered with redwinged blackbirds, making all nature vocal with the joyous life and beauty of their wild, warbling notes. These all belonged to me as well as to Col. Edward Lloyd, and, whether they did or not, I greatly enjoyed them."

Estrangement and alienation enter into the most intimate of relationships, the family. Here, where people are at their closest to one another, the very form taken by the ties that bind them, breed antagonisms. For these family ties are conditioned by and reflect the power of money and private property in the outside world. As Engels puts it in *The Origin of the Family, Private Property, and the State:*

Marriage is conditioned by the class position of the parties and is to that extent always a marriage of convenience. . . . This marriage of convenience turns often enough into crassest prostitution —sometimes of both partners, but far more commonly of the woman, who only differs from the ordinary courtesan in that she does not let out her body on piecework, as a wage-worker, but sells it once and for all into slavery. . . . The wife became the head servant, excluded from all participation in social production. . . . The modern individual family is founded on the open or concealed domestic slavery of the wife; and modern society is a mass composed of these individual families as its molecules. In the great majority of cases today, at least in the possessing classes, the husband is obliged to earn a living and support his family, and that in itself gives him a position of supremacy, without any need for special legal titles and privileges.[8]

Thus the seeds of estrangement are inherent in the family under capitalism. That it also affects the children from infancy has been amply documented by Freud, and a host of novelists and playwrights. Freud showed courage and made history in forcing society to accept such unpleasant truths. Yet the creative writers in many cases show an insight into realities that Freud lacks; they trace the social and economic roots of the problem, where Freud schematizes it as an eternal battle of the id, ego, superego, penis-envy, "Oedipus Complex" and so on. Engels shows us why the bourgeois family relationship inevitably encourages prostitution and adultery, and also why such escapes by both husband and wife from the estrangement of love in the family cannot satisfy the need they express.

A passage in Marx's philosophical manuscripts throws light upon the naturalism in regard to sex that has preoccupied literature for at least the past half century; the dwelling in detail on prostitution, on the sex organs and on the physical act of intercourse. Much of this emphasis rose as a derisive attack upon moral hypocrisy and exposure of the corruption behind the bourgeois facade of "wedded bliss." And while there should be no side of life closed to art, the point is that this art also shows, unwittingly, what has been lost to alienation. To point derisively to prostitution or the sheerly physical sex act as the "real facts" of love is really to imply that an entire area of human relationships has been eroded; the complex relationships of mutual growth, aid and affectionate understanding of which the sex act is but the base. Marx writes:

As a result man (the worker) no longer feels himself to be freely active in any but his animal functions—eating, drinking, procreating, or at most in his dwelling and in dressing-up, etc.; and in his human functions he no longer feels himself to be anything but an animal. What is animal becomes human and what is human becomes animal.

This applies not only to the worker but to all classes of society. Alienation in man's "human" life—that is, his social life, his work—causes him to lose the possibility of his growth through it and his discovery of himself in it. For this "human" life has turned into the jungle animal life of a war for survival. And so, the "animal" functions, like the physical act of sexual intercourse, become the only ones in which he finds himself to be "human," although the level is driven down to the animal. Marx continues: "Certainly eating, drinking, procreating, etc., are also genuinely human functions. But in the abstraction which separates them from the sphere of all other human activity and turns them into sole and ultimate ends, they are animal."

We can relate to this a passage from another essay:

The relation of man to woman is the most natural relation of human being to human being. It therefore reveals the extent to which man's natural behavior has become human, or the extent to which the human essence in him has become a natural essence —the extent to which his human nature has become nature to him. In this relationship is revealed, too, the extent to which man's need has become a human need; the extent to which, therefore, the other person as a person has become for him a need—the ex-

tent to which he in his individual existence has become a social
being.[9]

The alienation Marx describes in analytic terms is the
underlying theme of a host of literary works. For if one of the
triumphal achievements of 19th and 20th century world
literature is the breadth of its social panorama, presenting so
to speak the living history of the time, a necessary accompaniment to this was its penetration into internal or subjective
life, exploring the psychologies shaped by the swift transformations of social life and the problems and dilemmas they
brought forth. Characteristic of the greatest writers was their
stubborn fidelity to reality, and readiness to explore heretofore trackless areas of social behavior and the mind. It is both
the direct light thrown on contemporary history and the probing into the depths of mental conflict that give the literature
of the age its unique sensibility. And part of this discovered
reality is the growing cancer of alienation corrupting the most
intimate of human relationships.

Thus Balzac, in *Eugenie Grandet*, presents a classic portrayal of the early 19th century miserly mind, money-obsessed,
exchanging for this miraculous possession its life and humanity. Old Grandet fits Marx's comment that since money
appears to command everything, it is the "master" of everything, and so, "when I have the master I have the servant and
do not need his servant." Starting with the bargain purchase
of confiscated church lands, Grandet becomes one of the
wealthiest men in France. Yet he continues to live with the
frugality of a peasant, doling out butter to his family by the
ounce and sugar by the grain. The tyranny money holds over
him transforms into his tyranny over his wife and daughter.

He is genuinely attached to them, but for them to have
desires not compatible with his hoarding of wealth means to
him that they are trying to destroy him, and so he destroys
the potential happiness of both of them. As a final irony,

when his wealth passes into the hands of the daughter whom he has crushed, she neither wants it nor knows what to do with it.

In *Father Goriot*, Balzac shows another side of the picture. Here the father lives only for his two daughters, who marry into aristocratic society. And yet this very act which he has fostered alienates them from him. In their new surroundings, they are ashamed of his low-class origins. And the more they have to come back to him to exact more money from him, for in the life they live money is everything, the more they resent and despise him.

Flaubert in *Madame Bovary* and Tolstoi in *Anna Karenina*, each in his own way, shows the hopeless and, in the end, destructive search by a woman for a genuine love relationship which the conditions of middle-class married life deny her.

Dreiser, in *An American Tragedy*, shows how the social education in the "good life"—a life based on the good of having money—alienates a human being from his own humanity. Clyde Griffiths, whose parents conduct a religious mission to the poor, soon discovers that their moral pattern of redemption in the next world and poverty in this one, is unworkable in the rough life of an American city. As a bell-hop in a hotel he discovers the difference between the lives of the poor and rich. A wealthy uncle offers Clyde a job in his factory. There he and one of the workers fall in love. They have an affair, and the girl becomes pregnant.

Meanwhile, as a rich man's nephew, Clyde gains entrance into the upper strata of society, with a taste of luxury and the prospect of marriage into this circle. Now the girl he has loved becomes an obstacle. Her pregnancy condemns him to the bleak life of a "poor relation." They go rowing, the boat over-turns, and she drowns. He has not physically killed her but the longing to have her out of the way paralyzed him when he could have saved her. He is convicted of murder and executed. Thus Dreiser shows society self-righteously condemning Clyde as an evil-doer, while unable to face the fact that he has only embraced the idea of the "good" which this same society has taught him every day, not in its professed morality but in its actual practice. Whatever the crime Clyde committed, the far greater crime is that which robbed Clyde of his humanity.

Dreiser could never accept the existentialist answer that the "criminal" was only a response to the "absurdity" or inherent "cruelty" of life. The problem was a social one and he sought a social answer. Thus in an essay in the book, *The Color of a Great City* (1923), he takes up another aspect of alienated humanity, that of children of unmarried mothers left at the door of foundling homes.

We are so dull. Sometimes it requires ten thousand or ten million repetitions to make us understand. "Here is a condition. What will you do about it? Here is a condition. What will you do about it? Here is a condition. What will you do about it?" That is the question each tragedy propounds, and finally we wake and listen. Then slowly some better way is discovered, some theory developed. We find often that there is an answer to some questions, at least if we have to remake ourselves, society, the face of the world, to get it.[10]

We get here a clue to why Dreiser, near the end of his life, embraced Marxism.

If Marxist economics shows that not only must the working class struggle for its daily livelihood, but that the owners of capital are condemned to a cut-throat competitive struggle, so the psychology of alienation is that if the poor have one kind of misery, the well-to-do have another. The poor struggle for the little surplus above the barest necessities that will enable them to live like human beings. The well-to-do have amassed a great surplus and find that in the process they have incomprehensibly been stripped of their humanity.

A profound study of inter-family alienation is Eugene O'Neill's play, *Long Day's Journey Into Night* (1939-41). Set in the decade before the First World War, it shows an outwardly prosperous and happy family rent by fierce and apparently baffling antagonisms. The father, James Tyrone, a retired actor who has been financially successful, harasses the family by penny-pinching miserliness. The mother, who had once been a beautiful woman, is a drug addict slipping toward insanity. The older son, James Tyrone Jr., is a jobless alcoholic and frequenter of brothels. The younger son, Edmund, who hopes to become a writer and possesses genuine poetic gifts, has gone to sea and returned, a consumptive.

As the play begins, the three men go off to the doctor for reports of the final tests made of Edmund's disease, and come back with the confirmation that he has tuberculosis, and must go to a sanitarium. This explodes a series of revelations that almost shatters the family. At the end the three men attain some common ground, the fellowship of misery, as they helplessly watch the mother drift off the edge of sanity.

The drama proceeds through the clash of personality. Scene by scene the characters turn themselves inside out, exposing new strata of a family history covering two generations. We are first aware of the father's money obsession. He goes about the house turning off the electric lights. Why should his hard-earned cash go to the electric power company? The older son, even before the visit to the doctor, accuses the father of crying poverty so that Edmund would be sent to a state sanitarium instead of getting better care at a private one. And we become aware of the mother's alcoholism and drug addiction, which she all too transparently tries to hide and excuses on the grounds of her terrible pains and headaches. She protests that she has never really been well since the birth of her youngest son, with the hint that here again the father's penuriousness was to blame. Had he gotten a better doctor for her confinement, instead of a "bargain" doctor, she might not have suffered so badly, and turned to drugs.

The father seems at first to be the villain of the piece. But then, near the end of the play, his own story unfolds. When he was a boy, his family had immigrated from starving Ireland. In America his father had deserted them, leaving the mother to support the children, working as a charwoman, never earning enough for a full meal. At the age of ten, he had gone to work in a shop for 50 cents a week. And so, he confesses, perhaps the "power of a dollar" had burnt itself into his mind too deeply.

He too had alienated part of himself by the commercial sacrifice of his own talent. Having developed a consuming love for the stage, he had become a promising actor. Playing Shakespeare, he was spoken of as a successor to the great Booth. But then he had made a sensational success starring in a tawdry melodrama. (Eugene O'Neill's father, on whom James Tyrone is based, had made such a hit in *The Count of Monte Cristo*.) And year in and year out he toured the country in this role, earning a large and sure income he could never bring himself to halt. He became a celebrity but his real talent went down the drain.

The mother had been a pretty but timid girl, brought up in a convent school. She had wished to become a nun, but the Mother Superior had advised her to postpone the decision for a year, to learn whether she really had the vocation. In that year she had met the matinee idol, James Tyrone, and fallen in love with him. Then came disillusion. Her visions of a glamorous, happy life were replaced by the actuality of a life of exhausting tours, moving from one cheap hotel to another, never having a settled home and the opportunity to bring up her children as she wanted. How could the man she loved do this to her? But his love was overpowered by the fear of poverty. To break out of the trap she was in was inconceivable. Family life was poisoned by his irrational terror of "dying in the poorhouse," the purchase of a "bargain" house that nobody liked, losses in swindles into which he was tempted by his dollar obsession, the resort to the "bargain" doctor when her second boy was born. And so, out of her pain and wretchedness, she sought relief in drugs.

The older son, deeply attached to the mother, watching her degeneration and powerless to halt it, had built up a fierce hatred for the father and had turned to alcohol and whoring, becoming, in the father's bitter words, the "family tramp." Toward his younger brother he had developed ambiguous feelings, affectionately hoping that he would break out of the father's grip, yet resenting that he was the "mother's darling," that he had talents which seemed to mock his own wasted life. And the younger son, the gifted writer, wanting family love desperately, feels rebuffed and alone, estranged even from his mother. For she has drifted too far out of reality to recognize his illness and his needs. He must remain "her darling baby."

In facing and thinking through the problem of what had happened to the Tyrone family, so much like his own, O'Neill has arrived at a profound objective truth. The play becomes a revealing chapter of the life of Irish immigrant families in America, and an insight further into the contradictions met by every wave of immigrants. At great privation they had come from poverty-stricken countries to the "land of opportunity." There was opportunity, but the price was the sacrifice of one's humanity to the fight for the "dollar," in which many were ground down and the few who succeeded found that its fruits were bitter.

The tragedy develops like classic Greek drama, but with "fate" or the "gods" replaced by the living social pattern in which money, as Marx says, "functions as the almighty being." O'Neill shows how in the father, the thought of money is so ever-present that even when he seems to recognize its control over him, he has not freed himself. Baited about his miserliness over the choice of a sanitarium for his afflicted son, he retorts, go to any sanitarium, pick the best, spend whatever money it demands! Then he adds, "within reason." And, hardly aware of what he is doing, he notices a lit electric bulb in a corner of the room and turns it off. O'Neill brings the drama to an inexpressibly moving conclusion with the mother's final degeneration. She flees, in her mind, back to the past, to the last time in which she was unalloyedly happy, to the time of the decision which was to cause her ruin. Speaking to herself, unaware of the three silently listening men, from whom she is now in mental flight, she is again in her adolescence. She had wanted to be a nun, but the Mother Superior had told her to wait a year. How could so wise a woman have given her such bad advice? For in that year she had met and married the handsome and famous actor, James Tyrone. "We were happy—for a time."

Marxism is often falsely accused of setting up a one-to-one, mechanistic relationship between the economic base of society and the ideas and thoughts in people's minds. As Engels wrote in a letter, "It is not that the economic position is the *cause and alone active*, while everything else only has a passive effect. There is, rather, interaction on the basis of the economic necessity, which *ultimately* always asserts itself." And part of O'Neill's greatness is that out of his own insight, he traces this complicated process of interaction, with economics as a decisive force. There is the migration from poverty and oppression in Ireland; then the poverty and harsh marketplace reality in the new world. The father's money obsession, his never-ending nightmare of being driven back to the deprivation in his childhood, becomes the key to his alienation from his talented self, and to the estrangement between himself and his wife, even as they love one another.

And since he, the bread-winner, the decision-maker, represents the harsh world of reality, her estrangement becomes an estrangement from reality itself, so that she finally seeks refuge in delusions. This estrangement of the mother, in turn, destroys the older son, who watches it with impotent horror, and whose capacity for love is consumed in the despairing attachment to his mother. All this inflicts incurable wounds in the younger son, the artist. Thus we see how, through all the complexities of human relationships, "private property" becomes the generating force of alienation in private life.

In outlining the relationship between "private property" and alienation, Marx by the same reasoning showed that alienation is not the all-embracing truth of modern life. Just as exploitation incites a struggle against it, so alienation incites a struggle against it, sometimes instinctive, like a reflex of self-preservation, and sometimes with a full awareness of the problem. In his economic and philosophical manuscripts Marx outlines the counterforce to alienation which we can call the humanization of human relations; the development of a way of life that is built on the kinship of human beings, where each finds in his connections to the others the ground for his own growth as a human being. The "others" become necessary to and a part of his own mind and life, instead of inimical and hostile. As he understands the humanity of others, they teach him and reveal his own humanity. Put in other words, the task is to live as a social human being. Marx writes: "The human essence of nature first exists only for social man; for only here does nature exist for him as a bond with man—as his existence for the other and the other's existence for him—as the life-element of the human world; only here does nature exist as the foundation of his own human existence."

It is through labor, the social process of changing the world for human use, Marx says, that the qualities of the outer world, of people and nature, have been disclosed, and that the outer, objective world, has "educated" the subjective world of man's thought, senses and perceptions. "The forming of the five senses is a labor of the entire history of the world down to the present." Private property, through the alienation that is organic to it, splits apart the subjective and objective world, so that human longings and the need for fulfillment find no satisfaction in the outer world. It has turned alien and hostile. To "objectivize" the world means to restore the true subject-object relationship, to recover the outer world of nature and people as the field in which human beings can discover what is in them. "The objectification of the human essence both in its theoretical and practical aspects is required to make man's *sense human,* as well as to create the *human sense* corresponding to the entire wealth of human and natural substance."

An "established society"—that is, a society without the anarchy of private ownership of the means of production, and without class exploitation—can devote all its energies to the mastery of nature, the discovery of its laws and their application to human use and freedom. By the same token, this "established" society, which takes from "private property" its wealth of productive powers but eliminates its antagonisms, can enable man to flower in all his senses in response to the richness of the world about him. It becomes a humanized world, furthering his growth and giving scope to his powers.

Just as resulting from the movement of *private property,* of its wealth as well as its poverty—or of its material and spiritual wealth and poverty—the budding society finds to hand all the material for this development: so established society produces man in this entire richness of his being—produces the *rich* man *profoundly endowed with all senses*—as its enduring reality.[11]

This does not mean, however, that the growth of people "rich" in humanity must await a classless society. In one of his theses on Feuerbach, Marx criticizes mechanical material-ism. "The materialist doctrine that men are products of cir-cumstances and upbringing, and that, therefore, changed men are products of other circumstances and changed upbringing, forgets that it is men that change circumstances and that the educator himself needs educating." So men find that in the struggle against private property, which is property as ex-ploitation, this struggle must be carried on socially. If at first they come together for seemingly merely practical reasons, they discover other qualities through their collective activity; a common humanity, a revelation of hitherto unperceived qualities in others, and in themselves. Thus Marx wrote in 1844 of workers' organization, at a time when it was in its relative infancy, and communist and socialist ideas were prac-tically synonymous with organization itself:

When communist workmen associate with one another, theory, propaganda, etc., is their first end. But at the same time, as a result of this association, they acquire a new need—the need for society—and what appears as a means becomes an end. You can observe this practical process in its most splendid results whenever you see French socialist workers together. Such things as smoking, drinking, eating, etc., are no longer means of contact or means that bring together. Company, association, and conversation, which again has society as its end, are enough for them; the brotherhood of man is no mere phrase with them, but a fact of life, and the nobility of man shines upon us from their work-hardened bodies.[12]

During the century and longer in which working-class or-ganizations have become everywhere a powerful historical force, these organizations have necessarily been subjected to the contradictions and corruptive forces of capitalist society itself. There has been direct and indirect bribery, bureaucratic leadership, a labor "aristocracy" indifferent to the plight of others unorganized or unemployed, the self-seeking character-istic of bourgeois morality. Yet through all its vicissitudes, its forward thrusts met by new obstacles and open or insidious attack, the working class inevitably relearns, on a constantly broadening arena, its fundamental principle of strength, which is the opposite to the guiding principle of bourgeois life. This is that no section of it can have interests separated from or opposed to the interests of the working class as a whole. Propaganda, bribes and threats, all are used to drive the working class from this position. If one sector makes an economic gain, it is advised and warned to think of itself first and ignore others. If labor exercising the power of its unity makes economic gains on a wider sector, it is warned to "stay out of politics" or out of such matters as racism and discrimination. If it makes progress on the national political front, it is warned to stay out of international affairs, to close its eyes to hidden or open colonial exploitation, to seek no ties with the working class of other countries. With a tacit understanding of the genuine social morality of Marxism and socialism, every such step of the working-class movement is assailed as "communist influenced." Similarly if a white man joins a Negro picket line for jobs and civil rights, the suspicion is advanced that he must surely be a "communist." To act in a truly human way is to become, according to the prevalent witch-hunt definition, a monster.

Alienation is a genuine psychological phenomenon and at the same time a subjective falsification of outer reality and a denial of the possibilities of life. When a new order is in struggle against or replacing the old, the latter may see the representatives of the new as monsters, but the new does not necessarily see the old in that way. A more rational and realistic view of life is also a stride in humanization. So Shakespeare offers deeply understanding and human portraits of the old order of arrogant, ambitious and warring aristocrats, even while he shows them as a menace to the peace and unity of a

nation. Maxim Gorky presents profoundly revealing, humanized portrayals of the middle class showing how they destroy
themselves as human beings while exploiting the peasantry.
The Negroes in America have no such pervasive "monster"
image of the white people as the white racists have of the
Negro. An ideological struggle for progress is not a struggle
of one form of alienation against another, but a struggle of
humanization against alienation. A step in humanization is a
discovery of truth. A graphic example is given in "Testament
of a Transplanted White Southerner" by Calvin Kytle, in the
Saturday Review (May 30, 1964):

> But even though I am not yet emancipated, I do know what it
> means to have a Negro as a friend. It means, for one thing, that
> I can never again think of the "Negro problem" as an "economic
> problem" or as a "social problem" which is the way even the most
> liberal professors in the South were teaching it in the Thirties and
> Forties. Once you've come to know a Negro as an individual, the
> race problem becomes purely a human problem; you can never
> again see an act of discrimination without reacting as if to a per-
> sonal hurt. . . . They are making me come to terms with myself—
> to integrate, if you please, my behavior with my principles, or
> otherwise to know myself for a hypocrite.

The struggle for civil rights and for equality of the Negro
in America has provided particularly rich experiences in the
humanization of human relations. On the one hand, the
murders of both Negroes and white civil rights workers in
Mississippi and elsewhere, with the murderers apparently pro-
tected by the institutions supposedly dedicated to protect
people against murder, only bring out in glaring violence
what has long been apparent in the speeches of racists; that
it is they, clamoring of Negro "inferiority," who are themselves inferior, impoverished minds alienated from their own
humanity. And on the other hand, when white people join
Negroes in a movement for what is really their common

democratic interest, this becomes a new stage in the humanization of their relations. As Marx says, what appeared to be
a "means," becomes an "end." People formerly separate discover their common human experiences and problems, how
much akin they are as human beings, how rewarding their
association can be. They discover sources of strength in themselves they did not know they possessed.

It is literally true that in this humanization of reality, one
sees, hears, perceives and "senses" differently. On the broad
panorama of world history, this process of humanization of
nature and social relations is recorded in the arts. The arts
are developments of the human senses, and their means of
expression, like language, drawing, coloring, shaping, building, creating patterns of musical tones, are products too of
human labor and social intercourse. They serve as tools for
the sensory exploration of the outer world, for thinking about
the world and for probing the inner life that outer reality
evokes. The very style in which a novelist or poet writes, an
artist paints or a musician composes reveals his response to
nature and people. The arts of one age are not necessarily
greater than those of previous ages, but they are necessarily
different, revealing how a new stage in the mastery of nature
and the more rational organization of society has led to a new
stage of human sensibility.

Art by its very nature is a social activity, although it can
be put to anti-social uses. It is a social activity because its
language and other means of expression are a socially created
heritage, and because the artist, like the scientist, even though
he does his work generally in seclusion, is motivated by some
form of social consciousness. The basic problems he deals
with in his art are those raised before him by society, and
his completed work becomes a social possession. There are
situations of course when official society does not welcome

the discoveries of art, or demands degrading or anti-human work. But for an artist to make a principle of working for himself alone is to present his individual rebellion against such demands as an eternal "law" of hostility between the artist and society. Of course an artist works for himself. But the result is art to the extent that what he discovers in himself is also a discovery for others in themselves. Great artists have always been great educators of people, in the sense of opening their eyes, developing their perceptions, altering their responses to the world about them in such a way that the world seems to be a more human place in which to live. Of art, as of daily life, Marx's statement is profoundly true: "the senses of the social man are different from the senses of the non-social man."

Thus art is a force in the humanization of reality. The state of human and social development in the world of its times places a limit on sensibility beyond which it cannot go, but it explores to the full what is then possible, giving it the objective form of an "art work" to make it a social possession and a permanent record of a stage in human growth. It was impossible for an art serving the medieval European aristocracy to show the peasantry as equal in human qualities to the feudal lords, although the folk poetry and art demonstrated this humanity. When a Shakespeare or a Cervantes can disclose the human depths in the common people, it is a sign that the feudal ideology has become obsolete. And so we can find expressed in art every stage in the humanization of human relations, just as we can find reflected every form of alienation.

In such writers as Balzac, Tolstoi, Dreiser and O'Neill, who have depicted the process of alienation in bourgeois society, there is no accompanying alienation on the part of the writers themselves. As they depict it, alienation is a form of human suffering or self-destruction, and they thereby reveal the alienated themselves as understandable human beings through whom the reader learns something about himself. They show how the forces at work in society are reflected in conflicts internal to the individual.

With the crisis in the 20th century, however, we enter a new stage where side by side with the humanized portrayal of alienated lives, a literature appears which expresses the writer's own alienation. These conflicting currents will often appear side by side in the same artist. Behind this expression of alienation lies a deepening subjectivism. The artist's absorption in his internal or subjective life begins to overwhelm his view of others, who take on a hostile, monstrous or fearsome appearance. The "humanization" dwindles to the artist's own longings, fears and frustrations, often poignantly revealed, while his outer-world outlook reveals only what he is estranged from, finding in it no ties to or common ground with his own being.

A writer, for example, who can no longer see alienation as an objective social phenomenon, as Balzac, Dreiser and O'Neill do, but views the entire world in terms of his own alienation, is the Czech, Franz Kafka (1883-1924). His extraordinary poetic gift is put wholly at the service of expressing the awesome, nightmarish horror with which he regards the world of maturity and "official society." In the novel *The Trial*, it is law and justice—not any particular or class-inspired miscarriage of them but law and justice themselves —that appear as a frightening, inexplicable and omnipotent force, destroying people. In the novel *The Castle*, it is all "official society" that appears as a monstrous bureaucracy, indifferent to human beings and at the gate of which they clamor in vain. In the story *Metamorphosis*, it is his own family from which the individual finds himself hopelessly alienated. The symbolic presentation of this takes the form of a young man waking up one morning to find that he has turned into a cockroach. His family at first tries to care for him as if he were their own, but soon regards him with loathing and horror and in the end brings about his death.

Kafka is not an existentialist. Yet the fact that the existentialists today put him high among their prophetic figures indicates to how great an extent the growth of alienation as a widespread social-psychological phenomenon is organically connected to the rise of existentialism as a philosophy. This does not mean that existentialism preaches alienation. On the contrary, it advances itself as a counter to alienation. But as this study has tried to show, existentialism is not a philosophy in the sense of a more or less rational structure of thought which tries to put into some order what is known about the real world. It starts as a frame of mind, which then tries to rationalize itself in philosophical terms. This frame of mind is that of a person in a prisonhouse death cell awaiting execution, or of one told that his days are numbered because of an incurable disease. He feels alone in his predicament, no help can come to him from outside, nothing he has learned about science or history makes any sense, and he must find whatever solace or affirmation he can within himself. It is because existentialism revolves about a frame of mind that such terms have become popular in discussing it as the "existentialist anxiety" or the "existentialist predicament." The existentialist sees this frame of mind as eternal truth, a glimpse of the awesome reality of existence, a recognition that the fact of death makes the world and life "absurd."

But this frame of mind, the feeling of lonely impotence in the face of an implacably hostile or indifferent universe, is not "eternal truth"; it is, rather, an awareness of an alienation socially created, rising on the heels of capitalism, with its dominating competitiveness or war of "all against all," intensifying after each successive crisis. Thus the existentialist's "predicament" is really his revulsion against the world of capitalism, combined with his rationalizing away of any means of understanding it as such, and so of coping with it. Existentialism, then, is not alienation. It is the awareness of alienation, accepting it as the eternal condition of people in society, and it tries to combat it by going—in mind—out of society. And since truly fruitful human ties, and the "humanization" of social relations, are the real counterforce to alienation, the existentialist may be described as one who tries to recover his humanity by rejecting the very path through which it can develop or grow.

The existentialist solutions are as varied as the philosophers. Kierkegaard's was to abandon reason and secular hopes for faith in the supernatural. Before God, he said, all men are in the wrong. Nietzsche's was the assertion of the individual "will to power" and prophecy of the "superman." Heidegger's was a primitivistic awareness of "being" as "emergence." This primitivism included a social ignorance that led him to welcome the Nazi blackshirts, arms production and panzer divisions as the liberation of the world from regimentation and the machine. Jaspers' was the advice to give to the "Caesar" of the masses-run world what it demanded, while preserving philosophy as a private freedom. Camus' was to scorn the absurd world, and find freedom in a commitment without hope. Sartre's was to see freedom as solely internal, resting on independence from any outer compulsion, including that which asserted not merely the possibility but the necessity of human cooperation. And most revelatory in their own writings is how little affirmation they do find, how deeply troubled they are.

Existentialism came late to the United States, and germane to this is the fact that disillusion with capitalism came late. Through most of the 19th century—perhaps because of the "open West" and the fact that the most intense exploitation took the "peculiar" form of Negro enslavement—there was the widespread conviction that the country had no basically antagonistic classes, that it was potentially a great democratic brotherhood, that certain evils like money speculation, profit-obsession, low wages, slavery, political corruption, could be removed like alien growths. Near the end of the century different views began to emerge. They can be found in Henry Adams' (1838-1918) autobiography, *The Education of Henry Adams*. It records his growing awareness that his country is exploitative, capitalist and imperialist. By rights, he admits, he should have been a Marxist, but he was barred from socialism, he says, by "some narrow trait of the New England nature." And so, after a struggle with himself, he gave up his belief in the democratic America of the founding fathers, for "submission to capitalism." He adds, speaking of himself, "of all forms of society or government, this was the one he liked least." But since the country was capitalist, "it had to be run by capital and capitalistic methods."[13] And so he is alienated from his own country, serving it in the spirit, as he says, of a "serf" of the bankers, and alienated from his own life work, the study and teaching of history. From history, he concludes, nothing is to be learned except that the world has been running down, through mechanistic, physical forces, since the middle ages, and he can find his humanity only in a mental return to the medieval cathedral.

Adams circulated his book privately in 1907, feeling that most people would find it strange and shocking. This disillusion however rose in intensity among a host of minds after the First World War, with the crafty bargaining peace that parcelled out African and other colonies among the victors, and with the anti-labor hysteria of the 1920's. American democracy seemed alienated from itself. The very government which presumably the people had created, loomed over them as an alien force, indifferent and even hostile to them, against which they felt impotent. Against this background, American literature began to embrace not only the awareness of alienation in society but the expression of the artist's own alienation. And with the renewed disillusion after the Second World War, which was followed by the "cold war," the appeal of existentialist answers began to arise.

ALIENATION AS A LITERARY STYLE:
F. Scott Fitzgerald and T. S. Eliot

Much of the radically new and startling quality of the literary trends in the decades of the First World War and the 1920's came from its expression, not of a humanized relation to the outer world, nor of a humanized view of an alienated situation, but of the artist's personal alienation. This appears in the style itself. To illustrate what is offered here as the difference between "humanized" and "alienated" styles, this is a humanized landscape from Thoreau's *A Week on the Concord and Merrimac River:*

The sun-setting presumed all men at leisure and in a contemplative mood; but the farmer's boy only whistled the more thoughtfully as he drove his cows home from pasture, and the teamster refrained from cracking his whip, and guided his team with a subdued voice. The last vestiges of daylight at length disappeared, and as we rowed silently along with our backs toward home through the darkness, only a few stars being visible, we had little to say, but sat absorbed in thought, or in silence listened to the monotonous sound of the oars.[1]

A literary description, like a painted one, is no simple enumeration of data but a human involvement with nature or the outside world. Thus it embodies, by implication, a human portrait, or state of human life. While the scene Thoreau describes is not a particularly spectacular one, we feel in it—precisely for that reason, perhaps—the writer's intimate response to nature, the opening up of his senses caught in words that also open up our senses, and the way in which his heightened sensitivity causes nature to flow, so to speak, into his mind and body, so that it becomes part of and an extension of his own being. It is nature "humanized." Writing is a tool of perception and thought about life, the style of which is shaped by the perceptions themselves. The approach of Thoreau is not "old-fashioned"; it will remain in fashion so long as people can feel this companionship with the world outside them, accepting it as a place for their own growth as human beings.

In contrast, alienated writing presents the outer world as cold, hostile, forbidding, inimical, reflecting the observer's own fear, unrest and desolation. A typical "alienated" image is this from F. Scott Fitzgerald's story, *The Diamond as Big as the Ritz*: "The Montana sunset lay between two mountains like a gigantic bruise from which dark arteries spread themselves over a poisoned sky." Even a practically imageless language can express alienation, through a deliberate emphasis on sound, making the words appear to be concrete objects, bereft of their function as instruments of perception, as in this passage, typical of the entire play, from Gertrude Stein's *Four Saints in Three Acts*:

It is very easy in winter to remember spring and summer it is very easy in winter to remember spring and winter and summer it is very easy easy in winter to remember summer spring and winter it is very easy in winter to remember spring and summer and winter.[2]

The obsessively driving rhythms, sound repetitions and interchange of word orders remove from the words any effect they might have in evoking a humanized response to the outer world.

In poetry, the opening of Robert Frost's sonnet, "Range-Finding," in the book *Mountain Interval* (1916)[3] illustrates humanized writing:

> The battle rent a cobweb diamond-strung
> And cut a flower beside a ground bird's nest
> Before it stained a single human breast.
> The stricken flower bent double and so hung.
> And still the bird revisited her young.
> A butterfly its fall had dispossessed
> A moment sought in air its flower of rest,
> Then lightly stooped to it and fluttering clung.

In contrast is the alienated imagery in the opening of Robert Lowell's "Where the Rainbow Ends," from the book *Lord Weary's Castle* (1946):[4]

> I saw the sky descending, black and white,
> Not blue, on Boston where the winters wore
> The skulls to jack-o'-lanterns on the slates,
> And hunger's skin-and-bone retrievers tore
> The chickadee and shrike.

In T. S. Eliot's *Ash Wednesday* (1930)[5] images of nature alienated are used symbolically:

> In the last desert between the last blue rocks
> The desert in the garden the garden in the desert
> Of drouth spitting from the mouth the withered apple seed.

Alienated writing is not bad or inexpert writing; in fact the examples cited are distinguished by the fine craftmanship. It is not a deliberate contrivance of the artist to annoy his audience. Of course such deliberate "shock" effects can be found in many lesser writers and other artists who took up the various "new trends" of the 1910's and 1920's and the games dignified with the title of "experiments with language." These are trivia swept away in the passage of not too long a time. It is true that manifestos of these "new trends" represented them as a "revolution in language," with the implication that the traditional language had been "used up" and it was necessary to concoct a new one.

However, the style inspired by alienation represents a particular psychology, engendered by a social crisis which the artist has allowed to disrupt the individual ties to the world about him and throw him back upon himself. It is not inevitable that the crisis should produce this alienation, nor is the style due to the fact that the scenes described in such writings are themselves sad or desolate. Frost's "Range-Finding," with its humanized images, is a bitter comment on the inhumanity of war, and here is a humanized depiction of a desolate scene from John Steinbeck's novel *The Grapes of Wrath* (1939):[6]

On a night the wind loosened a shingle and flipped it to the ground. The next wind pried into the hole where the shingle had been, lifted off three, and the next, a dozen. The midday sun burned through the hole and threw a glaring spot on the floor. The wild cats crept in from the fields at night, but they did not mew at the doorstep any more. They moved like shadows of a cloud across the moon, into the rooms to hunt the mice. And on windy days the doors banged, and the ragged curtains fluttered in the broken windows.

The mortgage-holding banks have taken over the land and driven out the people. Yet in this "landscape" the human presence is felt; the undoing of people's work by nature uncontrolled evokes the people who have carried on a dogged struggle to make the world habitable and who will continue this struggle.

Behind the radically different and, for a time, shocking styles of alienated expression lay a psychology that was also a view of life, an implied philosophy, different from that of Frost, for all his frequently pessimistic observations, or that of Steinbeck, for all his grief over human destruction. One of the dismal failures of most of the criticism which accompanied the new trends was its refusal to come to grips with their view and put it into a critical context of what was actually going on in real life. Instead, the myth was propagated that this was the "art of the future" and the viewpoint behind it, so clearly a product of the crisis of the times, was hailed as the "new vision," the discovery of "truth," and the path to the liberation of art.

An alienated style is not to be confused with the deliberate grotesquerie and mock brutality of social-minded, humanist satiric artists like Swift in *Gulliver's Travels* or Daumier in his caricatures, where the imagery itself contains clues to the audience to "undistort the distortions," and perceive the realistic, human view advanced behind the comic mask. But the distinction is not always hard and fast. In the imagery of alienation in F. Scott Fitzgerald, we have a transitional or borderline style, moving from humanist satire to the irony of alienation where the artist feels that the whole world is an absurd "joke" on him.

Fitzgerald stands out in American literary history as the writer who brilliantly caught the tone and temper of the "jazz-age 'twenties." There was a side of America to which the term "jazz age" had no application; the mining towns of the South and West, the city centers of huge monopoly industries, the labor unions through which workers sought human conditions of work but were barred by armies of thugs backed by money-corrupted courts and police.

The "jazz age" applied to strata of American life enjoying war-born prosperity, providing unlimited money for speculators and glowing opportunities for the youth graduated of high-status colleges. They could become junior executives in the mushrooming corporations or writers selling their talents to produce publicity and advertising copy. One could enjoy the cornucopia if one put aside the moral principles still being piously taught in schools, and these were readily discarded. There was a tacit acceptance of the collapse of the "American Dream" of a great, unselfish humanitarian classless democracy breaking ground to the future; indeed, a dream that had never been a reality. America was accepted as the land of "big money," which determined its international and internal politics.

In this milieu, morality and humanitarianism were assumed to be hypocrisy. Patriotism was a fake. Power and profit had guided both the prosecution of the war and the making of the peace. There was less resentment of this than an acceptance of it as a guide to life. Moralists were associated with the bigots and opportunists who had barred the manufacture and sale of alcoholic liquor through a constitutional amendment being flouted by the most respectable citizens, with this in turn expanding the underworld of organized gangsterism.

This was the "jazz age" milieu. The money to be made served no purpose unless one spent it on status display, "conspicuous consumption," or diversions provided by a garish "entertainment industry." In this milieu alienation was rife, for prosperity demanded a sacrifice of humanity, and the bought pleasures took on empty, subhuman or mindless forms.

There was an added note of hysteria in the effort to wipe certain realities out of consciousness. A socialist revolution had taken place in Tsarist Russia, and our land of democracy, along with its former war allies—and enemies—was doing its utmost to strangle it. At home, in official circles, there was a frantic fear of the spread of socialist ideas among the workers. This motivated ruthless attacks upon labor unions and the wholesale arrest of militant labor leaders and political radicals in contemptuous disregard of their constitutional rights. The fact that the war had brought tens of thousands of Negroes out of peonage on the Southern plantations into the army and the factories—though under conditions of brutal segregation—had created a "problem," the answer to which was a rising tide of racism.

F. Scott Fitzgerald was of this milieu, and at the same time critically detached from it. He expressed its "hard-boiled," disillusioned attitude through the deliberate use of alienated imagery, to which he added his own light and sardonic wit. In the story, "May Day" (1920),[7] he describes the parades of returning soldiers through the New York City streets.

There had been a war fought and won and the great city of the conquering people was crossed with triumphal arches and vivid with thrown flowers of white, red, and rose. All through the long spring days the returning soldiers marched up the chief highway behind the strump of drums and the joyous, resonant wind of the brasses, while merchants and clerks left their bickerings and figurings and, crowding to the windows, turned their white-bunched faces gravely upon the passing battalions.

Never had there been such splendor in the great city, for the victorious war had brought plenty in its train, and the merchants had flocked thither from the South and West with their households to taste of all the luscious feasts and witness the lavish entertainment prepared—and to buy for their women furs against the next winter and bags of golden mesh and varicolored slippers of silk and silver and rose satin and cloth of gold.

The array of data is such that a Keats might make into a sumptuous feast for the senses. But the effect here is one of bleakness and inhumanity. This is subtly done, through the interweaving of the patriotic motifs with motifs of commerce, merchandising, wealth, conspicuous display.

So it is with the search for "entertainment," as in the party scene in *The Great Gatsby* (1925):[8]

One of the girls in yellow was playing the piano, and beside her stood a tall, black-haired young lady from a famous chorus, engaged in song. She had drunk a large quantity of champagne, and during the course of the song she had decided, ineptly, that everything was very, very sad—she was not only singing, she was weeping too. Whenever there was a pause in the song she filled it with gasping, broken sobs, and then took the lyric again in a quavering soprano. The tears coursed down her cheeks—not freely, however, for when they came into contact with her heavily beaded eyelashes they assumed an inky color, and pursued the rest of their way in slow black rivulets. A humorous suggestion was made that she sing the notes on her face, whereupon she threw up her hands, sank into a chair, and went off into a deep, vinous sleep.

This again is a deliberate assumption of alienation. We see people vividly, but cannot feel them as people, with an inner life. It is as if they are from a world of strangers. And in both this and the previous excerpt, in depicting the estrangement of the people from one another, or their alienation from their own humanity, Fitzgerald expresses also his own detachment from them.

Fitzgerald sometimes thought of himself as a socialist, like the hero in his first novel, *This Side of Paradise* (1920),[9] Amory Blaine, who says:

This is the first time in my life that I've argued socialism. It's the only panacea that I know. I'm restless. My whole generation is restless. I'm sick of a system where the richest man gets the most beautiful girl if he wants her, where the artist without an income has to sell his talents to a button manufacturer.

But he never carried this belief to the point of political activity, or of trying to discover how the other side of America lived and thought. His style of alienation was not all of his response to life, but rather the tone of the milieu which he captured so deftly, and looked upon so ironically. But it was himself that he was also surveying in this tone. He was never able to develop successfully the humanist side of his writing.

In the 1930's, when strong democratic forces were aroused in American life and the genuine, human face of the working class emerged in the broadest national consciousness, Fitzgerald's life was ravaged by the mental and physical illness of himself and his wife. In an autobiographical sketch he wrote in 1936, "The Crack Up,"[10] he says, "my political conscience had scarcely existed for ten years except as an element of irony in my stuff." Now, he says, he is giving even this up. He will live at enmity with the world. He will put a sign, "Beware the Dog," above his door. And he adds the heartrending line, "I will try to be a correct animal though, and if you throw me a bone with enough meat on it I may even lick your hand." He died in 1940 at the age of 44, a great but unfulfilled talent.

In contrast to F. Scott Fitzgerald, T. S. Eliot's alienation from the surrounding world is almost total. All of modern life, all society, revolts him. His disdain is especially intense for the common people, and for the forces that, as he sees them, impelled the masses into motion on the field of history; romanticism, science, democracy, industrialization. His thinking is reactionary in the fullest sense of the world; not only anti-democratic, but seeking refuge in the mind of an earlier age, antedating modern "evils." A prime word of scorn in his vocabulary is "secular" or "secularism," whether referring to art or to thought; that is, an attention to real life as it is with a humanist interest in social welfare and progress. In the remarkable and comparatively early poems, *The Love Song of J. Alfred Prufrock* and *Portrait of a Lady*, there are moving humanist portrayals of desolation with something of a Henry James objectivity. But after this, in his poems, plays and essays, it is rare to find an image which expresses tenderness toward any aspect of life or nature about him. One would look in vain for any portrayal other than his own anguish with which the reader can feel kinship.

Eliot sees the world around him as a rack on which he is being tortured. He wrote in a symposium, *Faith that Illuminates* (1935): "The whole of modern literature is corrupted by what I call Secularism . . . it is simply unaware of, simply cannot understand the meaning of, the primacy of the supernatural over the natural life: of something which I assume to be our primacy concern."[11] But one cannot write about a supernatural which one has not experienced. The ancient portrayals of the gods or spirits were portrayals of human beings or animals, sometimes stylized or distorted to give them a ritual, other than real, symbolism. Dante filled his Hell, Purgatory and Heaven with Italian scenery. Eliot, loathing his contemporary world, finds solace in past literature, the experience of which is more real to him than living experience. In *The Waste Land*,[12] the recalled memories of these fragments of past poetry, with their humanism intimated even when parodied, intensify the desolation of the images reflecting his alienation.

> *But at my back in a cold blast I hear*
> *The rattle of the bones, and chuckle spread from ear to ear.*
> *A rat crept softly through the vegetation*
> *Dragging its slimy belly upon the bank*
> *While I was fishing in the dull canal*
> *On a winter evening round behind the gashouse*
> *Musing on the king my brother's wreck*
> *And on the king my father's death before him.*

The allusions are to Marvell's

> *But at my back I always hear*
> *Time's winged chariot hurrying near*

and to Shakespeare's *The Tempest*:

> *Sitting on a bank,*
> *Weeping again the king my father's wrack*

So it is when Eliot, as in *The Waste Land*, records common speech as mindless prattle. His ear is fine, and yet the image evoked is one of alienation. He does not see or feel the common people as human beings at all. They are repulsive to him, and he makes them so to the reader.

Now Albert's coming back, make yourself a bit smart.
He'll want to know what you done with that money he gave you
To get yourself some teeth. He did, I was there.
You have them all out, Lil, and get a nice set,
He said, I swear, I can't bear to look at you.

Eliot comes closest to genuine feeling—and genuine poetry —when he expresses directly his own terrible loneliness and fear, the fear of one who has severed all ties to his fellow men and so finds nothing in himself. An example is this poignant passage in *East Coker*, from *Four Quartets*:[13]

O dark dark dark. They all go into the dark.
The vacant interstellar spaces, the vacant into the vacant,
The captains, merchant bankers, eminent men of letters,
The generous patrons of art, the statesmen and the rulers. . . .
Or as, when an underground train, in the tube, stops too long
*   between stations*
And the conversation rises and slowly fades into silence
And you see behind every face the mental emptiness deepen
Leaving only the growing terror of nothing to think about;

This is humanized writing, in contrast to the alienation Eliot reveals when writing of the outer world. And we are close here to what can be called the "existentialist situation"; a fear of death so intense because life is drained of meaning.

In two respects, however, Eliot differs from the existentialist view, and his views and influence can rather be called "pre-existentialist," in that they created a fallow ground for the philosophy. In existentialism, religious as well as atheist, there is a revulsion against dogma and anything that presumes on "authority." In this rejection it finds its "freedom." And there is, occasionally, a relish and joy in life itself.

Where existentialism takes a "romantic" view of the world it calls "absurd," Eliot's view goes toward the "classical." He has, in his almost total alienation, nothing of even the limited existentialist joy in life or response to its appeal. It was said here earlier that one would look in vain in his work for a credible, rounded human portrayal with a credible inner life, except when he drops the pose of being a modern St. Thomas Aquinas and reveals his own inner fears and torment. This is true even of one of Eliot's great "heroes," Becket in *Murder in the Cathedral*,[14] who is not a flesh-and-blood human being, but a mouthpiece for Eliot's dogma. In the following passage, for example, Becket is talking about his earlier, more secular years:

> *Thirty years ago, I searched all the ways*
> *That lead to pleasure, advancement and praise.*
> *Delight in sense, in learning and in thought,*
> *Music and philosophy, curiosity,*
> *The purple bullfinch in the lilac tree,*
> *The tiltyard skill, the strategy of chess,*
> *Love in the garden, singing to the instrument*
> *Were all things equally desirable.*

But the image is still an alienated one. There is no joy in life even in these remembered pleasures. The purple bullfinch in the lilac tree is purely ornamental, nothing like Milton's lark singing in the dappled dawn. Compare these lines to a passage from Henry Vaughan, the 17th century English mystical religious poet who is one of Eliot's great admirations. To Vaughan, the world of nature was only a clothing and symbol for the presence of God, and yet there is a real ecstasy in his response to nature. (The same contrast to Vaughan would be true of Robert Lowell's religious and alienated poetry.)

> *hark! in what rings*
> *And hymning circulations the quick world*
> *Awakes and sings!*
> *The rising winds,*
> *And falling springs,*
> *Birds, beasts, all things*
> *Adore him in their kinds.*

Thus all is hurled
In sacred hymns and order; the great chime
And symphony of Nature.

To Eliot's frigid dogma, however, a worship of God that
unites with a St. Francis-like humanism, a love for nature
itself—not to speak of a religion concerned over the miseries
of human beings in the real world, and the struggle for progress—is a contaminated religion. A central influence on Eliot's
thought was that of T. E. Hulme, an English militarist and
proto-fascist philosopher killed in the First World War. In
his posthumously published *Speculations*, Hulme had denounced the "romanticism" of believing that man was "an
infinite reservoir of possibilities," and that by rearranging
society "you will get Progress." The enthusiasm for liberty,
he said, was a delusion. He himself propounded what he
called the "classical" idea; that "Man is an extraordinarily
fixed and limited animal whose nature is absolutely constant.
It is only by tradition and organization that anything decent
can be got out of him."[15] To Eliot this book of Hulme's was
the beginning and end of wisdom. In his essay *Second
Thoughts About Humanism* (1928), in which Eliot criticizes
"religious humanists," he quotes these words of Hulme as
sacred authority.

I hold the religious conception of ultimate values to be right,
the humanist wrong. . . . What is important, is what nobody seems
to realize—the dogmas like that of Original Sin, which are the
closest expression of the categories of the religious attitude. That
man is in no sense perfect, but a wretched creature, who can yet
apprehend perfection. It is not, then, that I put up with dogma
for the sake of the sentiment, but that I may possibly swallow the
sentiment for the sake of the dogma.[16]

All "liberal theologians," Eliot says, "would do well to
ponder" these words. Humanism, love of life, care for the woe
of others, beliefs in progress are sentimentalities, that have

nothing to do with religion, and therefore with truth. At best they might be tolerated as sugar-coating for the pill of dogma, which is truth. There is no human progress. There is only imperfection and perfection, and perfection is God. Humanism involves hope for the future, love for one's fellow human beings, a rational and thinking mind applied to life and the world. And Eliot demands the abandonment of hope, love and thought. He writes in *East Coker*:

> *I said to my soul, be still, and wait without hope*
> *For hope would be hope for the wrong thing; wait without*
>   *love*
> *For love would be love of the wrong thing; there is yet faith*
> *But the faith and the love and the hope are all in the*
>   *waiting.*
> *Wait without thought, for you are not ready for thought:*

There is irony here. Eliot believes in what he calls an "intellectual aristocracy." But where Nietzsche saw the "elite" or leaders as the breakers of rules, as supermen in contrast to the mass of people following a "slave morality," Eliot counsels his "elite" to accept a slave mentality; namely, that they give over their mind and art to outside "authority"—in thought, to religious dogma, in government, to monarchy, in poetry, to "classicism." His "classicism," moreover, has nothing to do with the traditions and achievements of classical literature and art. For if classicism implies a certain order, clarity and rationality, these came out of what the great classical artists had discovered in life itself. Eliot's "classicism" is closer to "neoclassicism"; that is, the achievement of rhetorical clarity and order, with only so much of life permitted as can filter into this arbitrary order and precision. It is like finding "freedom" in self-imposed confinement. Eliot can propose this because, to him, human beings are slaves. Wisdom lies in admitting it and in giving up futile, heretical endeavors to know the world, not to speak of reshaping it. His world view is summarized in this speech of Thomas Becket, in *Murder in the Cathedral*:

> *We do not know know very much of the future*
> *Except that from generation to generation*
> *The same things happen again and again.* . . .
> . . . *Only*
> *The fool, fixed in his folly, may think*
> *He can turn the wheel on which he turns.*

Even existentialism, for all its comparable disdain for science and the possibility of knowing and commanding reality —"man turning the wheel"—rebels against this passive obedience. Though Camus, in his image of Sisyphus perpetually rolling the rock uphill, sees life as much like Eliot's wheel, he would say that a human being, while being turned by the wheel, could express his scorn for it. Eliot strips man of even this rebellious gesture.

And so it is with Eliot's view of the artist. The poet, he says, to produce true poetry, must accept blind authority. While he impresses readers with his seemingly vast knowledge of poetry, and talks with awe of "heritage" and "tradition," he interprets this tradition to make it a tail for his poetic kite. A poet, he says, simply takes over a body of thought handed to him and gives it eloquent rhetoric. His job is not to think. In the essay, "Shakespeare and the Stoicism of Seneca" (1927), he describes two of the most courageous thinkers about life among the great poets, Dante and Shakespeare, as writers who simply and mindlessly added "emotion" to the authoritative thought of their time. Dante took his, Eliot says, from St. Thomas Aquinas; Shakespeare, from Montaigne.

I can see no reason for believing that either Dante or Shakespeare did any thinking of his own. . . . The difference between Shakespeare and Dante is that Dante had one coherent system of thought behind him; but that was just his luck, and from the point of view of poetry is an irrelevant accident. It happened that at

Dante's time thought was orderly and strong and beautiful, and
that it was concentrated in one man of the greatest genius. . . .
You can hardly say that Dante believed, or did not believe, the
Thomist philosophy; you can hardly say that Shakespeare believed,
or did not believe, the mixed and muddled scepticism of the
Renaissance. If Shakespeare had written according to a better
philosophy, he would have written worse poetry. It was his business to express the greatest emotional intensity of his time, based
on whatever his time happened to think. Poetry is not a substitute for philosophy or theology or religion. . . .[17]

Eliot argues like a medieval scholastic, whose structure of
logic is built on unreal, irrational premises, and who must,
above all, never test his thought by any light it may throw
upon real life. Everything is put into precise categories. The
bee's job is to make honey, the spider's to spin webs, the
philosopher's to make logic, the poet's to make emotion
with language. Poetry is, by definition, alienation.

Of course poetry is not a substitute for philosophy, just as
it is not a substitute for science or politics. But philosophy,
science, politics, poetry and all art are different forms of
thinking about life, and stimulate one another. If Dante took
ideas from St. Thomas Aquinas, he also added to them a
realistic, devastating attack upon the corruption of court and
church in his time that was not his teacher's thinking, and
provided the human data that makes his poetry so great.
Shakespeare too taught philosophers more than he learned
from them. Others of his time, like Ben Jonson, were polished
masters of language. But the very richness and variety of
Shakespeare's use of language and the multitude of human
types whom he first brought into the social consciousness of
literature shows how profoundly he studied life. His greatness
lay in his ability to challenge the illusions of his time with the
realities. In a period of firm belief in absolute monarchy,
there was no greater critic of the corruptions that were part
of court life than Shakespeare. Eliot's view of the poet's role,

however, is that of an exalted writer of advertising copy. Let the boss give him the "message," and he will clothe it in "emotion."

In the 1930's, Eliot's thought, with its contempt for democracy and the human potentiality, its upholding of "authority," its scorn of the possibility of improving human welfare, came as close to fascism as it could without actually supporting Hitler and the Third Reich. In fact, in "The Idea of a Christian Society" (1939), his stated difference with fascism allows room for the belief that had it made its peace with the Church—as Franco did in Spain—he would have welcomed it.

The fundamental objection to fascist doctrine, the one which we conceal from ourselves because it might condemn ourselves, is that it is pagan. There are other objections too, in the political and economic sphere, but they are not objections that we can make with dignity until we set our own affairs in order. There are still other objections, to oppression and violence and cruelty, but however strongly we feel, these are objections to means and not ends.[18]

And the fact is that the theological dogma of the 13th century, which he praises as "orderly," "strong" and "beautiful," was likewise enforced then with frightful cruelty, violence and oppression.

The influence exercised by Eliot on poetry and criticism was bolstered by his consummate mastery of rhetoric, his fine ear for sound, his economy and precision, his calculated exactness when he wanted it and calculated ambiguity when he wanted it. His style raised an "anti-romantic" banner which, intensified by his alienated "shock" imagery and combined with his sweeping rejection of and attack upon the industrial world made him appear to be a rebel. Even those who recognized this fake "rebellion" as an anti-humanist "new conservatism" sometimes felt that his craftsmanship was a liberation of poetry.

There is, of course, much to learn from a fine craftsman.

What was insufficiently realized was how much the "fine tool" Eliot had fashioned, and the Eliot cult exalted both in poetry and in criticism, had narrowed the uses and scope of poetry. The Eliot pseudo-classicism, which had served so well the needs of his own alienation and substituted echoes, symbols and myths of past cultures for the scrutiny of how people lived, became a new academicism. The most important reason for its appeal and influence, over and above the craft itself, was its assurance that, with this method, one could be a ranking poet without any need to plunge into life at all. Alienation was a virtue.

As a result, a vast amount of anemic poetry was produced, impeccable in its rhetorical polish, but with a dreary didactic substance of philosophical platitudes dressed up in symbolical imagery. Any myth sufficed to supply this imagery, so long as it had nothing to do with life today or the actual world of human strivings. Similarly the Eliot approach also assured critics that they too could evade reality and need only analyze rhetorical subtleties and track down symbolic meanings, as if poetry or art were a kind of cryptogram. To combine attitudes of rebellion with a flight from social problems and even political reaction proved an enticing path, wherever reaction in real life showed strength. What Eliot provided was a lesson in how to be "daring" and at the same time, "safe."

The Eliot cult grew to major proportions in American university life when the "cold war" followed the end of the Second World War. Its fraternity members were poets, critics and university instructors, often all three in one; an ideal combination for mutual praise, putting each other's works in anthologies, and instructing the young in their pre-eminence.

In 1949 the cultists felt strong enough, with the "cold war" tide, to engineer the Bollingen award for poetry to one of their "father" figures, Ezra Pound. Pound's reputation had been won for finely sensitive translation, imitation, quotation and parody of old styles, so that reading him was like a literary trip through a collection of Italian Renaissance, Provencal, Chinese and ancient Greek exhibits. To this he added an attack upon the modern world based on an economic theory dredged up from the Middle Ages, declaiming against "usury" and the printing of paper money, calling for a "strong man," and accompanying this with a mindless stream of vituperation, a "daring" use of obscenities, and an anti-Semitism worse than Eliot's. All this could be dismissed as crack-pot, were it not so obviously fascist, and during the war he became an open propagandist for fascism on the Italian radio. The Bollingen award to a man saved from conviction for treason only on the ground that he was insane, was a consciously reactionary affirmation that talent with words made literary greatness, however infantile the mind behind them, giving notice to young writers that to be "accepted" they had better discard any leanings toward social responsibility.

It is sad that in the turn against the Eliot cult in the late 1950's and early 1960's, so much of the "rebellion" against it retained his contempt for social awareness and his elitist scorn of the mass of humanity, merely substituting the existentialist outlook for his pseudo-classicism.

CONFLICT BETWEEN HUMANIZATION AND ALIENATION: *William Faulkner*

William Faulkner, like T. S. Eliot, finds an answer to the hatred he feels for the corruptions in the capitalist world, by embracing an ideology more reactionary than that of capitalism. Unable to discern, either through economic-historical knowledge or basic human attachments, the reality of class forces, or the contradiction between basic democratic traditions and the violent, ruthless debasement of these traditions by rampant property interests, both seek escape in a mythical harmonious past, from which the present seems to them to be a degeneration. Eliot finds this "order" and "beauty" in the European Middle Ages, ridden by disease, poverty, the Inquisition and heretic burning. Faulkner finds it in the slave-holding South before the Civil War. Both are writers of extraordinary gifts.

As stylists, Faulkner and Eliot are diametrical opposites. The difference is not only that Faulkner writes novels and stories, while Eliot writes poetry and criticism. Faulkner creates characters who have a time, place and history. Eliot even in his plays creates characters who are only transparent mouthpieces for dogmatic argument. Faulkner's words are like vibrating nerve-ends, soaking in all the sensuous aspects of the outer world, arranged in sequences that abandon all pretense to rational order or logic, in almost endless chains of sense impression or inner monologues. Eliot's words are like concrete objects to be arranged in orderly, disciplined patterns, evoking subjective feelings but not responsive to the outer world, possessing a reality of their own consonant with the cold face he turns to the world about him. They become a mask of alienation behind which lurks his own loneliness and anguish. Faulkner writes with a rich humanization of reality. Yet in him too there is alienation.

Most of Faulkner's writings have a definite locale; the Southern states, and most often Mississippi, in which of all the former slave-holding states there was in Faulkner's own lifetime the most brutal exploitation, terrorization and pauperization of the Negro population, the accompanying pauperization of a large section of the white population, the worst educational system, the highest illiteracy and the most flagrant corruption of courts, justice and democratic processes, with even a pretence at justice replaced often by naked violence and murder. These are all reflected in his writings, thus giving them considerable substance as a portrayal of American life. But they are reflected as in a highly distorted mirror.

The guiding spirit of Faulkner's thought, the well-spring of his irrationality, is a virulent nationalism based on a mythical nation, one that never existed. This is the Civil War Southern Confederacy, which was not a nation but a part of the United States split off by an oligarchy of slave owners, whose aim was to keep the Negro slaves in bondage and to combat the growing opposition to slavery among their own, indigenous, white non-slaveholding population. As Herbert Aptheker writes in *Toward Negro Freedom*:

He who seeks to understand the reasons for the ultimate collapse of the Confederacy will find them not only in the military might of the North, but, in an essential respect, in the highly unpopular character of that government. The Southern masses opposed the Bourbon regime and it was this opposition, of the poor whites and of the Negro slaves, that contributed largely to its downfall.[1]

It was after the Civil War that the myth arose, becoming more romanticized as the actual history slipped into the past. It was that the South had been a homogeneous, unified "nation" based on paternal land relationships, with the Negroes obediently serving their "betters" and in turn being taken care of by their kindly masters; a society cultured like a "Greek democracy" and free from commercialism until the mercenary hordes of Northern capitalism had invaded it. In actual fact it was as money-minded and profit-seeking a society as any, run by the cotton industry, with the slaves' lives ruthlessly wasted and a traffic in human bodies more horrible than had ever existed in ancient slave-holding societies, on top of which was a parasitical class whose "culture" was largely dueling, woman-chasing, drinking and gambling. There was more true culture produced in the poetry and music of the slaves. One of the first inspired American composers, Louis Moreau Gottschalk, was born in New Orleans, but he freed the few slaves he had inherited and fervently supported the Union in the Civil War. But as Thomas Wolfe writes in *The Hills Beyond*:[2]

In a curious way, the war became no longer a thing finished and done with, a thing to be put aside and forgotten as belonging to the buried past, but a dead fact charged with new vitality, and one to be cherished more dearly than life itself. The mythology which this gave rise to acquired in time the force of an almost supernatural sanction. It became a kind of folk-religion. And under its soothing, other-worldly spell, the South began to turn its face away from the hard and ugly realities of daily living that confronted it on every hand, and escaped into the soft dream of vanished glories —imagined glories—glories that had never been.

Faulkner, beginning to write in the middle 1920's, publishing a series of impressive novels and short stories in the 1930's and attaining an almost sanctified status in the 1950's, was the first writer to apply a major literary talent to the elaboration of this myth. He presents it not historically, but

largely through the mind and thought of present-day descendants of the old Southern slave-holding gentry. These are the
"heroes," the "good" figures of his books, with whom he deals
most warmly, whom he sees in most human terms, both when
describing their degeneration, as with the Compsons in *The
Sound and the Fury*, and when making them his own spokes-
men, as with Gavin Stevens in *Light in August, Intruder in
the Dust*, and other books.

Faulkner developed a genealogy for this gentry, extending
back for more than a century, intertwining families like the
Compsons, McCaslins, Edmonds', de Spains, Sartoris', High-
towers, so that in any novel or short story he could pick and
spin out one or another thread. One is reminded of Balzac's
Human Comedy, a novelistic panorama of French society in
which characters appear from book to book, or Zola's Rougon-
Macquart series. But in comparison, Balzac and Zola give us
the human and psychological life within an actual history,
throwing light on this history. Faulkner's panorama has no
such social-realistic character. His perception and grasp of immediate reality has genius, and is done with a passionate involvement greater than Zola's and even perhaps than Balzac's.
He almost sucks life into his books. But the social and psychological reality he absorbs in his books must first be, so to
speak, "digested" by the myth of the gentry making a last,
gallant stand against the hated onrush of capitalism. The eye
for reality supplies the detail. The myth tends to supply whatever organizing form there is, and this form, based on an
irrational subjectivity, tends to fall apart.

Just as Faulkner's style is so much made up of inner mono-
logue, so his novels tend to be monologues on a grand scale.
The Faulkner monologue shuttles between present and past.
It differs considerably from the stream of consciousness of
James Joyce, Marcel Proust and Virginia Woolf, where there
is a certain naturalism, an attempt to trace the actual thought,

perception and memory process. Faulkner's monologue is his
own irrationality put into the mind of the people he writes
about, and the monologues of these figures merge with his
own as narrator, which also shuttles between present and past.
It is sometimes quite difficult for the reader to know just what
Faulkner is talking about.

It is through the distorting lenses of the gentry's eyes that
Faulkner views the other strata of southern society. In his last
novel, *The Rievers* (1962),[3] written shortly before his death,
he defines "intelligence" as "the ability to cope with environment: which means to accept environment yet still retain at
least something of personal liberty." To accept environment,
or reality, then, is not altogether a virtue. Reality to him is
the dreary world of capitalism, replacing the noble and feudal
past. The gentry cannot cope with the mercenary, capitalist
environment unless they make compromises. If they don't,
they die tragic deaths. The Snopeses, the mercenary class
risen from the poor whites, who are replacing the gentry in
political life, can cope with this environment, because they
think like intelligent animals that prey on others; rats, for
example. The Negroes cannot cope at all with a white man's
environment, whether the cultured one of the old gentry or
the brutal one of the modern marketplace. Consequently they
need the white man to guide them and think for them. They
can cope magnificently, however, with "primitive" environ-
ments, like the kitchen, the nursery, the barns, the fields, the
stables, the hunting grounds. Like the existentialists, Faulkner combines a revulsion against the mores of capitalism with
a blindness to the history and workings of capitalism. His
mind seems untouched by any knowledge of the real history
of what he writes of as history.

Thus Faulkner, ignorant of African history, does not know
that the myth of the "primitive Negro" was a rationalization
of the depopulation of Africa by the slave trade, just as racism

in general is a rationalization of the brutal competitiveness of bourgeois life. He does not understand that the old land-holding and slave-holding gentry represented not a pre-capitalist order but a part of capitalism, and that whatever illusions they had of themselves as a kind of landed aristoc-racy was based on their unwillingness to admit where their money came from. So, many of the old gentry looked kindly on their slave house servants, coachmen, musicians and wet nurses, and even had children by them, while leaving to their overseers the brutal business of driving and whipping the slave laborers in the fields. Faulkner does not understand that when he warns the "North" to "keep its hands off the South," he is playing the game of the most reactionary Northern business interests, who want a reservoir of cheap labor in the South and prize the anti-labor votes of the Southern racist politicians.

Faulkner is always aware that the central question in Southern life is the relation between white and non-white. But he views this through the myth of the once-happy rela-tionship between the old gentry and their colored slaves. Today, as in the past, he says, only the gentry really under-stand the Negro. The whites have the mentality that makes them masters. The Negroes are good servants, even wonderful ones, who are contented with very little; perhaps an occasional piece of discarded finery. They may even be excused from service if they fall sick, provided the illness does not last long enough to cause the masters serious inconvenience.

These childlike primitives don't really want freedom, or the vote, or to live like the white people. As long as they make no demands for civil rights and are loyal to the white masters they are admirable, even noble people, close to nature, like the primitive worshippers of old nature gods. Examples are Dilsey, the cook, her husband, Roskus, and her son Luster, who take care of the Compson family in *The Sound and the Fury*, or Lucas Beauchamp in *Intruder in the Dust*, proud to count himself as one of the McCaslin family, whom his own family had served. These, to Faulkner, are "good" Negroes. The "bad" ones are those who seek independence and want to live in some ways like white people.

There also are "good" and "bad" whites. The latter are the poor whites who have swarmed into landownership, business and politics along with the decadence of the old gentry, and who are brutal, grasping and money-obsessed; the Snopes family, for example, who figure in *The Hamlet* and other novels. The "good" are the gentry, so long as they remember their traditions and do not betray them by turning into people like the Snopeses, as Jason Compson does in *The Sound and the Fury*.

In defiance of all that science teaches, Faulkner is acutely "blood" conscious. The old Southern gentry are to him a "homogeneous" people, Anglo-Saxon, unlike the Northerners, contaminated by immigrants, or what he calls, in *Intruder in the Dust*, the "coastal spew of Europe." The Negroes are also a "homogeneous" people, so long as there is no "mixed blood." "Blood" homogeneity is good. "Mixed blood" is dangerous. As to the most rabid racist, so to Faulkner, even a touch of "black" ancestry makes a person a Negro. And the danger comes because these two kinds of "blood" are incompatible. Thus Gavin Stevens, the gentleman, analyzes Joe Christmas, in *Light in August* (1932).[4] Joe Christmas can pass for a white man. But he has Negro "blood," and this causes his downfall. He murders a white woman, is tracked down by bloodhounds, and finally shot and killed. Stevens says: "The black blood drove him first to the Negro cabin. And then the white blood drove him out of there, as it was the black blood which snatched up the pistol and the white blood which would not let him fire it."

The labor struggles of the "depression" 1930's were an important education for the American people. When working people, white and Negro, were moving history actively, collectively and consciously, the awareness grew that among them, not among the great corporations and their servants, was to be found the real America. The link was seen between the monopoly corporations and fascism. The racist psychology was recognized for what it was, as irrational, inhuman and serving only the cause of exploitation. The spotlight of truth picked out the festering sores of lynchings, chain gangs and other brutalities toward the Negro people in the South. It was not that the South had a monopoly on racism, segregation and denial of human rights to the Negroes. What became evident, however, was that there, where the corruption was most violent, the life of the white people as well was most blighted, and there could be seen the focal point of an infection that was blighting democracy throughout the entire country.

All that this upheaval did to Faulkner was to put him on the defensive. He held on to his myth. In the novel, *Intruder in the Dust*[5] (1948), a Negro, Lucas Beauchamp, is saved from a false accusation of murdering a white man, and from being lynched, through the efforts of the "good" white people, who include the sixteen-year-old nephew of Gavin Stevens. Lucas Beauchamp has "white blood," his father being the illegitimate son of the master whom he had served as a slave. He shows this "white blood" in his scorn for the "white trash," who are not "gentry." What Faulkner finds admirable in him is that he remains fundamentally a "Negro," never attempting to rise out of a squalid life, exhibiting the primary virtue of the "race"; the "capacity to wait and endure and survive." It is the Southern gentry, Faulkner says, who will elevate the Negro. For they are homogeneous people, Anglo-Saxons, and the Second World War has shown that the people of Europe, "except for Anglo-Saxons, actively fear and distrust personal liberty." Gavin Stevens, as Faulkner's mouthpiece, says that the gentry should combine their economic and political and cultural privileges with the Negro's capacity to suffer and endure.

Then we would prevail; together we would present a front not only impregnable but not even to be threatened by a mass of people who no longer have anything in common save a frantic greed for money and a basic fear of a failure of national character which they hide from one another behind a loud lip-service to a flag.

Faulkner ignores the fact—which does not fit his myth-picture of the Negro—that the Negroes themselves are carrying on the fight for their human rights. To him this movement is a product of "theorists and fanatics and private and personal avengers." He warns the North to keep its hands off. "We are in the position of the Germans after 1933 who had no other alternative between being either a Nazi or a Jew." Faulkner still waves this strange national flag, that of a mythical nation of beneficent homogeneous Anglo-Saxon slave-owners and their homogeneous Negro bondsmen living in peace and happiness on the land, each mutually serving the other, up to the barbaric invasion of Northern, mixed-blood capitalism. And this nation, he says, will yet win its independence. How this nation will live Faulkner doesn't consider, for he probably regards economics as a capitalist invention.

Yet, what establishes Faulkner as an artist is the core of reality which he depicts so vividly, while he weaves his myth about it. This reality is the decline of the gentry; their inability to cope with the world about them and to save themselves. He cannot see that there is a new life stirring in the South, of which the gentry can be a part, without having to become grasping merchants or sharp swindlers. And so his portrayal takes on the tone of an awesome requiem, not only for the inept, impotent, disappearing gentry but for the Old South itself. He is a nationalist not for a land which is struggling for independence but for a nation which never existed and which he sees as dead. The living descendants of the old plantation owners are haunted by the ghosts of their dead ancestors, who are more real than the living. Thus in *Absalom, Absalom!*[6] (1936) he writes of "the deep South dead since 1865, and peopled with garrulous outraged baffled ghosts." Of the young Quentin Compson he says, he "was still too young to deserve to be a ghost and yet having to be one for all that."

In the Compson family, as described in *The Sound and the Fury*, the father is no businessman, and must sell his land piece by piece to keep up genteel appearances. One last piece goes so that his son Quentin can be sent to Harvard. The mother is a querulous, self-centered invalid. Quentin has a close to incestuous attachment to his sister, Candace. At Harvard he commits suicide. Another son, Benjamin, is feeble-minded, and must be fed and cared for by a young Negro. Candace tries to escape from family, lineage, traditions and the small-town South itself through sexual affairs and marriages that waste her life. The son Jason, who takes over the family reins when the father dies, turns into a hard, shrewd, grasping speculator, the opposite in spirit to the gentry. He becomes, spiritually, kin to the "Snopes's." The novel is perhaps Faulkner's best, because in it social-psychological reality takes precedence over myth.

None of Faulkner's characters does any rational thinking; that is, faces a problem with some objectivity, analyzing it, bringing to bear on it some tested social knowledge and experience, and weighing the consequences of a decision. Even Gavin Stevens, who in his role as a spokesman must appear to do some general thinking, starts with his passions and then attempts to rationalize them in myth-generalizations. Faulkner gives his characters a "mind" through his masterful inner monologues, so "true" in speech rhythms and sensuous data that the reader tends to overlook the fact that this is Faulkner speaking. He himself thinks with his passions, with his loves and hates, and so we get his attitudes in the mixture of humanization and alienation that characterizes his style.

The story, "That Evening Sun" (1931),[7] which is part of the Compson "saga," opens with a description of a street in Jefferson, Mississippi. Typical of Faulkner, it evokes all the senses: sight, sound, touch, smell.

Monday is no different from any other weekday in Jefferson now. The streets are paved now, and the telephone and electric companies are cutting down more and more of the shade trees— the water oaks, the maples and locusts and elms—to make room for iron poles bearing clusters of bloated and ghostly and bloodless grapes, and we have a city laundry which makes the rounds on Monday morning, gathering the bundles of clothes into bright-colored, specially-made motor cars: the soiled wearing of a whole week now flees apparitionlike behind alert and irritable electric horns, with a long diminishing noise of rubber and asphalt like tearing silk, and even the Negro women who still take in white people's washing after the old custom, fetch and deliver it in automobiles.

But, "fifteen years ago," Faulkner writes, laundry was collected by Negro women differently.

Nancy would set her bundle on the top of her head, then upon the bundle in turn she would set the black straw sailor hat which she wore winter and summer. She was tall, with a high, sad face shrunken a little where her teeth were missing. Sometimes we would go a part of the way down the lane and across the pasture with her, to watch the balanced bundle and the hat that never bobbed nor wavered, even when she walked down into the ditch and up the other side and stooped through the fence.

The first paragraph is full of the imagery of alienation. The shade trees have been replaced by electric lights on iron poles that look like "bloated and ghostly and bloodless grapes." The electric horns are "irritable," and the motorcars make a sound like "tearing silk." The second paragraph quoted is a "humanized" description. The hat balanced on top of the bundle could, from a derisive point of view, be made grotesquely funny, but Faulkner's description arouses a warm feeling for the woman. So, through imagery alone, through the alternation of alienated and humanized sensitivities, Faulkner's thought is conveyed; his revulsion against the vulgarized, mechanized and industrialized life that has replaced the old ways.

When we come to Nancy's husband, Jesus, the picture is again an alienated one. To Faulkner he is not a man but a monster, obsessed with killing. In the descriptions of him, the razor image recurs. "Jesus was in the kitchen, sitting behind the stove, with his razor scar on his black face like a piece of dirty string." Later, Nancy says of him, "I ain't seen him, and I ain't going to see him again but once more, with that razor in his mouth." And this monster-image, not a man but a walking razor, is to Faulkner the counterpart of Jesus's rebelliousness. Earlier in the story, Jesus had muttered, "I can't hang around white man's kitchen. But white man can hang around mine. White man can come in my house, but I can't stop him. When white man want to come in my house, I ain't got no house. I can't stop him, but he can't kick me outen it. He can't do that." Any sympathy this statement of the case might arouse in the reader is rubbed out by reiteration that Jesus is a killer. And it is not with conscious plan, of course, that Faulkner had described Nancy as having a "high, sad face sunken a little," while that of Jesus was a "black" face with a "razor" scar, which looked like a piece of "dirty string." A human response brings one kind of imagery to mind; an alienated response, compounded of fear and hatred, brings up another kind.

Faulkner's humor is aimed largely at the "poor whites," the small farmers and artisans like the Bundrens of *As I Lay*

Dying, or the descendants of this class who, avid for land
and money, have now become a power in economic and political life like the Varners and Snopeses of *The Hamlet.* The
humor has a wild grotesquerie, playing on the people's idiocy,
their avaricious cunning, and their lack of any feeling for
one another. Thus in *As I Lay Dying,* one son, "a good carpenter," is sawing boards for his dying mother's coffin, outside her bedroom window, while another son is out hunting
a prospective dollar.

In *The Hamlet,*[8] Eula Varner, fat and dim-witted, is sent
to school because the school itself is a "Varner enterprise,"
and Will Varner "would have insisted that his daughter at-
tend it, for a while at least, just as he would have insisted
upon collecting the final odd cent of an interest calculation."
Later, Eula surprises the family, who thought she had some
kind of stomach trouble, by giving birth to a child, illegitimate of course. As her brother Jody stands over her, demanding to know who made her pregnant, and she answers, "Stop
shoving me. I don't feel good," her mother cries: "I'll fix
him. I'll fix both of them. Turning up pregnant and yelling
and cursing here in the house while I am trying to take a
nap!"

Faulkner's humor is his defense against these people. He
has a lingering affection for them because they are his people,
of his South, his "nation," and yet fears them because in their
animal-like cunning, their single-minded avarice unchecked
by any gentlemanly standards, they are taking over the land.
It was, according to the "myth," the Northern "invasion"
which broke the power of the high-minded, cultured planta-
tion-owning gentry and let these poor whites loose to devour
everything. And so he laughs at them, as an assertion of his
difference from them, his superiority over their idiocy even
while their idiocy puts him at their mercy. In this way one

might write of a pet animal, knowing that it can at any time snarl, and bite.

And yet Faulkner does not really know these people, for their mindlessness is a projection of his own fears. Quite a different view of them is provided by Erskine Caldwell in *God's Little Acre* (1933) or in the stories of *Kneel to the Rising Sun* (1935), or in *You Have Seen Their Faces* (1937). For missing from Faulkner is any portrayal of people in humanized social relationships. In the years of the Great Depression, other writers found mutual strength and fellow feeling in ordinary working people coming together on a common problem, but not Faulkner. Take this moving passage from Steinbeck's *The Grapes of Wrath*. Steinback is addressing the abstract "bank" which has driven the Oklahoma farmers from their land.

Here "I lost my land" is changed; a cell is split and from its splitting grows the thing you hate—"We lost *our* land." The danger is here, for two men are not as lonely and perplexed as one. And from this first "we" there grows a still more dangerous thing: "I have a little food" plus "I have none." If from this problem the sum is "We have a little food," the thing is on its way, the movement has direction. Only a little multiplication now, and this land, this tractor, are ours. The two men squatting in a ditch, the little fire, the side-meat stewing in a single pot, the silent stone-eyed women; behind, the children listening with their souls to words their minds do not understand. The night draws down. The baby has a cold. Here, take this blanket. It's wool. It was my mother's blanket—take it for the baby. This is the thing to bomb. This is the beginning—from "I" to "we."

These dispossessed Oklahoma farmers, in whom Steinbeck reveals such humanization of relations, are the social counterparts of the poor whites whom Faulkner describes, sometimes affectionately, as idiots.

ALIENATION AND REBELLION
TO NOWHERE: *John Dos Passos*
and Henry Miller

In the works of John Dos Passos, alienation takes a different form from that in Eliot or Faulkner. As with Eliot, alienation dominates his style, but there is no assumption of the role of a theologian, demanding a turn to the "supernatural" and denouncing interest in the "secular." Dos Passos is a completely secular and political-minded novelist. As with Faulkner, his writing strikes roots deep in the American land, but he does not suffer from Faulkner's narrow vision and attachment to a mythical past.

Dos Passos puts American capitalism into the witness box like a brilliant prosecuting attorney, making it confess to and document the exploitation, avarice, cruelty, deception, hypocrisy, thievery, bribery, murder, "every man for himself" selfishness, waste of talent and lives, that lay behind its accumulation of wealth. He does this as a clear-eyed social historian. But the heat of his furious attack on society generates no warmth toward his characters as human beings. They have no inner life commensurate to the outer world he depicts. If in their appearance, manners and acts they are true types of the time, in their inner life they converge to one type: the quickly disillusioned who find life repellent and loathsome, who die inside long before they die physically.

Alienation dominated Dos Passos' style in his works of the

1920's, like *Manhattan Transfer* (1925).[1] The first scene is a hospital, where a baby is born.

The nurse, holding the basket at arm's length as if it were a bedpan, opened the door to a big dry hot room with greenish distempered walls where in the air tinctured with smells of alcohol and iodoform hung writhing a faint sourish squalling from other baskets along the wall. As she set her basket down she glanced into it with pursed-up lips. The newborn baby squirmed in the cottonwood feebly like a knot of earthworms.

The husband visits the wife in the hospital: "Rows of beds under bilious gaslight, a sick smell of restlessly stirring bedclothes, faces fat, lean, yellow, white; that's her. Susie's yellow hair lay in a lose coil round her little white face that looked shriveled and twisted."

Such alienation permeates the style of Dos Passos' most impressive work, his trilogy *U.S.A.*,[2] made up of *The 42nd Parallel* (1930), *1919* (1932) and *The Big Money* (1936). This work has the structural skeleton for an epic of American society from the beginning of the 20th century to the execution of Sacco and Vanzetti in 1927. Setting off the stories of his invented characters are 26 interspersed "thumbnail" biographical sketches of actual historical personages—political figures like Theodore Roosevelt, William Jennings Bryan and Woodrow Wilson; working-class leaders like Eugene V. Debs, Joe Hill and "Big Bill" Heywood; social critics and thinkers like Randolph Bourne, John Reed and Thorstein Veblen; millionaires and industrialists like Andrew Carnegie, J. P. Morgan, and Henry Ford; artistic figures like Isadora Duncan and Frank Lloyd Wright; scientists and inventors like Charles Steinmetz, Luther Burbank, and the Wright brothers. These caustic and brilliant sketches are brought to a climax of moral denunciation in the symbolic biography of "The Unknown Soldier."

Scattered throughout the book are "Newsreels" made up

of newspaper headlines, fragments of news stories, verses of popular songs, conveying the sensationalism and manufactured hysteria with which the press and "mass communications" tried to shape the public mind. Also scattered throughout are passages called "The Camera Eye," fragments of talk and sense impression, not part of any narrative but conveying the tone and feeling of common speech, like a "Greek Chorus" of the common people announcing its presence but with nothing to say.

Dos Passos creates twelve main characters whose life stories run through the trilogy, the writer breaking off one thread to take up another. Each is told as if it were an independent novel, although the central figure of one will appear as a secondary figure in another, affording interesting contrasts between a person as he sees himself and as others see him. It is an unusual, imaginative approach to the social novel which deeply interested the French existentialist writers, and its influence can be seen in Sartre's *Paths to Freedom*.

So close does *U.S.A.* come to being one of the great American social novels that its failure and the subsequent bleakness of Dos Passos' work must be considered a tragedy of our culture. It is not a failure of talent or skill, but a philosophical failure, and a failure of the humanism that a novel of such scope demands for its fulfillment. Dos Passos took from Marx his analysis of capitalist society, but not his confidence in the masses of people, based on the historical knowledge that at strategic times and places they had carried through transforming social changes. Or, we can say, there was not enough human warmth and light in Dos Passos for this aspect of Marx's thought to kindle into illuminating flame.

The invented characters are drawn from a considerable range of American life. There is J. Ward Moorehouse, who creates the first big "public relations" institution engaged in masking the dirty operations of big business under shining "public images." There is Charley Anderson, a World War flier, with an inventive mind, who rises to affluence in the growing postwar aircraft industry, learning in the process that underhand financial manipulations are more profitable than inventive skills. On the other hand, there are the radicals; Fainy McCreary, who works with Haywood's I.W.W. and then goes off to Mexico, and Ben Compton and Mary French, who are involved in the postwar labor battles and then in the fight to save Sacco and Vanzetti. But whatever humanity any of them might have tends to be drowned in the writer's own alienation.

We can appreciate the satiric value of an alienated style when applied to the milieu of J. Ward Moorehouse, although it keeps us from seeing that even such people are not altogether strangers or monsters.

They called up the Staple house and talked to the nightnurse who said that Mrs. Staple was resting more easily, that she'd been given an opiate and was sleeping quietly as a child, and Gertrude told her that when her mother woke to tell her she was spending the night with her friend Jane English and that she'd be home as soon as the blizzard let them get a car on the road. Then she called up Jane English and told her that she was distracted with grief and had taken a room at the Fort Pitt to be alone. And if her mother called to tell her she was asleep. Then they called up the Fort Pitt and reserved a room in her name. Then they went up to bed. Ward was very happy and decided that he loved her very much and she seemed to have done this sort of thing before because the first thing she said was: "We don't want to make this a shotgun wedding, do we, darling?"

But it is this way with everybody in the book. The radicals see the world through alienated eyes, lead loveless and joyless lives, act as if driven by a self-destructive mania to a miserable martyrdom.

They drank and drank and ate free lunch and drank some more, all the time rye with beer chasers, and the man from up San Ja-

cinto way had a telephone number and called up some girls and
they bought a bottle of whiskey and went out to their apartment,
and the rancher from up San Jacinto way sat with a girl on each
knee singing *My wife has gone to the country*. Mac just sat belch-
ing in a corner with his head dangling over his chest; then suddenly he felt bitterly angry and got to his feet upsetting a table
with a glass vase on it.

"McCreary," he said, "this is no place for a class-conscious rebel.
I'm a wobbly, damn you. . . . I'm goin' out and get in this free-
speech fight."

The other McCreary went on singing and paid no attention.
Mac went out and slammed the door. One of the girls followed
him out jabbering about the broken vase, but he pushed her in the
face and went out into the quiet street.

None of the radicals in real life whom Dos Passos writes
about, like Debs or Haywood or John Reed, led such bleak
lives. Theirs were the exhilaration of moving with history,
the joys of human contact and the discovery of human potentialities including one's own, the gratifications of loving
and being loved. Near the end of the trilogy, as part of "The
Camera Eye," Dos Passos quotes part of Vanzetti's moving
last letter, and says, "the old American speech of the haters
of oppression is new tonight in the mouth of an old woman
from Pittsburgh, of a husky boilermaker from Frisco who
hopped freights clear from the Coast to come here, in the
mouth of a Back Bay social worker, in the mouth of an Italian
printer, of a hobo from Arkansas." But none of Dos Passos'
characters speak like that or share Vanzetti's humanity.

Dos Passos is most eloquent when writing of defeat and
death. A memorable section is the death of the sailor, Joe
Williams, in a drunken brawl. Even more so is the death
of Charley Anderson. Estranged from his high-society wife,
he has been driving, drunk, with a kept woman, and has
smashed up his car. To his hospital deathbed comes a stream
of acquaintances and associates, asking him for money, asking
him to sign a power of attorney, asking him if he has made

a will. Half in a stupor, he says, "Say, nurse, it's like a run on a bank." A few minutes afterwards he falls away into nothingness.

And through and above these death scenes is the dominating theme that America is a "beaten nation." It is both said directly, and given overwhelming weight by the narratives and the images and style. Reaction is triumphant, the forces of chicanery, exploitation, deceit and destruction are all-powerful. With this as his conclusion, there was no other path for Dos Passos, despite his social awareness, but downward. And that was where Dos Passos went, justifying himself by berating every movement for social progress as not meriting any man's confidence. He foreshadows the hatred of capitalism combined with disillusion in progress that would take an existentialist form in the 1950's.

An even more direct link between the two generations of "disillusion," that which followed the First World War and that which followed the Second, is provided by Henry Miller. For while he is of the generation of Fitzgerald, Eliot, Faulkner and Dos Passos, he did not burst into the broad American literary consciousness until the late 1950's and early 1960's. His books like *Tropic of Cancer* (1934)[3] and *Tropic of Capricorn* (1939)[4] had been barred from publication or sale in the United States as pornography. The lifting of the ban generated tremendous literary excitement, the books becoming best-sellers and Miller being praised by otherwise responsible critics as one of the greatest of living writers.

The excitement was not solely one of belated discovery. The form that Miller's "revolt" took, as one of the "disillusioned" after the First World War, was much like that of the self-named "beat generation" after the Second World War. It was as much a way of life as a way of writing, a defiant, vituperative resignation from society with the writing serving as an autobiographical manifesto for his behavior.

Born in 1891, Miller was reared in Brooklyn, N.Y., and supported himself by various odd jobs until 1924, when he decided to devote himself to writing. In 1930 he made Paris his home, writing while struggling against hunger and poverty, and returned to the United States after the war broke out, in 1940.

The pathos of impotence underlies the bravado of Henry Miller's declaration of war against the whole world, and is admitted in the utter, self-revelatory frankness with which he writes. Perhaps we cannot quite call it impotence, because he did produce a series of books. But there is a tacit surrender in their formlessness, raising seriously the question of what permanence they might have beyond their impact as "sensations." The process of organizing experience into an art form involves a certain minimum of self-criticism, which in the big artists becomes the ability to get out of their own skin and embrace a sweep of life. Miller, however, relies wholly on his remarkable "gift for gab." We think of the kind of book we might have gotten had there been a real Don Quixote, and instead of Cervantes' narrative, we had only the diary of the brave if addle-headed Don.

Miller tries to put a good face on his surrender. He says, "I have made a silent compact with myself not to change a line of what I write." Turgenev and Dostoievsky had their perfections, "but in Van Gogh's letters there is a perfection beyond either of these. It is the triumph of the individual over art." But Van Gogh did not substitute writing letters for painting pictures, and the letters are those of a man engaged in a successful, if harrowing, struggle to create solid works of art. Yet here too Miller strikes a note that would resound in the 1960's, and not only in literature but also in painting and music, as in the derisive joking of "pop art" and in "indeterminate" music. The artist sacrifices his future to the impact of the moment, and the underlying thought is, if the world has no future, why worry about the future of an art work?

What is Miller's "triumph"? He reiterates that he has renounced the bondage to a demanding world, and has found freedom. "I don't ask to go back to America, to be put in double harness again, to work the treadmill. No, I prefer to be a poor man of Europe. God knows, I am poor enough; it only remains to be a man." This is in *Tropic of Cancer*. Shortly after, we learn that his dubious "freedom" involves ghost-writing theses for incompetent writers, and composing publicity pamphlets for a house of prostitution.

To be free of society is to be free like an animal. The animal can go where it wants but is everywhere prey to hunger and enemies. Miller glimpses this. "I made up my mind that I would hold on to nothing, that I would expect nothing, that henceforth I would live as an animal, a beast of prey, a rover, a plunderer. Even if war were declared, and it were my lot to go, I would grab the bayonet and plunge it, plunge it up to the hilt." He makes love like an animal, and bravely describes it down to the last clinical detail. This is his battle against society, against the prudes and philistines. But it is also his surrender to a loss of humanity. For to see a woman as more than an immediate sex object, to see her as a human being with her own needs, is to become involved, to acknowledge demands on oneself. Miller wants human relationships but is afraid to pay the price, and so declaims in justification, "People are like lice—they get under your skin and bury themselves there. You scratch and scratch until the blood comes, but you can't get permanently deloused."

Whatever permanence Miller's art may lack, it is certainly significant as a social phenomenon and "type response" of our times. For Miller's was one that many others were making, and would make in the 50's more than the 30's. It is that one must renounce society in order to gain one's own hu-

manity. And the value of his frankness is that we can find
in his books—if we look—how humanity shrinks in these
terms. His heart will go out to a beggar, a prostitute, a sick
dog. Thus, he finds in himself love for humanity and asserts
his own. But he can learn of massacres, mass starvation, disasters elsewhere, not under his nose, and he gloats that he
remains unmoved. "I am inoculated against every disease,
every calamity, every sorrow and misery. It's the culmination
of a life of fortitude." But this "fortitude" is a calculated
self-centredness, which he can only justify by claiming that
all the world is equally bestial, and he alone has the courage
to say so. What he also reveals is the anguish in which this
leaves him. In *Tropic of Capricorn* he cries, "Now it dawns
on me with full clarity: *you are alone in the world.*" It is
bitter to be alone. And again in *Tropic of Cancer*, he cries,
"My world of human beings had perished; I was utterly alone
in the world and for friends I had the streets, and the streets
spoke to me in that sad, bitter language compounded of human misery, yearning, regret, failure, wasted effort."

To really live is to live in the world that includes society.
The more a person cuts himself off from any knowledge of
it, the more he renounces it, the more irrational and frightful
are the blows it delivers. Miller fights back by cursing it.
Realizing, perhaps unconsciously, the impotence of such a
verbal attack, he bolsters the words with violence and every
obscene insult in his vocabulary. "The world needs to be
blown to smithereens." And again, in *Tropic of Capricorn*,
"I want to annihilate the whole earth. It's a huge piece of
stale cheese with maggots festering inside it. F - - - it! Blow
it to hell! Kill, kill, kill: Kill them all, Jews and Gentiles,
young and old, good and bad. . . ."

Like an existentialist—Miller comes as close as one can to
existentialism without using the terminology—he cannot refrain from sweeping generalizations about history, making a

virtue out of his ignorance. Napoleon was "the last big man of Europe." Or he will suddenly fall in love with primitive society and the middle ages. There was a "glorious light" in the land, he says, and "then came the scientific age and darkness fell over the land"—the darkness in Miller's mind, his retreat into infantilism. It prevents him from seeing what beacon lights of human strivings and progress there are in the world along with the evils he so vituperatively reports, and it blights the poet in him.

Miller the poet is bright, sensitive, curious, observant, full of vitality, and the pity is that Miller the mind gives the poet so little to work with. He swings between a passionate welcome to life and furious revulsion against it, between a humanized and an alienated response to the same object. He can present beautiful, humanized portrayals of Paris. "Indigo sky swept clear of fleecy clouds, gaunt trees infinitely extended, their black boughs gesticulating like a sleepwalker." And again:

The rain had stopped and the sun breaking through the soapy clouds touched the glistening rubble of roofs with a cold fire. I recall now how the driver leaned out and looked up the river toward Passy way. Such a healthy, simple approving glance, as if he were saying to himself: "Ah, spring is coming!" And God knows, when spring comes to Paris the humblest mortal alive must feel that he dwells in paradise. But it was not only this—it was the intimacy with which his eyes rested upon the scene. It was *his* Paris.

And the same Paris can be presented in the most alienated light. "Paris is like a whore." And again:

In the blue of an electric dawn the peanut shells look wan and crumpled; along the beach at Montparnasse the water lilies bend and break. When the tide is on the ebb and only a few syphilitic mermaids are left stranded in the muck, the Dome looks like a shooting gallery that's been struck by a cyclone. Everything is slowly dribbling back to the sewer. For about an hour there is a deathlike calm during which the vomit is mopped up. Suddenly the trees begin to screech. . . . The moment has come to void the last bagful of urine. The day is sneaking in like a leper.

It is a different kind of alienated vision from Eliot's, Faulkner's or Dos Passos'. Miller's alienation is a weapon of attack and defense, part of the war he fights, in the course of which he must consciously constrict his own humanity. He hurls his words connoting sex, dirt, disease and drains like a small boy hurling mud balls at the wall of a school building. It is a strange revolt for "freedom," which leaves him incessantly plucking off the tentacles that the world he renounces keeps laying on him.

What brings Miller to an existentialist position is his search for some human basis for living, which he can assert in the face of a world he regards as inimical and absurd. If he is not an existentialist, this is only because it is an explicit philosophy and he does not bother with philosophies. In *The Colossus of Maroussi*,[5] written in 1940, describing his visit to Greece, he expresses the existentialist view very succinctly. A Frenchwoman, wife of a shopkeeper, annoys him with her remarks in favor of civilization, and out comes his stream of vituperation:

Madame, I am thinking of you now, of that sweet and fetid stench of the past which you throw off. . . . You are the black satin ghost of everything which refuses to die a natural death. . . . You are the white of a rotten egg. You stink.

Madame, there are always two paths to take: one back towards the comforts and security of death, the other forward to nowhere.

"Forward to nowhere" is the key phrase. It also summarizes Miller's "rebellion," and the "rebellion" of the "beat generation" of writers in the 1950's, who hailed Miller as their spiritual godfather. Around such figures the shallow concept has been propagated of the artist as perpetual "rebel," asserting the perpetual "nonconformism" of art.

The truth is that rebellions are made in real life, not in art. They occur when conditions for the mass of people become intolerable, and the institutions under which they live, instead of assisting their progress, stifle it. What art has done is progressively to humanize the world and the relations among people in it; to make men aware of their own potentialities, to reveal the pathways for many-sided growth and expose the destructive forces that impede this growth. Its main line of achievement has thus ever been on the side of the forces for freedom and progress. In this sense, we can call the artist a "rebel," but the rebellion is not outside society. Rather, it puts the artist in close relations to the forces in society making for forward movement. To see art as "permanent rebellion" is to place the artist in permanent alienation from his fellow human beings. It undermines the potentialities of art itself, by constricting the artist's own humanity. Alienated art is still art, but it is art announcing its own imminent death.

The fact that an art which prides itself on its "permanent rebellion" and on thumbing its nose at society, is honored, praised and rewarded by this very society, where any criticism of its real exploitive relations is looked upon as dangerous and even treasonable, indicates how empty this show of rebellion is. When those who uphold the status quo cannot pretend that it offers any vistas of human progress, they can be quite satisfied with a "rebellion" that reviles it but marches "forward to nowhere." Yet there is a kind of abject admission of its own despair in itself that society shows in the praise and even acclaim it gives to writers like Henry Miller and his numerous progeny of the 1950's. For what these writers can be described as doing, figuratively, in their gloating naturalism of coition, perversion, toilet, drug addiction and mental and bodily dissolution, is forcing this society to eat its own excrement, as if to admit that this is its truth.

210 REBELLION TO NOWHERE

Perhaps the book that can best be cited, if not admired, as a classic example is William Burroughs' *Naked Lunch* (1959).[6] Where Henry Miller's ramblings at least showed him and people he met in some open-air and real-life surroundings, the "stream of talk" of this book takes the form of the fantasy-stream-of-consciousness of a narcotics addict. It achieves a brutal humor in its portrayal of how the mind and body can destroy themselves, doing this with such intensity that to read it becomes a kind of training in masochism. It makes some gestures at an attack upon political reaction, with the content of a boy thumbing his nose or derisively opening his fly. It abounds of course in intensely alienated imagery: "Smell of chili houses and dank overcoats and atrophied testicles. . . . A heaving sea of air hammers in the purple brown dusk tainted with rotten metal smell of sewer gas." The author is talented. One of the characteristics, however, of this talent which dwells in alienation is that each successive writer makes his predecessor look like a noble figure, even an esteemed classic. Thus compared to William Burroughs, even Henry Miller appears to be a humanist.

COLD WAR, RELIGIOUS REVIVAL
AND FAMILY ALIENATION:
William Styron, J. D. Salinger
and Edward Albee

Though only some art is social-minded, all art has social significance. No matter how purely internal an artist's exploration may be, the inner conflicts he reveals are engendered by real conflicts and problems in the world outside him. The difference is that a social-minded art is created with awareness of the connections between "inner" and "outer," while the artist lacking such awareness sees the outer world as mysterious, unreal or incomprehensible, turns inward for reality, and finds this also mysterious. Yet in its sensitivity this art serves as a social document, recording among often bizarre, murky and pessimistic conclusions, the existence of a real problem in people's minds; a psychological situation that is socially and historically created regardless of what the artist himself believes to be its origin.

When the United States emerged from the First World War into the "Boom," literature disclosed that all was not well with the American people or American democracy. If it showed little or no knowledge of the "underprivileged," it reflected the truth that unrest among the "underprivileged" is paralleled by unrest among the "privileged," that such prosperity brought not happiness, but a troubling awareness that life had few satisfactions.

Then came the movement in the arts known as the "proletarian 'thirties,'" which it is the fashion today to deride or ignore, as if this movement had been a perverse conspiracy to coerce art into political attitudes. Yet, in a comparatively short time, a glowing page was written in American literary history; not only by comparatively young writers who grew with this movement, like Jack Conroy, Albert Maltz, Thomas Bell, Lillian Hellman, Clifford Odets and Richard Wright, but also by others who joined hands with it, like John Steinbeck in *The Grapes of Wrath*, Carl Sandburg in *The People, Yes*, Ernest Hemingway in *For Whom the Bell Tolls*, Erskine Caldwell in the story collection *Kneel to the Rising Sun*, Thomas Wolfe in *You Can't Go Home Again*, Langston Hughes in *The Ways of White Folks*. But more important than any single work was the general spirit of social-mindedness that re-entered American literature.

This was not the product of any esthetic manifesto, although the movement itself roused searching discussions of art and its relation to society. What occurred in the arts was called into being by the social consciousness of the era. This was shaped by three great struggles: that of labor for the right to organize unions in the great monopoly industries; that against racism; and that against fascism in both its international and local manifestations. From this widespread consciousness and activity two demands confronted writers and other artists. One was to catch up with what was happening among the majority of American people, the working people, and get to know and understand them. The other was to try to learn the nature of the forces at work in the world that affected the artist whether or not he knew of their existence. Observing and joining with the people in motion, the writers responded with confidence in American democracy and in the future.

The Second World War came, and then, in the late 1940's and 1950's, a sharp turn in literary direction; a flight from social-mindedness and a disillusion with progress, now taking a conscious existentialist expression. Within this the lineaments appear of the "disillusioned 'twenties" but on a new level. Again there is American prosperity, and the country is playing an openly powerful role on the world scene. Again there is the disclosure that all is not well, with a sense of frustration and unhappiness the more pervading because its origins seem again mysterious and an act of fate, or of the "tragedy of life."

And here, too, the clue to what happens in the mind is provided by what happens in life. Such a clue is provided by David Riesman in the 1960 preface to the paperback edition of his book, *The Lonely Crowd*, which had first appeared eleven years before.

The postwar increase in the size and opulence of the middle class pushed the residual poor and unorganized still further away from political influence. . . . In 1948 political imagination and flexibility, even though rare, could still be reasonably hoped for. . . . Before Korea and McCarthy, foreign policy could still be debated, though of course not without pressure from jingos, and a story in *Time* or the *New York Times* about Morocco or Pakistan was not almost invariably "angled" in terms of the Cold War and the American bases. We had not yet put ourselves by domestic exploitation of the struggle with world Communism into the bi-partisan deep freeze of the last ten years.[1]

In the ten years after 1948, he says, the political climate became more "oppressive" and more "terrifying."

Much of the literature which embraces or approaches existentialism deals with what Riesman calls, in another context, "the malaise of the privileged." What is new, contrasted with the literature after the First World War, is that the sense of crisis reaches an almost hysterical intensity. Far more acute and widespread is the alienation disclosed in family and social relationships, and the impossibility of one person to know another is advanced as an undying truth of life. People are shown clawing at each other in a disorderly, absurd and violence-ridden world. Sexual violence, physical brutality, homosexuality, suicide and murder, all in a death-haunted setting, recur as dominant themes. The physical aspects of sex are described with virtuoso elaboration and cogent to this is Marx's insight: when what is human in life turns into the "animal," or when the humanized psychological ties among people are disrupted by the hostility of alienation, then the "animal" becomes "human," and it is in himself as an animal that the despairing human being seeks his own humanity.

An example of the new tone of writing is this passage from Tennessee Williams' play, Cat on a Hot Tin Roof,[2] which, produced in 1955, won a Pulitzer Prize and was made into a motion picture. The play portrays a family in Mississippi. The father, "Big Daddy," is one of the wealthiest landowners in the state. Sixty-five years old, he is dying of cancer. One of his sons, Gooper, with his wife and five children, stays in the house, waiting for the father to die. All six fawn on the old man in the hope of inheriting the major part of his wealth. "Big Daddy" however favors his other son, Brick, who, in revulsion against what he sees as the "mendaciousness" of life, has withdrawn from society and turned to alcohol. He is married but feels homosexual impulses. "Big Daddy" is speaking about his wife, "Big Mama," and Gooper's family, to Brick.

Think of all the lies I got to put up with!—Pretenses! Ain't that mendacity? Having to pretend stuff you don't think or feel or have any idea of? Having for instance to pretend I care for Big Mama! I haven't been able to stand the sight, sound or smell of that

woman for forty years now!—even when I laid her!—regular as a
piston. . . . Pretend to love that son of a bitch Gooper and his
wife Mae and those five same screechers out there like parrots in
a jungle? Jesus! Can't stand to look at 'em! . . . I've lived with
mendacity! Why can't you live with it? Hell, you got to live with
it, there's nothing else to live with except mendacity, is there?

We can recognize Big Daddy as a financially successful
descendant of Faulkner's Snopeses, Varners and Jason Compson, also of Mississippi. There is a latent social insight which
Williams does not pursue, in the fact that this drained and
baffled character, owner of 28,000 acres of fertile land, is a
prototype of those who in real life dominate the politics of
the state, practically pick the legislators, deny civil rights
to the Negro, organize "White Citizens Councils," and influence national policies. What is new, if we compare this
to Faulkner's kind of speech, is the concentrated violence
and obscenity—itself a form of violence—in the language of
alienation. The tone is authentic but the concentration is
Williams's, and of the age.

In this and the earlier plays which made Tennessee
Williams's reputation, there had been at least an implied
understanding that his characters and their problems were
the product of a specific social and historical situation. The
trend in the 'fifties, however, was for the writer, himself increasingly subjective, to treat his characters' problems as also
purely subjective, their alienation reflecting an "eternal human condition" or in other words, the "existentialist predicament."

An example is William Styron. His novel, *Lie Down in
Darkness* (1951)[3] can be called an excellent production from
the "Faulkner workshop," with Styron, in such aspects as
lucidity and formal control, excelling the master. He tells of
a Virginia family much like Faulkner's Compsons of Mississippi in *The Sound and the Fury*. The mother, who has

brought to her marriage her family riches, is a cold, puritanical woman. The father is repelled by her, has an affair with another man's wife, and also smothers his daughter with an unhealthy excess of affection. The daughter responds to this and forms a league with the father against the embittered mother. But the daughter wants to break away from the entire stifling milieu. She does this first through an affair with a young student, then marriage to a New York artist whose life she finds she cannot share, and finally a series of despairing sexual attachments until she commits suicide.

Styron shows himself an excellent stylist and craftsman in his interior monologues and shuttling back and forth in time. This particular approach to the form of the novel, starting with the closing situation and then looking back in the past to throw light upon it, has become increasingly used in the 'fifties, perhaps because it is so close to a psychoanalytic process. Styron however proves to be an excellent psychologist, for although the father-daughter situation is one much discussed by Freud, Styron's treatment does not read like a mechanical psychoanalytic case history.

Yet Faulkner's novel has far more significance. He gives his picture of family degeneration—also using motifs of defiance through promiscuity, incest and suicide—an epical and historical character, even if it is through his distorted picture of American social history. Styron does not share Faulkner's myth of the old South. Politically, he is more liberal. But Faulkner, even in his subjective mistreatment of history, had traced some links between what was going on in his characters' minds and what was going on outside of them. Thus his picture of degeneration is part of American social history. Styron, however, in abandoning the Faulkner myth, does not replace it with a truer social picture. He only narrows his focus.

Styron's short novel, *The Long March* (1952),[4] has the

distinction of being one of the few novels registering the actual impact on the American mind of the Korean war. In the course of this war a hysteria was whipped up such as had not been found necessary in the Second World War. In that anti-fascist war, there had been no policy of answering fascist brutality with like brutality and inhumanity. But now, under the assurance that the struggle was against communism and communism was by its very nature the worst barbarism, every barbaric tactic was justified. Overlooked was the fact that our ally, whose government we were supposedly defending, was a notorious dictator and swindler. The Nazis, who had been condemned for ruthlessly carrying the war to civilians, were outdone by napalm bombs that incinerated fields, towns and people. In the anti-fascist war, the aim had been to train an enlightened soldier. Now a soldier had to be trained to be a single-minded killer. Herbert Aptheker, in *American Foreign Policy and the Cold War* (1962), quotes a report by John Osborne in *Life* magazine that we are "forcing on our men in the field acts and actions of the utmost savagery."[5]

Styron's novelette is set in a marine training camp in the United States. The Korean war is only briefly mentioned as going on at the time. What he does picture is the new carelessness of human life and brutality in the military training. At the beginning, eight men are killed during target practice by a shell that falls short, the shell being from a shipment that was known to be probably defective. The rest of the story is of a forced march of 36 miles, which the men had not been trained for adequately, ordered by the commander, Colonel Templeton. He is a martinet, whose militarism has a "priestlike, religious fervor." A Captain Mannix, who hates both militarism and the Colonel, protests against the march but goes through with it, despite a hurt foot, determined to show that he can take any ordeal. Finally he explodes in

wrath against the Colonel, and is cited to be court-martialed
and sent to Korea.

Significant is Styron's description of Mannix: "The man
with the back unbreakable, the soul of pity—where was he
now, great unshatterable vessel of longing, lost in the night,
astray at mid-century in the never-endingness of war?" Like
Camus's Sisyphus, Mannix rolls the rock of militarism while
scorning it, and this broadens to a symbol of Styron's hatred
of war while feeling that man is eternally condemned to it.

It is but a step from this to the existentialist position of
Styron's following major novel, Set This House On Fire
(1960).[6] It is a psychological story of a murder. The slain
man, Mason Flagg, is a monster for whom one feels no sympathies. He is a wealthy, egocentric sadist and sexual pervert
who lives in an elegant Italian villa and goes through the
motions of being a patron of the arts. The killer, Cass Kin-
solving, is a talented, basically goodhearted painter, but di-
rectionless and an alcoholic. He finds in Flagg first a patron
and then a destroyer. He kills Flagg partly because of his
outrage at the lives Flagg has wrecked, partly to free himself
from the humiliating servitude into which Flagg had forced
him. Flagg's death is ascribed by the police to suicide. At the
end, Cass is back in the United States, peacefully bringing
up his family, doing newspaper cartoons. He writes to a
friend, who happens to know the real events:

Now I suppose I should tell you that through some sort of
suffering I had reached grace, and how at that moment I knew it,
but this would not be true, because at that moment I didn't really
know what I had reached or found. I wish I could tell you that I
had found some belief, some rock, and that here on this rock anything might prevail—that here madness might become reason, and
grief joy, and no, yes. And even death itself death no longer, but a
resurrection.

But to be truthful, you see, I can only tell you this: that as for
being and nothingness, the one thing I did know was that to

choose between them was simply to choose being, not for the sake of being, or even the love of being, much less the desire to be forever—but in the hope of being what I could be for a time. This would be an ecstasy.

It is a completely existentialist statement. A human being is faced with the two millstones of being and nothingness, between which society is ground away. The world is madness and tragedy. The individual makes his decision for life, by asserting his scorn for the world, and if his bid for freedom demands that he kill another, that is what he must do.

The novel has much that is sharp, true and satiric to say about the glittering flimsiness of the modern art world, as well as of the American movie colony making pictures in Europe. And the problem affecting the life of an artist, touched on in the novel, is a real one: the fact that prosperous and powerful America seems to offer to its people only the shoddiest values by which to live, dehumanized conformity to commercial success and a hardening of the heart to the plight of another. Yet the only answer the book offers is to find a partial integrity by withdrawing into a private life as little touched as possible by social affairs. Since the world is a jungle, the individual frees himself from it by an act of jungle violence.

What of the youth in this jungle? An answer appears in the works of J. D. Salinger. The remarkable success, both here and abroad, of Catcher in the Rye,[7] a modest novel exhibiting no epic ambitions or outlandish formal experiments, indicates how vital an achievement it is for an artist to bring into social consciousness a new psychology shaped by contemporary history.

The narrator of Catcher in the Rye, Holden Caulfield, is the son of a wealthy New York City lawyer. Holden's parents have apparently denied him nothing that money can buy. His weekly allowance would probably feed a poor family for a month. He has none of the worries of a working-class youth about getting a job. He sees his future as settled, in some white-collar, junior executive post, saying that he'd be working "in some office, making a lot of dough, and riding to work in cabs and Madison Avenue buses, and reading newspapers and playing bridge all the time and going to the movies." He attends a rather exclusive, expensive college-preparatory school in Pennsylvania. The story opens in the week before Christmas, sometime in the late 1940's. Holden knows that he is about to be expelled from school. This will be his fourth such expulsion.

Holden does not know what he wants out of life, and he has no confidence in anything parents or teachers tell him. He has no interest in his studies, except for literature, in which he has discovered that he might have a gift. He finds his schoolmates repulsive. He finds the girls he dates frightening or repulsive. The presumed object of such a date, in school slang, is to "give her the time," and the boys like to boast of their sexual prowess. Holden, however, like practically all of the others, is not an accomplished seducer. He hates New York City, with its taxicabs, and Madison Avenue buses, "with the drivers and all always yelling at you to get to the rear door, and being introduced to phony guys that call the Lunts angels, and going up and down in elevators when you just want to go outside, and guys fitting your pants all the time at Brooks." It is a clear picture of psychological estrangement. The items themselves, in Holden's picture of his allotted future or of New York City, are not innately repellent, and Salinger does not clothe them in Faulkner's deliberately repellent imagery. The impression is that Holden's outpouring of complaints is only an expression of an unrest within him, the real nature of which he knows he doesn't know.

The family expects Holden home in four days, for the

Christmas holidays, and since he knows that he is to be expelled, he decides to spend these four days in a wild splurge in New York City. His adventures in these four days are a bleak summary of the standard methods of purchasing a "good time"; visiting a night club, getting drunk at a bar, having a prostitute in a hotel room supplied by an elevator-operator pimp, trying to pick up a girl in a dance hall, seeing a Broadway "hit." It is all dust and ashes and, in his desperation, Holden cries that he's "lonesome as hell. No kidding." He is lost, frightened, and there is no one whose advice he can trust.

He visits an English teacher who had once given him some friendly encouragement. The teacher welcomes him, but gives him a lecture on how education will tell him "what size mind he has," and offers him a precept from the psychoanalyst, Wilhelm Stekel, namely that instead of aiming to "die nobly" for a cause, he should "live humbly" for a cause. Nothing is further from the mark, so far as answering Holden's needs is concerned. He knows of no cause for which he would want either to "die nobly" or "live humbly." To Holden's disgust the teacher follows this with homosexual advances—the sick offering to cure the sick. Holden's alienation is complete. His parents, teachers and, in fact, all who are beyond his generation, are in another world, mentally and spiritually. There is no communication. His schoolmates are repulsive to him. The one person to whom he can speak openheartedly, who can "talk his language," is his younger sister Phoebe, but she looks up to him, and cannot help him.

What is the problem in this sixteen-year-old's mind? It is not family. Though he thinks of his parents as of another world, though nothing they say means anything to him, nothing he says means anything to them, he is fond of them. Among his teachers, there are some he would like as persons, if he did not feel so distant from them. The problem is the world as a whole, as he sees it. He feels estranged from his elders because the world is theirs, one they have shaped and that he does not want to enter. Salinger documents this social world most perceptively though he draws no theoretical conclusions nor analyzes its driving forces.

A key word in Holden's vocabulary is "phony." It is his moral standard. "Bad" is "phony." And everything he sees about him is "phony." On the very first page of his narrative occurs the word "prostitute." Holden is talking of his brother, "D.B.," whom he had admired more than anyone else in the world. D.B., Holden says, had been a "terrific" writer, but had gone to Hollywood to write for the movies, and become "a prostitute." Holden is now convinced that the entire world of his milieu is a "racket," or "phony." Nobody believes or practices the morality he preaches. Everybody is a prostitute. The counterpart to this "phony" world, the other side of its fearful, forbidding character, is war. Like every teen-age boy in the "cold war" period, he knows that the army is awaiting him to turn him into a killer, an army rotten with black-market corruption and dirty politics. It terrifies him, and yet to speak of his terror would be to lay himself open to the charge of cowardice. But he is not a coward. He says to himself that he could not stand it if he had to go to war. The army is phony. Its anti-fascism in the last war was phony. He's glad, in a way, he says, that the atom bomb was invented. If there ever is another war, he says, he will volunteer to sit right on top of the bomb.

We learn that Holden's parents have resorted to the standard method for "curing" someone who, with all the good things of life available to him, does not "adjust." They send him to a psychoanalyst. At the end of his story, Holden seems to feel that he has changed somewhat. After spilling out everything on his mind he feels he now "misses" the schoolmates and others whom he had found repulsive. He recognizes his yearning for human companionship, and is willing to lower his standards. But there is still no confidence in psychoanalysis. For the analyst keeps asking him, Holden says, what he intends to do in the Fall. Holden answers, how can he know until he does it? And one is left with the implication that there is no school of psychoanalysis prepared to show people what to do to change a world where everything is a "racket," and how to tear out the roots of war. That would not be "adjustment."

Earlier studies of alienation in the family, and estrangement of sons and daughters from the parents, had probed into the complex tensions and resentments among the parents and shown their repercussions on the children. We have seen this in O'Neill's *Long Day's Journey Into Night*, and in Styron's *Lie Down in Darkness*. It is this kind of family situation which Freud had examined, and on which he built his theory of the "Oedipus Complex." What is new in Salinger is that the alienation he depicts among children is not rooted in any particular inter-family relation. The roots are in present-day society, and the alienation is between one entire generation and another. Here Salinger has hit upon a social truth reflected also in the fact that much contemporary psychoanalysis is moving from Freudianism, giving Oedipus back to the ancient Greeks and going in for existentialism. This does not mean of course that existentialism has any sounder ideology than Freudianism.

Put succinctly, what is in the mind of Salinger's children, adolescents and people in their early maturity, is that the world is a horrible one to grow up into, and they shrink from entering it even as they grow up into it. They believe nothing their elders tell them or, by implication, that the accumulated social knowledge of "education" tells them. The younger ones look to brothers and sisters for companionship, confidence and learning, not to their parents. The older ones are highly sophisticated, can analyze their parents and themselves, know that society is hopelessly corrupt and search desperately for some way out.

The picture Salinger gives in *Catcher in the Rye* is further developed in the history of the Glass family, as depicted in several stories including *Franny and Zooey*.[8] Of the seven Glass children one was killed in the Second World War. The oldest, Seymour, a man of brilliant intellectual promise, kills himself in 1948, shortly after his marriage. Another son, Buddy, a talented writer, is attached to a college, but lives withdrawn from social life. A son, Waker, becomes a Catholic priest, although the family, with the mother Irish and the father Jewish, is not especially religious. A daughter, Boo Boo, is married, has three children, and is alarmed to discover that, for all she has learned from psychological tracts about parents and children, her progeny baffle her. A son Zachary (called Zooey) is a television and stage actor. About 25 years old in 1955, he does not know what to make of himself, for he is repelled by the commercialism and shallowness of the theatre. Another daughter, Franny, about 20 years old, is going to college, has little confidence in anything she is taught there, and suffers a nervous breakdown. Both Franny and Zooey are flirting with religious answers, including Zen Buddhism.

The Glass children are of an unusual mold, for their parents were successful vaudeville entertainers who gave them a sophisticated home life, and the children themselves, in turn, had all been famous as "quiz kids" on radio programs. They are not only precociously bright, but also know that the surrounding world regards them as "freakish" or "not normal." But they are untroubled by this, for to them the world of "normalcy" is freakish, grotesque, corrupt, a world in which a human being cannot grow. They want no part of it. And yet their precocity and sophistication do not alter their typicality, for their estrangement from the world into which the inexorable process of growth pushes them is shared by countless other "bright" children.

Typical is their attitude to their parents, as dwelt on in *Franny and Zooey*. There is no "father-hatred" or "mother-hatred" or Oedipus or Electra complex. They have read all about this, or learned about it from psychoanalysts, and discounted any such impulses in themselves. They feel real affection for their parents. But there is no problem important to them about which they will consult their parents. They feel, even in their bafflement, a superior wisdom, as if their parents' minds had been shaped by an earlier world in which things had been much simpler. They will choose one of their own, a brother or sister, as a mentor. Thus Holden Caulfield still looks up to his brother "D.B." more than to anyone else, although "D.B." has become a literary "prostitute." To the Glass children, Seymour had been their chosen mentor, and now that he is dead, Buddy moves into the role. Two years younger than Seymour, Buddy is, in 1955, about 36 years old. But he has kept himself as clear from the world of conventional maturity as possible. A writer, he calls himself a "literary whore" and remains aloof from literary circles. A teacher, he has renounced the college degree within his grasp. He shudders from anything that looks like a "career."

The long story, *Seymour: An Introduction*,[9] purports to be the first step in a portrayal of his dead brother, written by Buddy Glass, and yet it can also be taken as a presentation of Buddy's—and Salinger's—own principles of writing. There is an almost fiercely eloquent assertion of the need for absolute integrity. "The true artist-seer, the heavenly fool who can and does produce beauty, is mainly dazzled to death by his own scruples, the blinding shapes and colors of his own sacred human conscience." But it is a search for a purely inward integrity, with no regard for the kind of adventures in life and relations to other people that can provide the material and ideas to be handled with integrity. There is no hint of the equally important truth that it is not this kind of purity alone, but the scope of what is handled with purity, that makes the artist. And with this inward concentration on "no compromise," there is the understandable accompaniment of an almost obsessive purist fear that something he writes will be considered "compromising," "imitative" or "facile"; that he will scornfully be called, not a "writer," but a "writer of rattling good stories." This obsession could be carried to the point of self-destruction.

The attitude of the Glass children to their parents is one of affection and condescension. It is almost as if they, the children, were the "old ones," and the parents, the "innocents." They are amazed and happy when a parent shows an insight which almost enables the two foreign worlds to meet. And their indictment of the world which their parents have prepared for them is like Holden Caulfield's. It is false, "phony," and also wields war and the H-Bomb. Zooey warns his mother against calling in some analyst who will "adjust" Franny to such things as "the joys of television, and *Life* magazine every Wednesday, and European travel, and the H-Bomb, and Presidential elections, and the front page of the *Times*, and the responsibilities of the Westport and Oyster Bay Parent-Teacher Association and God knows what else that's gloriously normal," because this, he says, will land her in a "nut ward," or send her to some mental monastery.

In the back of Zooey's mind is the fact that Seymour had consulted a psychoanalyst, had become "adjusted" to marriage into the "normal" upper middle-class world obsessed with clothes, furniture, lawns, appearances and status, and then in revulsion against it had shot himself. The central theme in Salinger is that this is an abhorrent world to grow up into, and anyone of sensitivity must guard himself against it.

This is even glimpsed by infants. Among the most captivating passages in Salinger's stories are those dealing with children three, four or five years of age, like Charles in the early story, "For Esme—with Love and Squalor," or Sybil Carpenter in "A Perfect Day for Bananafish," or Ramona in "Uncle Wiggily in Connecticut," or Lionel in "Down at the Dinghy." These children are not sweetly untroubled, unspoiled. If they are not yet hardened, maltreated, corrupted, twisted or utterly repelled by the world, they have already perceived its threatening character, and have begun, unconsciously, to erect their primitive defenses against it or express their resentment. From the age of two Lionel, now four years old, has been periodically hiding from his parents or running away from home. Ramona invents imaginary companions, and despite her mother's protestations insists passionately, almost as if her life depends on it, that each fantasy character is real, is at this moment in the room holding her hand or sleeping beside her in bed.

And each of the Glass children, brilliant and knowing as they all are, clings to some fetish. Seymour's suicide haunts them, for they know that it was due not to revulsion occasioned by a particular incident, or to mismating, but to something more fundamental. It was the world of "normalcy" that he found intolerable, the entire "grown-up" world. Buddy, at 36, pays the bills for Seymour's telephone in order to see the dead Seymour's name still in the phone book. Franny, in her breakdown, wants to "talk to Seymour," who is seven years dead. All have been attracted to various forms of religion, including Buddhism, and an unorthodox Russian Christian mysticism. Their differences from others of their generation is not so much their sharpness of mind, as an extra intensity. They feel their whole life is involved, and they want an answer they can live by without feeling compromised.

The turn of the Glass children to religious answers typifies the general religious revival that is now a growing part of American literary and intellectual life, and as a "solution" to the alienation that seems to pervade all social life, is closely connected to existentialism. This religious revival moves outside any particular church or theological dogma. It finds that science and material "progress" have brought the world to a crisis and seeks the solution to human conflicts in a personal revolution of the "spirit" or glimpse of the supernatural.

Jung carried psychoanalysis in this direction. The thesis of his *Modern Man in Search of a Soul* is that science, knowledge, reason, civilization and material progress only "do violence" to the "natural forces," which in turn "seek revenge," thus causing crises and upheavals.

Man has been aware of this danger since the earliest times, even in the most primitive stages of culture. It was to arm himself against this threat and to heal the damage done that he developed religious and magical practices. This is why the medicine-man is also the priest; he is the saviour of the body as well as the soul, and religions are systems of healing for psychic illness.[10]

This is history stood on its head, with its assumption that even in the most primitive times there was a systematized body of reason and scientific knowledge, against the threat of which man turned to magical practices and the witch-doctor. The truth is that within primitive magical practices themselves there was the drive to alter and master nature, and that each step beyond this, in the ability to live more rationally, with clearer knowledge of the laws of the outer world, led not to the imprisonment of the "natural forces" in man but to human freedom. Jung generalizes an entire history out of the fact that, in his own time, the mighty powers developed by science are misused in anarchistic money-grubbing, competition and war. He sees this not as a social problem, but as a "psychic illness," to be "cured" by returning to the "medicine man" in modern terms, or the

"living spirit" which "is eternally renewed and pursues its
goals in manifold and inconceivable ways throughout the history of mankind." This paean to the eternal "living spirit" has
an exalted sound, but in essence, it is an exaltation of ignorance; raising "natural forces" against reason enabled Jung to
accommodate himself to German fascism.

This is not to say that the "religious revival" or existentialism must necessarily follow Jung's path. From these movements have also come notable and frequent expressions of
abhorrence of fascism and activities against it. The question
raised here, however, is whether the full lessons have been
drawn from the phenomenon of fascism. Certainly, in the
cults in which Jung is so highly respected the connection
between his thought and his acceptance of fascism is ignored,
as similarly in the cases of Heidegger and Ezra Pound. In the
broadest sense, the question raised here is whether people
can live with an approach which sees an answer to a socially-
created crisis only in non-social terms; which sees the crisis
itself, and the "anxieties" it engenders, as purely a matter of
the "spirit."

Paul Tillich, an anti-fascist and existentialist theologian,
thus draws the connection between existentialism and the
religious attitude of today, which avoids doctrinal argument
and puts its faith in any religion.

> Religion is a matter of man's existential situation. We must
> start from below and not from above. We must start with man's
> experienced predicament and the questions implied in it; and we
> must proceed to the symbols which claim to contain the answer.
> But we must not start with the question of the being of God,
> which, if discussed in terms of the existence or non-existence of
> God, is in itself a lapse into a disastrous literalism.[11]

Typical of this modern religious thinking is its rejection
of the pre-"Enlightenment" religious dogma. We proceed
not from "above"—that is, revelation—but from "below," or

actual life. Yet, implied in it is the conviction that a "symbol" which does not relate to the outer world is "true," because it relates to human yearnings and tragic feelings. Subjectivity is truth. And this, itself, rests on the further, existentialist conviction that the actual world is absurd, meaningless or tragic, because no final answer can be given to the question of "what is being?" and that this is the "real problem," which cannot be solved through the operations of human beings in society upon the real world. "As myth and experience tell," Tillich writes, mankind is "in the state of universal, existential estrangement."[12]

In *Franny and Zooey*, Buddy Glass, in the course of a letter, mentions the influence on him of Zen Buddhism, with its theory of *satori*, namely being in a state of "pure consciousness" or "no knowledge."

D. T. Suzuki, a prolific modern expounder of Zen Buddhism, calls *satori* or "enlightenment" "not a conclusion to be reached by reasoning. . . . The *satori* experience is thus always characterized by irrationality, inexplicability and incommunicability."[13] What Zen, and *satori*, teach is that, through rigorous spiritual exercises, a person can be disciplined so that nothing will trouble him. Thus his anxieties disappear. Let fascism, poverty, the attacks of enemies, the blows of the world, all come. They cannot hurt, if one refuses to let them hurt. In this spirit Hamlet, anguished at his awakening to a world of falsehood and murder, suspecting that even the sweet Ophelia has become a tool of her father's cunning politics, cries to her, "Get thee to a nunnery!" But all Denmark could not be turned into a nunnery. Zen, of course, does not create actual monasteries. In the 20th century monastic walls are mental, a psychological barrier raised to ward off the blows of social reality.

In this spirit of simplifying the problems of life, Zen offers

the promise of happiness, or *tathata*, which Suzuki defines
as follows:

> *Tathata* is the viewing of things as they are: it is an affirmation
> through and through. I see a tree, and I state that it is a tree; I
> hear a bird sing and I say that a bird sings; a spade is a spade, and
> a mountain is a mountain; the fowls of the air fly and the flowers
> of the field bloom: these are statements of *tathata*. When a Zen
> master was asked, "What is everyday thought (*hsin*)?" he said, "I
> sleep when I am tired, I eat when I am hungry." This "everyday
> thought" is declared to be the ultimate Tao, the highest teaching
> of Buddhism.[14]

Analysis of Buddhism or its offshoot, Zen Buddhism, in
terms of its historical development and significance, is outside of the scope of this study. Buddhism, as one of the great
world religions, has played a historic role in the development
of human speculations about life and morality. But its historical significance is quite different from the role of Zen
Buddhism as a 20th century American cult. No ideology,
however fantastic, has not at one time had an intelligible
reason for being. In primitive magical beliefs about nature
spirits and how to "control" them, there was, for all the
nonsense, both a ritual for uniting the tribe for realistic tasks
and an accumulation of lore about the natural world. But
there is a difference between the magic of pre-scientific
periods, which indeed was the ground for the development
of science, and magic that persists as superstitions after genuine scientific methods and knowledge have been developed.
Superstitions, then, only rot the mind.

Similarly, a basic teaching of Buddhism, taken over by Zen,
is that happiness can come not from striving for more, but
from wanting less. Ordinary things yield great satisfactions
when perceived for what they are, and one can be content
with very little. Such a philosophy might have had a certain

validity in the feudal societies of India or China, with their luxuries, waste, bloody wars, power struggles, conniving politics and bureaucratic officialdom. Some people could then feel, in times of crisis, that neither wealth nor power was worth the effort; that one could be happier in a simple hut looking at a few blades of grass than to have luxuries and station shadowed by fear and insecurity. But even in feudal society, such teachings could have no meaning to peasants and serfs abducted into armies or whose fields were trampled by them, and who suffered famines. Can a naked and starving person be told to want even less?

So in our time, Zen Buddhism tells people, in effect, to lower their sights, to reduce their wants, to accept things as they are and find beauty there, to let nothing hostile to them affect them. There is an appealing truth in its urging that the most ordinary "things as they are" can be seen as beautiful and are capable of giving joy. Nevertheless, the modern world has put the need to "see things as they are" on a far higher plane than simple humanized perception. The awakening to things—seeing the world as it is, discerning the forces leading to human misery and those leading to human progress —demands a great deal of knowledge. Not to master this knowledge, not to enter into society and find social ways to apply it is to abandon humanity to crises, starvation and war. Thus Zen is really another version of the disillusion with progress which characterizes so much of the modern "rebellion." It says, like existentialism, that an individual must alienate himself from society in order to discover and affirm his own humanity. It offers the individual the refuge of a mental monastery.

The climax and conclusion of *Franny and Zooey* is what might be called an informal "depth analysis" by Zooey of Franny. He challenges her with her "mistake," which is to set up standards for others that are too high, too demanding, too exclusive; a mistake, he confesses, that he himself has made. She is, he says, a talented actress. And she should pursue her career regardless of the lesser integrity in her colleagues and the imperceptivity of many audiences. She can't just walk out on the results of her own hankerings, he says. "An artist's only concern is to shoot for some kind of perfection, and on his own terms, not anyone else's." Then, quoting Seymour, he tells her to act for the "Fat Lady" in the audience, this being a symbol for the common humanity to be found in everybody. This "Fat Lady," he says, is Christ. And Franny, now happy, relaxes. In the added symbolic touch that Zooey has addressed his mother as "Fatty," the acceptance of the "Fat Lady" implies that at least these two Glass children have bridged the abyss between the generations and made some peace with their mother. It is a touching scene.

The "lesson" is that in a social world drained of humanity, "phony" and breeding intellectual prostitution, peace and freedom can be found through pursuing artistic life with private integrity. And yet one wonders about this "adjustment." For the world of art is also a social world, demanding the collaboration of many minds and hands. To "shoot for perfection on one's own terms" is brave talk, but one must also learn and take from others. Collective integrity makes individual integrity more possible. And what is so obviously true of an art like acting is also true of what seems to be so purely personal and individual an art like writing. The great writers sought not "perfection," but to transmit clearly what they had learned from others and through their own engagement in society. The artist who withdraws from the troubles of his fellowmen, or sees himself in perpetual struggle against a hostile and "absurd" world, produces an alienated art. It is Salinger's achievement that he has and exhibits a breadth of sympathy, and has made explicit, so that we can think about it, a significant emerging aspect of our social reality. He writes about alienation, but he is not an alienated writer. The question is whether his views, which are so much like those of the Glass children, will permit him to attain, not "perfection," but growth.

School forms the background of some of Salinger's stories, but the inner life of the school or college is not a major factor in them, not even in *Catcher in the Rye*. School and the teaching faculty are lumped together with the rejected "old generation." However, in Edward Albee's *Who's Afraid of Virginia Woolf?*,[15] which was, by general critical agreement, the outstanding American play of the 1962-63 season, light is thrown on the opposite side of the pupil-teacher relation, namely on the teachers. Some critics argue that the play is simply an abstract or generalized psychological study which could just as well have been put in any other setting, and that its two main characters, George and Martha, are not to be taken as a typical faculty family. True, it would be hard to find a college professor and his wife who rail at each other in such a harsh, biting and abusive way, who make public such uninhibited revelations of each other's sex life. But this means only that Albee, following the style and temper of the 1950's and early 1960's, has given a violent and concentrated depiction of alienation, to the point of a "shock" assault upon the listener's feelings. A value of the play is that its psychological revelations are organically connected to a very real, historically emergent social situation.

The time covered by the play is almost its actual playing time, a few hours after Saturday midnight. George, 46, is a professor of history at a New England college; his wife Martha, 52, is the daughter of the president of the college. As the curtain rises, they are just returning from a faculty party at which they have done, like most of the others, rather heavy drinking. A few minutes after the opening, with fresh drinks in their hands, Martha says to George, "You make me puke!" A little while later he says, "And try to keep your clothes on. There aren't many more sickening sights than you with a couple of drinks in you and your skirt over your head, you know."

This is the comparatively mild beginning of a scorching wrangle that goes on for most of the three acts. In its course they knowledgeably draw upon the entire psychoanalytic arsenal for weapons to strike at one another, describing in detail each other's neuroses, hypocrises, illusions and failures. Each is like a fencer probing for a vital spot behind the other's hardboiled, sophisticated defense. During the first act, two visitors arrive, in response to Martha's invitation; Nick, a young instructor, new to the college, and his wife, Honey. Their appearance does not halt the duel between George and Martha. It is carried on with extra relish for having an audience, and the weapons are also turned to the psychological dissection of Nick and Honey.

The three acts are entitled "Fun and Games," "Walpurgis-nacht" and "The Exorcism." The titles, as the play itself gives them substance, take on an existentialist symbolism. "Fun and Games" is the desperate process of answering a tragically absurd reality by refusing to succumb, asserting one's strength by wielding a cruelly analytic knife upon others, while raising the protective shield of a pretended callousness to human suffering, including one's own. The victim is left with no secrets, no privacy, no unrevealed weakness or frailty, but all in the spirit of "fun." How else can one live, in a tragic world, but with fun and games? At one point George says to Nick, "I did run the History Department, for four years, during the war, but that was because everybody was away. Then . . . everybody came back . . . because nobody got killed. That's New England for you. Isn't that amazing? Not one single man in the whole place got his head shot off. That's pretty irrational."

The irony is bitter. George of course did not want to achieve promotion through someone's being killed. But the implication is that real life is like this, violently self-centered, where one advances by stepping over another, and human lives are held cheap.

In the second act, "Walpurgisnacht" or Witches' Sabbath, a climax is reached where the "game" has worn thin, the "fun" becomes serious, and the alienation in both couples is shown in gruesomely physical form. The sweet and prim young wife, Honey, is lying drunk in the bathroom, while Martha and Nick, with George's pretended blessing—it turns into an outburst of fury—go off to a frustrated copulation.

"Exorcism" is the resolution of conflict, the final facing of reality, the spiritual catharsis. George and Martha have finally fought out their duel. The truth emerges that she, the aggressor, is really the weaker. He is the stronger and her real protector. She knows she needs him, that she cannot live without him, but also that she will forever assail him. For, as the concluding lines reveal, she is terrified of the blankness of life. It is the existentialist theme. Reality is "absurd," cruel, meaningless, and bounded by the horror of death, which is so frightening because life has given nothing. The motif which runs through the play and supplies its title is a parody of "Who's afraid of the big bad wolf?" At the end, when George softly sings to Martha, "Who's afraid of Virginia Woolf . . ." she answers, "I . . . am . . . George . . . I . . . am. . . ." The truth we can glimpse however is not that life is absurd or meaningless, but that there are people whose lives, alienated from part of themselves, have become empty and meaningless. The "nothingness" of death is the spectre raised before them of the nothingness of their lives.

Albee has provided a genuine study in alienation; that is, of people who are as firmly attached to one another as they are hostile to one another, and whose hostility rises out of the conditions of their attachment. And indeed, the course of the play may be described as an existentialist psychoanalysis. Their bickering does not come out of the realization that they have made a "bad marriage," and that either has found a more satisfying relationship or "true love" elsewhere. They are emotionally bound to one another, they fit together, and yet the marriage has not grown because they have not grown as people. Out of the awareness of this lack in themselves they attack each other so savagely, though knowing that the counter-thrusts are also true and will strike home. She, the weaker one, tries to give imaginary substance to her life by inventing a son and speaking of him as if he were alive and grown up. George will permit her this fantasy so long as she does not go so far as to give it currency before others. When she does so, he feels he has to destroy the fantasy, however much it will hurt her. And in the "Exorcism" he does so, announcing to the guests that the child is dead, forcing Martha to accept the fact that he never existed, and to face reality. So at the end, when reality is faced, there is tenderness between the two.

Why do George and Martha lacerate each other, through each other? The play does not put the answer in the foreground, but provides enough clues to fill in the social situation. For both have lost their integrity under pressure, both are aware that they have sold themselves. A fifth character plays a central role in the play, although he never appears on the stage. He is Martha's father, the college president. His image emerges, in the course of the dialogue, rounded and clear. Here are some lines from the first act. "There are easier things in the world, if you happen to be teaching at a university, there are easier things than being married to the daughter of the president of that university. . . . Martha's father expects loyalty and devotion from his—staff. I was going to use another word." What emerges is that the father is a philistine to whom intellectual matters are a commodity; a college president of the type that has become increasingly prevalent, who runs an institution of supposed enlightenment and learning as if it were a business. He aims to turn out well-bred conformists with diplomas. He keeps a firm hand on his faculty. He wants nothing "controversial," nothing that might annoy potential donors, the politicians, the trustees, the local American Legion post. Martha has been his agent, losing her independence of mind. George has been his victim, losing his manhood.

Martha has used her position to play college politics. Her aim had been to marry a bright, ambitious professor who could please her father, be pushed up into an administrative post, and perhaps even succeed her father as president. But, she says derisively, "Maybe Georgie-boy didn't have the stuff." He was, she says, a "flop." George did not wish to demean himself by playing the game. And yet, he has let the father dominate him, to the point of giving up the publication of a controversial book. Though he has refused to play college politics he has surrendered his intellectual integrity. He is a historian, but he obviously no longer enjoys teaching history or carrying on further studies. He no longer has the capacity to make an honest intellectual contribution. He has not utterly demeaned himself in his own eyes, but what should have remained a passionate life interest has dwindled to just a "job." He is alienated from himself and from his gifts, just as a factory worker is alienated from his own labor, which gives him no satisfaction but looms over him like a hostile force.

Thus Albee has linked a genuine, significant social situation to his study of interfamily alienation. It needs only a little acquaintance with the times to supply what the play does not make explicit. This is the intellectual "deep freeze" of the "cold war," which has put free inquiry and debate in so many institutions of higher learning on ice.

In a *New York Times Sunday Magazine* article of August 4, 1963, entitled "How 'The Lost Cause' Was Lost," the eminent historian Henry Steele Commager suggests some of the reasons why the Southern Confederacy lost the Civil War. One, he says, was "the enslavement of the mind of a people," for any criticism of slavery was forbidden. "Whoever criticized slavery in the South was an enemy of society, a traitor to the Southern way of life." Commager then generalizes:

Now when you prevent the free discussion of the greatest of public issues, you prevent the discussion of almost all issues. When you drive out critics, you leave behind the noncritics. When you silence dissent, you assure only approval. When you intimidate criticism, you discourage the habit of critical inquiry. When you stop agitation, you guarantee complacency. We have learned in our own time the price that a society pays when it intimidates the liberal mind, when it silences criticism.

It is not the minor issues, Commager indicates, that are crucial in this way, but the "touchy" ones that affect wealth, power and authority, and question the very direction of national policy. They arouse the uneasy feeling that what is stifling progress and freedom is not some force outside the borders, but one within. The mighty become the wrathful judges of those who presume to judge them. Thus the tabooed questioning of slavery in the South during the Civil War is matched by the tabooed questioning of the "cold war" policies and few dare ask whether it is the American people who are threatened by the "Russians" or the business interests who feel their investments threatened in "undeveloped countries." As with slavery then, so with the "cold war" now, such questioning arouses a hysterical witch-hunt to destroy the questioner instead of answering the question. And it is not enough to say, as Commager does, that to stop agitation produces "complacency." It produces, rather, unrest and fear.

In 1960 John Steinbeck decided to rediscover the American people and what was on their mind by driving across the country, accompanied by his dog Charlie, in a small truck with living quarters in the rear. His findings are recorded in *Travels with Charley in Search of America* (1962).[16] Like everything Steinbeck writes, it is a genial and warmhearted book full of affection for people. Yet a desolate feeling pervades it, and a fear for the future of America. What has happened to the people, he asks? What has eroded their spirit of independence? "I had been keen to hear what the people thought politically. Those whom I had met did not talk about the subject, didn't seem to want to talk about it." He chats with a storekeeper in Minnesota, but as he says, it could have been anywhere. Steinbeck starts the conversation.

"It looks then as though the natural contentiousness of people had died. But I don't believe that. It'll just take another channel. Can you think, sir, of what that channel might be?"

"You mean where will they bust out?"

"Where do they bust out?"

I was not wrong, the twinkle was there, the precious, humorous twinkle. "Well, sir," he said, "we've got a murder now and then, or we can read about them. Then we've got the World Series. You can raise a wind any time over the Pirates or the Yankees, but I guess the best of all is we've got the Russians."

"Feelings pretty strong there?"

"Oh, sure! Hardly a day goes by somebody doesn't take a belt at the Russians." For some reason he was getting a little easier, even permitted himself a chuckle that could have turned to throat-clearing if he saw a bad reaction from me.

I asked, "Anybody know any Russians around here?"

And now he went all out and laughed. "Course not. That's why they're valuable. Nobody can find fault with you if you take out after the Russians."

Many things appear in this light colloquy; the extent to which the country has accepted as part of its thinking that we are in an undeclared war with "the Russians"; the storekeeper's awareness that there is something phony here; his fear of speaking his mind, where even a chuckle might be interpreted as a treasonable doubt; the awareness that this land of democracy and freedom has become haunted by spies and informers.

The same fears contaminate the halls of learning, and part of the price paid by society is psychological alienation in its intellectual life. The thinker and teacher is alienated from himself because his mind cannot freely pursue the logical course of his own thinking. This in turn disrupts his relations with those whom his job, presumably, is to teach to think. It is the effect of this alienated psychology upon personal life that Albee exposes with such brutal explicitness.

If art reflects a corrupt social situation, it need not necessarily be itself corrupted. As we have seen, there are critical and humanist portrayals of alienation. If Albee and Salinger have come close to existentialism, as a way station in the search for answers, they remain social minds with humanist sympathies, and give us at least an intimation of the social connections of the problem. They do not quite diagnose the disease through eyes that are themselves infected.

Both take their philosophy as seriously as they do their writing, and so with both, the question of the direction in which their philosophy will draw their writing is a central one. With Salinger, the fear is that his horror of corruption by a "marketplace" world will lead him to a kind of monastic withdrawal from the turbulence of social life itself, leaving his art less and less to work with. And Albee, in his play *Tiny Alice* (1964) seems to be taking the existentialist path which gives the question of "existence" and the "absurdity" of life precedence over all others.

242   COLD WAR AND FAMILY ALIENATION

Tiny Alice may be described as a "morality play" in the medieval sense, a dramatization of theology, except that its religiousness is existentialist, or anti-theological, much like Kierkegaard's. There is the attack on "worldliness," both in the form of the cunning, amoral lawyer who manipulates great funds of money and the Cardinal who is willing to betray his moral principles to get a sumptuous donation of money for the Church. As in his other plays, Albee pays no attention to other forms of devotion to the world, like trying to extend human knowledge of the world and helping human progress. The "hero," Brother Julian, is "unworldly." The question of "faith" is central. To take part in the affairs of the actual world is, to him, insanity. He had once been afflicted by doubts of God's existence, and had committed himself, consequently, to a mental institution. The "message" of the play is that there is a God, a force above the "absurd" universe in which people live, but not a God that anyone can comprehend, nothing like the God of "official" theology. To be embraced by God, a person must go through the most terrible suffering and anguish, including the loss of every shred of his previous faith and of hope itself, and also including death, like the crucified Christ.

Dare we hope that, having taken this flight into outer space, Albee will come back to earth?

13

ALIENATED EXPRESSION AND
EXISTENTIALIST ANSWERS

A. ACCEPTANCE OF ALIENATION: *John Updike and James Purdy*

To an increasing extent, alienation has become not only the subject matter but also the style of American writing. The world, and with it America, holds out no hope. Typical is the short poem, "Inauguration Day: January 1953,"[1] by Robert Lowell, who is by broad agreement of critics the outstanding American poet to come up after the Second World War. These are its closing lines:

> Ice, ice. Our wheels no longer move.
> Look, the fixed stars, all just alike
> as land-lack atoms, split apart,
> and the Republic summons Ike,
> the mausoleum in her heart.

The reference is clear to the atom bomb, but this, rather than protested, is accepted as only one example of the indifference of the universe. There is no denigration of President Eisenhower, but the intimation is that he is only a monument in a dead world to what were once bright hopes.

So it is in the novel, where the writer presumably gets out of his own skin. It is a commonplace today to talk of the "no hero" novel. This does not mean simply that the central character is a "little man," not one whose hand is on the lever of history. It means also that this "no hero" is defeated by a life so antagonistic, so impossible to understand and therefore cope with, that his struggles are only pathetic, impotent gestures. An example, by a writer of remarkable gifts, is *Rabbit, Run* (1960)[2] by John Updike.

The story is of a married man of 26, with a two-year-old child, who suddenly feels an overwhelming revulsion against the life he leads. He runs away with no idea of where to go or what to do, but only the panicky conviction that to stay is unbearable. He then returns to his home town, lives with a mistress for a while, is reconciled to his wife, who is pregnant, and then, after the child is born, runs again.

The situation is one of all-encompassing alienation, for Harry Angstrom, or "Rabbit," has no specific charges or complaints against his family or conditions of life. His wife tries to please him and his job seems to afford him a comfortable if not luxurious living. It is his own emptiness which conditions his alienated relations to others. The last time of real happiness that he can remember was in his adolescence, when he was the speedy star forward on his high school basketball team. The world is a forbidding place in which to grow up, and having had a taste of adulthood, his reaction is a frantic urge to flee. The details of the story do not matter for the purpose here. Updike shows the other characters as equally unhappy with themselves, with the partial exception of the short-time mistress, who has a sturdy, if almost desperately lonely, independence. She accuses Harry of self-centredness. "Why don't you look outside of your own pretty skin for a while?" The charge is true enough, but the implication of the novel is that this is a symptom, not a cause. Harry has no driving ambitions, he does not use people for his own advancement, he does not know what he wants. He is like a frightened child in a loveless world.

What is significant for the purpose here is the extent to

which this entire third-person novel is written in a style of
alienated reactions to the outer world, so that the only difference between Harry's estrangement and Updike's is Updike's awareness of it. He does not put his portrayal in a
social context which might throw light upon the problem,
but implies through the very narrative style that the world
is a forbidding one. When Harry meets his wife, just before
he runs away, he notices only that with the addition of
wrinkles, her mouth has become greedy, and her hair has
thinned, so he keeps thinking "of her skull under it." In
another context, the picture of a grandmother feeding her
grandson might be endearing. This however is how Updike
describes it:

His mother's glasses glitter as she leans in from her place on the
table with a spoon of smoking beans at the end of her fat curved
arm. Her face shows none of the worry she must be feeling about
why nobody comes for the boy and instead is narrowed, her face
a faceted beak, into one wish: that the boy eat. Her mouth is
focused into white crinkles.

When Harry first sees Ruth, "her upper lip pushes out a
little like an incipient blister . . . her hair, a kind of dirty
ginger color, is bundled in a roll at the back of her head."
He goes out in to the street. "In the white light faces wear
the American expression, eyes squinting and mouths sagging
open in a scowl, that makes them look as if they are about
to say something menacing and cruel."
  This is not Updike's calculated way of characterizing Harry
Angstrom. It reflects the imagery in the writer's own lens,
just as Renoir and Toulouse-Lautrec might paint the same
person with equal fidelity and yet in opposite manners. Even
nature is seen in an alienated way, as when Harry works as
a gardener.

Harry is caught in a tide of perfume, for behind him the breeze
has turned and washes down through a thick sloping bank of acrid
lily-of-the-valley leaves in which on that warm night a thousand

bells have ripened, the high ones on the stem still the bitter
sherbet green of canteloupe rind. . . . in the acres sheltered there
were dozens of great rectangular clumps like loaves of porous green
bread.

That Updike sees America today as a home of petrified
humanity is confirmed by his latest novel, *The Centaur*
(1963).[3] Why America is so bleak, he does not know. He
seems to ascribe it to the blind and meaningless movement
of life itself. There are humanist elements in *The Centaur*
but they only intensify the dominant feeling of Updike's
alienation.

The story recounts the death, at the age of 50, of George
Caldwell, a high-school teacher in a Pennsylvania town. It is
told largely through the eyes of his 15-year-old son, Peter,
although in the complex and finely handled shuttling forward
and back in time, which is part of the novel's technique, we
also know that Peter has later become a painter in New York.
We see George Caldwell as a soft-hearted and kindly figure,
wholly at a loss in a hard world run by self-centred people.
He feels a miserable failure, an object of ridicule to his pupils
and dismissed by his colleagues as a misfit. Indeed most of
the town thinks the same, but for a similar misfit, Dr. Apple-
ton. The businesslike and efficient principal of the school,
Zimmerman, despises him. Whatever Caldwell turns his
hands to ends in failure. When he offers kindliness, people
take advantage of him. After one such incident, he laments,
"A man like that would walk over your dead body to grab a
nickel. That's the kind of bastard I've done business with all
my life; they're too smart for me."

It is largely around Caldwell's figure that the writing takes
on a humanizing character. As for the rest, the town itself
and its businesslike citizens, with their children following in
their footsteps, the picture is one of the bleakest alienation;
in Updike's words, "a paralyzed patch of thankless alien
land." Here are the schoolchildren at a basketball game.

Adolescent boys as hideous and various as gargoyles, the lobes of their ears purple with the cold, press, eyes popping, mouths flapping, under the glowing overhead globes. Girls, rosy-cheeked, glad, motley and mostly ill-made, like vases turned by a preoccupied potter, are embedded, plaid-swaddled, in the hot push. Menacing, odorous, blind, the throng gives off a muted shuffling thunder, a flickeringly articulate tinkle: the voices of the young.

The author gives his story symbolic significance by paralleling his characters with figures from classical mythology. George Caldwell becomes Chiron, the centaur-teacher. Zimmerman is Zeus. Hummel, the garage owner, is Hephaestus. Mrs. Herzog, a domineering member of the school board, is Hera, and so on. But the effect of this symbolism is to abstract the picture of contemporary small-town America still further out of history, to give its bleakness a philosophic universality, to intimate that the world has not progressed from the primal raptures of the age of mythology but has merely decayed and hardened.

It is the Nietzschean view of civilization and science as not progress but decadence, expressed in *The Birth of Tragedy*. The belief that nature could be explained, Nietzsche says, and that knowledge was a "panacea," served to annihilate "myth," and "poetry was driven like a homeless being from her natural ideal soil." It is an enticing thought, until one reflects that the age in which men's minds were inspired by science and the possibility of systematically knowing and mastering the outer world, from the Renaissance and Shakespeare to the 20th century, produced more poetic riches than all the past ages put together. The reason for the bleak aspect that contemporary life takes on to so many has to be found, not in the forces for human progress, but in the answer to the question of why these forces seem to have ground to a halt.

In contrast to Updike, whose style is a view of the world through a lens of alienation, the equally gifted James Purdy assumes alienation as a matter-of-fact, "deadpan" manner, to become the clothing of his symbolism. The assumption is that the writer has disciplined himself to feel nothing, to be affected by nothing, to examine life on earth as if he were a sociological statistician from another planet. In Purdy's first novel, the effect is consciously comic, in the second, one of deep pathos.

The setting of *Malcom* (1959)[4] is New York City. The story is of a sheltered youth who has been mysteriously—and symbolically—abandoned by his father, and is induced by a passing astrologer to "enter life." "Life" consists of adventures among Bohemian artists or pseudo-artists and wealthy dilettantes. The atmosphere is one of utter strangeness, a calculated non-humanity, as if the novel were about another world where what appear to be people are robots. Events follow one another without any rational or meaningful connection, the characters prattle mindlessly without a spark of thought for anyone but themselves and bat each other like puppets in a Punch and Judy show. Here is a grotesquely "absurd" world, alienated from the reader because nothing in it can be related to the reader's own life and hopes, no figure is meant to awaken any emotional response in him, and everything has the fearful hostility of an "anxiety" nightmare. Malcom's patron makes arrangements for his funeral:

She had, for instance, ordered—even if she perhaps did not quite get—a quarter-ton of roses, and an equal amount of violets, so that Malcolm's last hours above earth were passed in a greenhouse of sweetness and foliage. . . .

She was greatly displeased, almost annihilated, however, that there was a ketchup factory in the nearby vicinity, and since the ketchup season was at its peak at the time of Malcolm's funeral, the burned saccharine smell of tomatoes struggled desperately with the evanescent perfume of violets and roses. . . .

The only flaw in the ceremony was the repeated insistence of the local coroner and the undertaker—later they were both silenced, it is said, by money—that there had been no corpse at all, and that nobody was buried in the ceremony.

This is comic writing, but without the force of social or realistic-minded satire, where a real situation is given a calculated "absurd" distortion so that the reader may turn it into sense, thereby getting a flashing insight into a truth of the real world. Its implication is that the real world, behind its pretenses at rationality, is equally "absurd," hostile to human yearnings for love, for warmth of human relations, for knowledge.

In Purdy's The Nephew (1960)[5] the tone is that of the quiet, twilight resignation of old people clinging to whatever support they can find in a life that is like a trackless waste. The novel is more realistic in manner, discarding the bizarre humor of Malcolm, but it is still essentially symbolical. The setting is a small Ohio town. The characters are old or middle-aged people, each with a secret unhappiness or frustration. Faye Laird, whose mother, with whom she lives, had broken up her love affair and intended marriage, is now a spinster school teacher in her middle forties. Willard Baker, the last descendant of a wealthy family whose beloved brother, a brilliant doctor, had been driven by scandal to drugs and suicide, is now an alcoholic and lives with a homosexual. Mrs. Barrington, a domineering, wealthy woman who had forced her husband to give up artistic aspirations for a law office, now knows that he didn't love her and no one loves her. Then, there is an old college professor, with the guilt-ridden memory of an affair with one of his students, whom he had later married, hastening the death of his first wife. He had once proclaimed Marxist ideas, but now recants to keep his job.

The two main characters are Alma and Boyd Mason, sister and brother, spinster and widower, who live together in their old age. Their lives had been given some meaning by their affection for an orphaned nephew, Cliff; a gentle, quiet-spoken lad, whom they had brought up. But he had been conscripted and sent to Korea, from where he was soon listed as missing in action. The two try to convince themselves that he will reappear. When his death is confirmed, Alma decides to put together a private memorial for Cliff, to keep his memory alive, by collecting whatever it was people in the town knew about him. Otherwise, she feels, his life would seem utterly meaningless, as if he had never lived, and their own lives, so much filled by him, would also lose all meaning. Such fond memories are a recovery of humanity in a desolate world that erodes it to nothingness.

Alma discovers, in her probing among people who knew Cliff, strange and even incomprehensible things about him. The shocking revelation comes reluctantly from Willard Baker that Cliff had hated the town, had hated the "charity" he was getting from Alma and Boyd, had been unhappy at his dependence upon them, had wanted to run away. Nobody really knows anybody else. Alma says, "There's so much we can never know about everything and everybody." Boyd says, 'We're all pretty much strangers to one another." But the consoling thought is that reality lies in one's own decision, and how one recreates another person for oneself. The important fact is not what Cliff was, but Alma's and Boyd's love for him.

This is the central thought of the novel, but there is a surrounding, highly subtle social symbolism. First, the town's main industry is a ketchup factory, and the heavy odor of cooked tomatoes and spices lingers disturbingly in the air all summer. But as Boyd says, "It's bread and butter to the people connected with the industry. This whole town would be broke without ketchup." In other words, this factory is the world of economics, of human labor producing commodities, from which the people of the novel shut themselves off, although they cannot ignore its presence.

Then, there is the reality that Cliff died in the Korean war. Alma "could not understand how, merely by his having put on Uncle Sam's clothes, he could go to that faraway Pacific place and never return." That is all she or anyone else thinks about the "police action" that cost a couple of million Korean lives, as well as about 40,000 American dead and twice as many wounded. Why was it fought? Is it, as the novel intimates, that these things just happen, that the forces which lead to wars and those involved in the decisions, exist, like the ketchup factory, in another sphere? Or is it that, to the great majority of Americans, there was a refusal to think about the war? For behind all its rationalizations was the uneasy feeling evoked by all the signs it bore of a country with human and democratic traditions fighting an inhuman colonial war, supporting a local dictator and protecting "private" investments. Intensifying this uneasiness was the fact that to question this was to risk being branded a "traitor." To this day, the Korean war remains "forbidden territory." Despite the numbers engaged in it, no novel has appeared examining it with the critical view that a host of novels have displayed toward the anti-fascist war.

This uneasiness may be connected to another symbolic touch in the book. It is Decoration Day, and Alma wants to repair and display the torn flag, Old Glory. "But the tear was not so easily repaired. . . . Other long-hidden snags and rents in the material suddenly asserted themselves, as in conspiracy with the first rent in the fabric, and soon Alma saw that what she held was a tissue of rotted cloth, impossible to mend."

And so there is an ambiguity to the book. On the one hand there is the existentialist view of life as absurd, with people portrayed as drifting particles of "being," seeking some meaning to their lives and stretching out hesitant tendrils to others. Nobody really knows anything about others or about reality. On the other hand there is the hint that the feeling of absurdity springs from the crisis of the American humanist and democratic traditions. And the question Purdy, like so many other brilliant and honest young writers must face, is whether the "crisis" is all there is to reality. Does not its very existence indicate a conflict between the forces of progress and those of reaction, which can be discerned if one looks for it?

B. LOST SOCIAL CONVICTIONS AND EXISTEN-

TIALISM: *Arthur Miller and Saul Bellow*

A distinction of Arthur Miller's plays is that their human conflicts are fought out against the background of the great social issues of the day. Yet instead of growing as a social playwright, he has turned to dwell increasingly on the individual "predicament" which only superficially appears to be also a social question. The latter, for all the intensity with which it is raised, seems at the end to be insoluble, while the culminating thought is the existentialist one of an "absurd" world in which the belief in human progress itself must be abandoned. The only possible solutions are private ones.

In *All My Sons* (1947), a small factory owner, Joe Keller, during the Second World War, sells defective airplane parts to the army. When exposure comes, he manages to put the blame on his partner, who is sent to jail. One of Joe's sons, an army flier, is reported "missing in action," and a climax of the play comes with the disclosure that this son, learning of his father's complicity, actually had killed himself. To the younger son, who also learns the truth, Joe pleads that he could not stand losing the business, which he had built with his life's blood and dreamed of handing on to his sons. Renounced by this son as well, he kills himself.

The play makes a strong statement about the shoddy ethics of business. Yet the motifs that will overwhelm Miller's social consciousness are already present here; the focusing of what appears to be a criticism of capitalism on the tribulations of the petty middle class, the recourse to suicide instead of any action to extirpate an evil, and the view of father-son alienation as due to a weakness or self-delusion on the father's part.

In *Death of a Salesman* (1949)[6] Miller presented what seemed on the surface to be another indictment of capitalism, with his picture of a salesman approaching 60 who has served an employer faithfully for more than half his life, and is now fired from his job. Willy Loman is thrown away, as he says, like a piece of orange peel. The indictment appears to charge capitalism with inhumanity. And yet as the play develops the inner life of the "salesman," the focus changes so that the fault lies only in Willy himself.

We gather this first when Willy is contrasted to his brother Ben, who boasts "When I was seventeen I walked into the jungle, and when I was twenty-one I walked out. And by God I was rich." Ben had offered Willy an opportunity to get rich with him, but Willy had pinned his hopes on being a salesman. Then there is his brother-in-law, Charlie, who is both successful in business and not alienated from his son, as Willy is from his own two sons. Willy's trouble, it seems, was that he did not go head-on into "free enterprise," namely becoming his own boss.

Willy's guilty weaknesses are further elaborated as the play builds to its dramatic climaxes. Why has a chasm opened between Willy and his oldest and idolized son, Biff? Why has Biff, now in his middle thirties, become an unhappy

wanderer, unable to get settled, and a thief? We learn that
Biff had once come into his father's hotel room, and found
him with a half-clothed woman. This had disillusioned Biff
in both his father and his father's kind of career.

The charge develops that Willy was a fraud, not only
perpetually deluding himself about salesmanship but im-
parting this delusion to his sons. "I'll get him a job selling.
He'll be big in no time." Willy's real bent was to work with
his hands or tools, rebuilding the back steps of his house,
planting a garden. But he refused to face what he really
was. And this is Biff's accusation. "We never told the truth
for ten minutes in this house!" Biff always resented the
pressure of his father's idealization of him. "I'm not a leader
of men, Willy, and neither are you . . . I'm just what I am,
that's all!" That Willy is a victim not of inhuman forces
running the outer world, but of his own delusions, is the
conclusion of the play. He drives his car to a deliberate
smash-up, killing himself. The reason is not, however, as
first intimated, that in this money-run world, he is worth
more "dead" than "alive," since he carries $20,000 life in-
surance. It is that he thinks this will restore Biff's love for
him. "He'll worship me for it. . . . Can you imagine that
magnificence with twenty thousand dollars in his pocket?"
Willy must cling to his illusions even if this demands killing himself.

The "successful" people, like Ben, Charlie and Loman's
employer are treated like apparitions from another world.
Had Miller given them some psychological substance, showing what "success" demands and what price it exacts, his
play would have filled its promise of being a social statement.
But it then would have been a different play. While Miller's
talent gives each individual scene a strong impact, the whole
adds up to confusion. The audience feels that something
profound has been said about the world it lives in, but what

it actually gathers is that we all are Willy Lomans, too weak-minded and gentle to cope with the exigencies of a harsh society. Richard Watts, Jr., writing of *Death of a Salesman*, says that Miller "is essentially a moralist, which makes the charge that he is some kind of orthodox left-wing economic determinist seem disproved immediately." Loman's real tragedy, Watts writes, "was not his failure in business or his discovery of the arrival of old age, but his surrender to false ideas of success."[7]

But if Loman's "immorality" is his unwillingness to face reality, this is also shared by the author. For Miller has not been faithful to his subject. He has not pursued it with the integrity of being willing to follow wherever it led him. When Dreiser wrote *An American Tragedy* he was no Marxist, which is what Watts means by "orthodox left-wing economic determinism." But he was true to his subjects, and a resolute realist. He showed that the "ideals of success" which killed Clyde Griffiths, however "false" one might call them, were those drummed into Clyde's head by the society he lived in, and were precisely those by which the successful people did gain "success." And long before this, in the character of Hurstwood in *Sister Carrie*, Dreiser showed that the same "ideals of success" and talents which bring a man wealth and high position, under altered conditions in the same society cannot put one dime in his pocket. What Dreiser showed trenchantly as a social flaw, Miller shows as a personal "error," which is why he can be praised with a complacency that nobody felt about Dreiser. Dreiser provided no more "answers" than Miller does. But Dreiser at least stated the problem clearly. And he later found the answer to his moral questions in Marxism, which, despite Watts' beliefs, makes morality a central concern.

The Crucible (1952), which dealt with the hysterical witch trials in Salem, Massachusetts, in the 1690's, was recognized without question as an implied and timely protest by Miller against the anti-Communist witch-hunts carried on by Senator Joseph McCarthy and by the House Committee on Un-American Activities, with the collaboration of the F.B.I. Yet, for all the honor deserved by this achievement, the fact remains that Miller's drama operated more as protest than as illumination. It did not throw any real light on the Salem trials, and the Salem setting only confused the issues in the present-day Inquisition.

The Salem trials were a desperate attempt by an oligarchy in a theocratic state, employing the barbarous medieval practices of torture and embracing the medieval superstitions about devils and witches, to hold back the tide of democracy, science and freedom of thought. But this real struggle does not enter with any dramatic force in Miller's play. We are given a fearsome picture of the weight of reaction, with tyrannical "hanging" judges supported by hypocritical clergymen and the malice of sexually frustrated daughters and female servants of the townspeople. The turning point which leads to the conviction of the hero, John Proctor, comes through a failure of communication with his wife. He has admitted an adulterous relation with the girl who is his chief accuser but his wife, who does not know he had admitted the truth, lies about it in the belief that it will save him.

Again, as in *Death of a Salesman*, the social issue is dulled, instead of sharpened, by the personal. And at the end, John Proctor is willing to save his life by signing a paper avowing a pact with the devil. But he is then asked to name other such devil-worshippers. This he will not do, and he is executed. In other words, Proctor's principles do not go so far as to combat the social barbarism of belief in witches and therefore witch-hunting. He will even bolster this evil with his own false statement. He will not however by further lies implicate others. Another "hero" of the play who challenges the Inquisition, the Reverend John Hale, himself believes that there are witches and has cheerfully consigned accused people to be burnt or hanged. His objection to the Salem trial is its disregard for what he considers fair evidence.

Had the drama centered about the issue of the free play of ideas, exposing the hysteria against witches as a means of holding back this tide, it would have been both historically deeper and more illuminating in its analogy to today. The Marxists persecuted in the witch-hunts of today are seeking their democratic right to debate their ideas in the public forum. Marxism to them is a scientific, philosophical and historical body of thought which addresses itself to existing problems that people are aware of regardless of what they think or know of Marxism. In the opinion of a host of leading world scientists, artists, writers and educators, it is impossible to understand the modern world without assimilating at least some of the insights of Marxism.

The attitude of the McCarthy investigations, of the House Committee on Un-American Activities and of the F.B.I., however, was that truth, science, validity of economic and historical views, had nothing to do with the problem. To question the inordinate power of the great corporations over the political and social life of the American people, including such matters as peace and war or their support of fascism, to question whether their drive for profit and for investments abroad served the welfare of the American people, to show "excessive" concern for the working people and the Negro victims of racism, was in their mind, "Un-American." To teach that capitalism was not eternal, that its institutions could be discarded just as those of slavery and feudalism had been, was by definition a "conspiracy" to overthrow America. America was not a democracy but a capitalism, and those who did not belive this were to them pariahs and traitors,

to be treated with the utmost barbarism. If democratic traditions or the Bill of Rights stood in the way of the witch-hunt,
they were to be disregarded.

There was not only a direct parallel but a conscious tie
to the operations of fascism, which had also used anti-
Communism in its march to power, destroying on the way
all democratic thought, activity and institutions. The American Inquisition attacked no fascist, racist or anti-labor groups,
although these were openly using methods of "force and
violence." Since it could find no actual crimes in its victims,
it used the weapons of blacklist to drive them from public
life, "contempt" to jail them, with a legally meaningless
but demagogically effective terminology that could embrace
a host of "New Dealers" it hated; "soft on communism,"
"subversive," "unreliable," "fellow-traveller." The new American "hero" was the informer, stool-pigeon and labor spy.

Against this wide-thrown net, Miller has objections. And
he will not personally be an informer, even against those with
whose ideas he now differs. But he fails to see the truth that
Commager and others have pointed out: the evil starts when
vested interests prohibit the free scrutiny of the realities of
life. The hysteria and tyrannical methods, which he portrays
so effectively, are results of this, not primary causes. And so
The Crucible, which might have been a great drama illuminating social, historical and human reality, dwindles to the
relatively narrow question of the propriety of the methods
of an Inquisition, and of just how far an individual will or
will not go in compliance.

In After the Fall, produced in 1964, Miller keeps only the
thinnest pretense of giving an objective character to the
working out of his personal problems. This transcendance of
the social by the personal is not simply due to the fact that
the play is transparently autobiographical. O'Neill's Long
Day's Journey into Night was also autobiographical. Yet

O'Neill, able to put himself in other people's shoes, could recreate his father, mother and brother as profoundly realized characters.

In Miller's play, all the characters but the central one, the lawyer Quentin, have the partial reality of existing only as Quentin remembers them in relation to his own problems. The traditional realistic dramatic form is expertly replaced by a stream-of-consciousness form, the play proceeding as a monologue by Quentin with the various scenes, fading into one another, being his recollections from different periods of his past. The content is that of an existentialist psycho-analysis, leading to an "adjustment" whereby social and political concerns are given up for private life. Of the social issues, one is represented by the German fascist death camps, like Auschwitz, with their millions of Jews and other victims. The other is that of the Inquisition carried on by the Congressional Committee on Un-American Activities.

The German concentration camp reappears throughout the play, its tower, sometimes lit up and sometimes darkened, looming above the stage. Quentin is terrified that people built such a house of slaughter. It is a stark reality of our time. As for socialism, he says, he once believed in it as an answer to such horrors, but now believes no more. Later, in Part One of the play, he says he feels a "strange complicity," and still later he says that something in him makes him feel like an "accomplice" in the slaughters. This "guilt" is a central motif of the play. It is an existentialist-sounding statement, like Sartre's, that each individual bears the responsibility for the world. And yet it demands further examination. What is the nature of this guilt? Is it that Quentin feels he should have taken a greater part in the fight against fascism? Is it that he should now be fighting against its renewed manifestations? Or is it that all people have something of the fascist, the killer, in them?

Any expectation that Miller intends to suggest the first two answers disappears when the theme of the Congressional witch-hunt committee enters, making up the dramatic heart of Part One of the play. Quentin, the lawyer, is not called up for investigation, but two of his friends are: Mickey and Lou, who have shared his socialist beliefs and his activity, along with Communists when the latter led the fight against fascism. Mickey is now disillusioned, bitterly anti-Communist and anti-Soviet Union. He despises the "Party," he says. He is ready to become an informer and cooperate with the Committee. He now considers his former colleagues his enemies. The reactionaries, he says, were right in everything "they said about us." He is also, he admits, terrified of the Committee.

Lou is also frightened, for the publicity means the end of his career. He asks Quentin to act as his lawyer. Quentin reluctantly agrees, for although Lou looks upon him as a friend, he is now against what Lou stands for. If Lou doesn't change, "I consign him to hell, because we are separate persons." When Lou takes Quentin out of his dilemma by jumping under a subway train, Quentin is relieved. "I hated the danger in it for myself," he says, for he wanted "to be a good American again." This accounts, he adds, for "the joy I felt now that my danger had spilled out on the railroad tracks." Again, as in his previous plays, Miller ends what seems to be a protest against reaction with suicide. The implication is that reaction must win.

The disillusionment of both Quentin and Mickey with the political Left does not spring out of any conviction that it does not live up to its principles, or that there are better ways of achieving progress and fighting reaction or fascism. The audience may think so at first, from the implied criticisms of the "Party," but what emerges from the play is the crucial fact that, by abandoning their associations, Mickey and Quentin are consciously abandoning faith in human progress.

They are collaborating with reaction, not because they think it is not reaction, and not because they are blind to the connections between the American Inquisition and its Hitler prototypes, but because they see reaction as all-powerful. It rules the world. It must triumph. The mass of people are corrupt. No hope can be placed in them. Every man must look out for himself. This is the explanation of the guilt and "complicity" that Quentin—and Arthur Miller—feel about the concentration camp. We are savages in a savage world. "No man lives who would not rather be the sole survivor of this place than all its finest victims!" Everybody, including us, has a murderer within him. "My brothers died here . . . but my brothers built this place; our hearts have cut these stones!"

Then how can this guilt be exorcised? The play's answer is that it cannot be. One must simply live with it, and find some hope, or relief, in "love." One must ignore the world and confine oneself to personal matters. It is put in existentialist terms. Near the beginning of the play, Quentin says that life was aimless to him, a place of "despair." But he then felt "hope" again. And this is traced in the central line of the play, dealing with Quentin's relations to his two wives and prospective third.

The first wife, Louise, appears to have been a rather strong personality, who felt that Quentin was too wrapped up in himself, failing to appreciate her possession of a mind of her own. Their separation arouses doubts in Quentin that he has the capacity to love, and he ascribes this to the childhood resentment he felt toward his mother, who had tyrannized over his kindly and gentle father. Quentin's experience with his second wife, Maggie—generally agreed to have been based on Miller's second wife, Marilyn Monroe—is what convinces him that he and everybody else have it in them to be a killer. This makes up most of the second and concluding part of the play. He had been attracted to her by her loveliness, naivete, whimsical vitality and high spirits, making her the opposite of his rather stern and intellectually demanding first wife. But what had seemed so engaging turned after marriage, as he tells it, into an irresponsible childishness, even brainlessness, and a constant bickering that made their relationship a hostile one. She finally kills herself with an overdose of sleeping pills. Quentin feels guilty about this. Perhaps he helped to kill her.

And so, a curious reversal occurs. Quentin's guilt about his second wife becomes the proof of his guilt, and everybody's guilt, about Auschwitz. And since this piled-up guilt is so overwhelming, like a pattern of the universe itself, the only thing to do is to live with it. We are all killers, the play says, and in spirit we all built Auschwitz. "And the wish to kill is never killed, but with some gift of courage one may look into its face when it appears, and with a stroke of love—as to an idiot in the house—forgive it; again and again . . . forever?" Holga, the woman with whom Quentin is now in love, appears above, saying "Hello!" and Quentin moves towards her. It is an existentialist answer, except that for the existentialist view of an "absurd" world, Miller substitutes that of an implacably reactionary world. All a man can do under this shadow is to find some personal happiness. Miller's self-analysis has successfully relieved his guilt about his second wife by turning it into "universal guilt" and his surrender to reaction by turning his fear into the "existentialist anxiety."

Saul Bellow also gives the reader his self-analysis and his adjustment. Probably every serious writer at some time or other has looked deep into himself and even examined his earliest childhood memories, with the results affecting his treatment of outer life. In the kind of work here compared to an existentialist self-analysis, however, the process of analysis becomes the finished work. So it was in Arthur Miller's

After the Fall, and so it is in Saul Bellow's novel *Herzog*
(1964).[8] Bellow follows a path similar to Miller's, from social
concerns to private life. But where Miller seems to have gone
through an anguished struggle, Bellow throws off social responsibility like an old coat.

In many ways, Bellow is the writer of the 'fifties closest to
Henry Miller. There are differences. Bellow is a much more
controlled writer than Miller and where Henry Miller seems
to write discursive memoirs, Bellow invents novelistic characters and situations. But as with Miller, his prime literary
gift is for a stream of brilliant and witty talk, enhanced with
vivid descriptive powers. In his two previous large-scale novels,
The Adventures of Augie March (1953)[9] and *Henderson the
Rain King* (1959),[10] the stream of talk took the form of a
fictional autobiography of his central character. In both books
there was an abundance of characters but no real characters
other than the central one, for although everyone was vividly
depicted, the characterizations tended toward the grotesque,
with no penetration to the human core which discloses the
kinship to others. In both books there were countless events
but nothing really happened in the novelistic sense, for without a clash of personages seen in depth there can be little
real drama.

The view that emerges from both novels is that the world
is absurd and the best a person can do is to protect himself
from it while laughing at it. *The Aventures of Augie March*
has something of the character of a farewell to social responsibility, for the hero spends some years as a labor organ-
izer before he decides that both this and politics are not his
calling. "My friend, I said to myself, relax and knock off
effort. The time is in the hands of mighty men to whom you
are like the single item in the mind of a chief of a great
Sears, Roebuck Company, and here you come, wishing to do
right. . . ." He ends up as an international trader cheerfully

carrying on illicit dealings, and his assertion of his freedom lies in his ability to laugh at everything. *Henderson the Rain King* is more symbolic-philosophical in manner, its hero being a wealthy man who is disgusted with Western civilization and tries to find the meaning of life in the rituals of a mythical African tribe. Its keynote is expressed in the beginning. "In an age of madness, to expect to be untouched by madness is a form of madness. But the pursuit of sanity can be a form of madness, too."

Herzog is different in form, written in the third person and exploring a single situation. But it is essentially, like the other two, a one-character novel; life as seen through the eyes of an estranged, withdrawn individual. Herzog is a professor of literature who had started a comprehensive history of romanticism, the first volume of which had been published and won him esteem among scholars at home and abroad. But he has now, in his middle forties, lost interest in the project, and also withdrawn from teaching. He has had two wives. He admits he mistreated the first, now divorced, but he occasionally visits the son he has had by her. The second, by whom he has had a daughter, has deceived him and run away with a man who posed as his best friend. He has a mistress who loves him and wants to marry him, but he does not want to become so closely involved with her.

There is little outer action in the novel. Herzog makes a trip to see his daughter, to whom he feels attached, and who is living with his divorced second wife and her lover. But this ends in the disaster of a car wreck, after which he resigns himself to separation from his daughter. He lives alone in a broken-down country house. His brothers are concerned with his withdrawal from normal life, and one of them suggests that he take psychiatric treatments. But Herzog refuses. The implication is that to be what people call "sane" or "normal" means only adjustment to a respectable conventional life that has no real values, and he, Herzog, must work out his own values.

The real action is internal, and here Bellow uses to the full his "gift for gab," or current of witty, ironic talk. This appears in Herzog's musings about his past life, and even more in the letters he continually writes. They are letters which he never finishes and never expects to mail. They are addressed to the living and to the long dead; to friends, enemies, statesmen, philosophers, writers, even to God. They raise whimsical and ironic queries about whether anything is really known about human life and happiness, and what is the answer to Death. They are the means through which Herzog works out his own solutions, which turn to a vaguely religious existentialism. As he himself says, "I go after reality with language. Perhaps I'd like to change it all into language." This does not mean that language is a tool for coming to grips with and thinking about reality, external and internal. Rather, Bellow's is the Heideggerian thought that language has a kind of power of reality of its own, for truth lies in the process of "questioning," not in any answers found. Thus subjectivity is truth. Herzog is trying to answer a social question, namely the values of life, by a withdrawal from society which through its very nature closes the door to the ability to discover the values of life. For it assumes self-centredness; what the values are "for me," aside from any relations to others.

While Bellow tries to make Herzog into a philosophical hero of our time, he is only lionizing a kind of meek, or self-pitying, self-centredness as against a driving, avaricious self-centredness. Herzog rationalizes away as human frailty whatever harm he has done to others, and bewails the insensitivity or malice others have shown to him. He thinks of people he knows, family and friends, either with an alienated revulsion or with detachment, as if to imply that even the well-meaning among them are in a strange world different from his, and can neither understand him nor make real contact with him. Like Henry Miller, he both yearns for love and fears getting too involved with people, or having to give as well as receive.

In a letter near the close, to Nietzsche, he agrees: "Rejecting mankind as it is, that ordinary, practical, thieving, stinking, unilluminated, sodden rabble, not only the laboring rabble, but even worse the 'educated rabble' with its books and concerts and lectures, its liberalism and its romantic theatrical 'loves' and 'passions'—it all deserves to die, it will die. Okay." But he does feel that Nietzsche is too uncompromising, and he, Herzog, has no aim to be a superman. He does not even want to be an "intellectual" for this will separate him from the common life. He says, "I mean to share with other human beings as much as possible." But this does not mean that he will interest himself in the troubles and oppression of other people; only that, having given up politics, he now gives up his intellectual life. His life, he says, has been a "convalescence" from "the illusion of improvement, the poison of hope." And if belief in social progress was a kind of disease, so, he now realizes, was his belief in writing about literature or teaching or thinking. He, Herzog, no longer wants anything. He is satisfied to put his mind to sleep, "to be just as it is willed, and for as long as I may remain in occupancy."

Bellow can be called the self-appointed clown of the American existentialist movement, in the sense that he laughs at his "no-hero" even as he kindles a warm glow about him. But he is not, in his humor, satirizing the existentialist frame of mind because he has nothing to replace it with. The world, to him, is "nonsense."

Clownishness takes over, to the author's own detriment, in Bellow's play, *The Last Analysis*, both in its stage version of 1964 and its subsequently revised published version. His "hero," Bummidge, is a sixty-year-old Jewish comedian who has made a fortune on stage and television, and who has been preyed upon by his scavenging wife, son, sister, aunt, other relatives, business associates, managers and mistress. In the play he goes through a kind of mock, part-Freudian, part-existentialist self-analysis, as a new kind of television attraction. Its conclusion is that the analysis and the world itself are nonsense. Bellow still writes wittily. But his characters are presented in so alienated a light that they lack the human substance even for good comedy. They are puppets delivering Bellow's funny lines. And so the play fails as both art and entertainment.

There is also an underlying cruelty in the play, felt in the derisive depiction of the cast of characters—all middle-class Jews—in their completely amoral, money-obsessed mentality. There is the germ of a theme here for a serious study of the contradictions and conflicts within an immigrant people, brought about by the price demanded for "success" in America. Eugene O'Neill showed how profoundly such a theme could be handled in *Long Day's Journey Into Night*. But O'Neill's humanism and social conscience are no longer the style of the time. Alienation is.

The motif which dominates *The Last Analysis*, Bellow's awareness of his ties to a Jewish ancestry from which he feels at the same time alienated, had been touched on in his earlier books, like *The Adventures of Augie March* and *Herzog*. And it is a motif found in a number of accomplished Jewish-American writers today. They represent the second or third generation of Jews who have passed through the process of "assimilation." This however, was not the "digestion" by the new world of the best and most living in the old Jewish cultural traditions. Rather, the newcomers "assimilated" the new ways of life and thought. Many saw this as a necessity, in order to throw off the parochial, mind-starving medievalism of old-country rituals. But the "new" was neither a Renaissance humanism nor an Age-of-Reason enlightenment; it was capitalism in its most grotesquely pragmatic stage, a society pervaded by the dust and ashes of alienation. There is a parallel to the thought James Baldwin raises in his question to the Negro people; do we want to be integrated in a burning house?

Jewish writers in the 1920's and 1930's, like Michael Gold in *Jews Without Money*, Clifford Odets in *Awake and Sing*, Henry Roth in *Call it Sleep*, had examined the question with a breath of human understanding and social awareness, pointing to a link between the Jewish people and what was most genuinely democratic and anti-exploitive in American life. But by the present generation of writers, alienation is accepted as a pervading law of life, removed from any social currents the awareness of which might throw light upon it. A dominant and recurrent motif in novels, stories and plays is that of people preying on one another; not as exploiters and exploited, but as in the prison of alienation, all "little" people who are blindly striving for elbow room and becoming in the process victims or victimizers. Bellow handled such a theme in his short novel, *The Victim* (1947).

Perhaps the most stylistically brilliant of this generation of writers who see American Jewish life in terms of total alienation is Bernard Malamud. In his first novel, *The Natural* (1952), there was no particularly Jewish motif. In a naturalistically documented fantasy, he dealt with the "American dream" sport, baseball, caustically showing the contrast between the naive hopes of the young of becoming a playing-field hero, a mighty swatter or strike-out king, and the dismal corruption permeating this commercial sport. And it was disillusion, not now with baseball but with all social promise, that he brought to his pictures of Jews in his novel *The Assistant* (1957) and the stories in *The Magic Barrel* (1950-

58) and in *Idiots First* (1950-63). Little people prey upon one another, not through any malice but because the blind forces of life seem to impel them, with the victimizers as helpless as the victims. And the utter lack in any of the characters of any wider consciousness than of what they do from day to day, is not realism. The meagre inner life which Malamud gives to his creations is the counterpart to his own failure to bring to bear any social-minded perspective upon the phenomenon of alienation. He surrenders to it as eternal and all-embracing truth. His consciousness differs from that of his characters only in that what they take with deadly seriousness, he views with detached irony. He feels a double alienation; that pervading American life, and that of a Jew bound to, yet hopelessly estranged from, his own ancestry and kin. There is no enemy, no outside force of human destruction, at which derisive laughter can be aimed. Life itself, as he sees it, is a bad joke played on all people.

And a question rises in respect to Malamud: how much of a career can he build on recounting this same joke? This is not aimed expressly at him. A man has to write as his deepest feelings dictate. But the conclusion suggests itself that alienation, as it engulfs the artist, so constricts the art that it can only lead to the death of art itself.

C. EXISTENTIALISM AND SOCIAL DEMANDS:

Norman Mailer and James Baldwin

Norman Mailer moved to existentialism along a path somewhat parallel to that of Arthur Miller; the path of a young socialist whose disillusion grows out of his despair at the apparent all-triumphant power of reaction. But where Miller seems to have made some sort of individual peace with the existing order, Mailer has continued to write as its implacable enemy. What is sad is that, in the course of the individual war he has declared on society, his great novelistic talents, which were those of a humanist and social-minded novelist, seem to be dribbling away.

The publication in 1948 of *The Naked and the Dead*[11] was a historic event in American literature. There had previously been thoughtfully realistic novels about the American army in the war. But *The Naked and the Dead* struck a new tone— the tone of the 1950's—in its obliteration of the "gallant knights in armor" view of the American soldier, its uncompromisingly truthful picture of what front-line combat means, and how soldiers actually lived, thought and spoke. Concentrating on one brief campaign, the conquest of an island in the Pacific, it tried to consider the battle in epic terms of the movement of history. In its fully rounded portrayals of a dozen soldiers and officers, with interspersed short biographies called "The Time Machine," it gave the impression of showing American society itself in uniform. And indeed the army of a nation at war is that nation itself turned inside out, with its secrets exposed. Furthermore, in the novels of this war, as of no other, the common soldier stood at the center, asking "Why was this necessary?"

Yet Mailer's view suffered from distortions, which became the more flagrant as he tried to give his canvas epic-historical proportions. His detail of army life, speech and fighting, based on his own experience, was magnificently true. In his views of the soldiers as people, however, with a history and a past, he not only borrowed techniques from Dos Passos, as in the "Time Machine" episodes, but seemed to be looking through Dos Passos's lens. Perhaps he would have seen them this way without Dos Passos, and his mainly humanist style contrasts with Dos Passos's embittered alienation. It is true as Mailer shows, that there were fascist-minded higher-ups in the American army that presumably were fighting fascism. But not true is the view of fascism as running the whole show and the democratic traditions as impotent and doomed. Yet it is this that the novel says, with cumulative impact.

The leading fascist types in the novel are two. Major General Edward Cummings has a keen, militaristic mind, is contemptuous of most people, and talks a kind of Nietzschean Hitlerism. "The only morality of the future is a power morality, and a man who cannot find his adjustment to it is doomed. There's one thing about power. It can flow only from the top down." The other is Sergeant Sam Croft, formerly in the National Guard, whose first victim had been a striking worker, shot in a "labor dispute." Mailer portrays him as a cold and practised killer, the kind of "good soldier," efficient platoon leader and tracker of men whom an army prizes.

The main anti-fascist is Lieutenant Robert Hearn, son of a well-off family and a Harvard graduate, who had taken part in left-wing political activity during the late 1930's, but had never felt at home in it. Mailer portrays him as already disillusioned, Dos Passos style. "All the bright young people of his youth had butted their heads, smashed against things until they got weaker and the things still stood." It is a jaundiced view considering the victories for American labor in the 1930's, and the fact that the fascist armies were now being dealt mortal blows. Hearn is ill at ease with the common soldiers, and tries to make friends through what he calls "tricks of buddying." Compared to Cummings his is a flabby mind, compared to Croft he is an inept soldier. These two hate him and engineer his death. Cummings sends him on a dangerous mission, and Croft, who has scouted ahead of the squad, lies to him about the position of the enemy and lets him walk into a Japanese bullet.

Of the common soldiers, one is Joe Goldstein, who wel-

comes the fact that he is in the army because Hitler persecuted the Jews. He tries to be a capable soldier and to make
friends with the others, although with the parochial view of
some Jews that all gentiles are anti-Semites, he feels estranged
from them. He has no views of what is going on in the world.
Another, Roy Gallagher, is a poor-boy anti-Semite, racist and
fascist, of the kind who joined Hitler's storm troopers. The
working class is represented by Red Valsen, a coal miner's
son, who might have come out of Dos Passos in the alienated life he has led, drifting from job to job or trampling
the roads. Most of the other soldiers are shown with vacant
minds.

There were, of course, such soldiers in the army. But they
do not represent the army as a whole. We get a better picture of the underlying companionship, fellow feeling, and
resentment of being "pushed around," in James Jones' *From
Here to Eternity*. This occurs despite the callow and adolescent political philosophy in Jones' book, and its hero shaped
in the movie tradition of crusader and outlaw; Humphrey
Bogart, John Garfield, George Raft, Gary Cooper. And we
get a still better picture in the hero, Yossarion, of Joseph
Heller's brilliant satire, *Catch 22*. Mailer, however, has already surrendered the American people to reaction.

Mailer's two subsequent novels, *Barbary Shore* (1951)
and *The Deer Park* (1955) retain his stylistic brilliance, but
as a novelist he has cut himself off from the source of his
strength, his social experience and sympathies. The first, set
in a Brooklyn boarding house, deals with a former Communist pursued by the F.B.I. The second purports to be a
picture of the movie-making milieu in California, and takes
up, inconclusively, the question of whether a blacklisted di-
rector should clear himself and resume his artistic career, by
informing on others. There is no fresh air in them, or breath
of life. Whatever interest they have is for the student of

Mailer's spiritual biography. They are symbolical novels, in which he is working out his own disillusion with the political left.

Mailer's subsequent existentialism is forthrightly expressed in his collection of essays and fragments, *Advertisements for Myself* (1959).[12] He admires Marx, from whom he takes the analysis of what he, Mailer, calls the "social cruelty" of capitalism, and he calls himself a "Marxian anarchist." What he fails to perceive is Marx's sense of history. Typical of Mailer's existentialism is that he sees among the mass of humanity only an enlightened "few," namely rebels like himself. The world war proved to him that most people are "murderous." He finds his freedom in his individual defiance of any convention. His rebellions include drug-taking, the flaunting of sex and individual acts of violence. His eyes are so turned inward that he can no longer see the real life around him.

In the main essay in the book, *The White Negro*, Mailer "praises" the Negro in a way to make most Negroes wish he had left them alone. Taking a term from Negro jazz colloquialisms, he calls himself a "hipster." The "hipster" is the Negro "outlaw." As a result of segregation and racist exploitation, Mailer says, all Negroes are "primitives" who have become "psychopaths" and individual rebels. How untrue this is, can be seen from the magnificent social humanity and warm, collective heroism displayed daily in the movement, South and North, for civil rights, democracy, education and the right to vote. But Mailer in his existentialist blindness can say, "the only courage, with rare exceptions, that we have been witness to, has been the isolated courage of isolated people." Portraying the Negroes as primitive, psychopathic, sex-minded, anarchistic rebels, he enlists himself with them, as the "white Negro." The "hipster," he says, is the "American existentialist." He, Mailer, by becoming a "hipster" has joined the new breed of "urban adventurers who drifted out at night looking for action with a black man's code to fit the facts." The "hipster," he says, "had absorbed the existentialist synapses of the Negro, and for practical purposes could be considered a white Negro."

Mailer's existentialism springs from a rather arrogant, elitist "despair" with the common people. Why don't they move? Why don't they see things as Mailer does? Why don't they demolish the society that so oppresses him? The fact is, as history shows, they have consistently moved for their own and all society's welfare, in their own good time. Fascism seemed to be winning victory after victory. But its armies were smashed, by what was primarily the heroism and the hatred of it by the common people over the world. Mailer was part of this, but he didn't have eyes to see it. It is a pity that a talent like Mailer's, which could flourish so well if he gave it rein to range over the realities of American life, should so blindly and wantonly destroy itself.

How far this self-destruction has gone may be seen in Mailer's latest novel, *An American Dream* (1965). It could be considered a projection in the form of a fictional narrative of the attitude towards life expressed in *Advertisements for Myself*; namely the view of the psychopath as representing sanity in an insane world, with a combination of sex and physical violence becoming the way in which a person asserts his independence of society. But it is more a set of symptoms than a successful work of art. Near its opening, its "hero," Stephen Rojack, is on the verge of committing suicide by jumping off a balcony ten stories above the street. Near the end, he is again on the verge of suicide, teetering on a parapet and almost jumping. In between, he visits his estranged wife, drags her out of bed and strangles her, the scene being described in the tone and style of an orgasm. He then goes into the maid's room, finds her on her bed half-naked, and rapes her, with an added touch of sexual perversion. He throws the body of his dead wife out of the window, almost killing a few more people. To the police, he claims that she killed herself. They soon gather the truth, however. Feeling cleansed and new-born because of his murder, and proud of his sexual prowess, he then has an affair with a night-club singer, boldly taking her away from the gangsters with whom she consorts, and also beating up a Negro singer who had been another of her lovers. He is cleared of murder charges through the influence of his father-in-law, who is a multi-millionaire with whole governments responsive to the wires he pulls. This tycoon had once committed incest with his daughter, was being spied upon by her, and wished her dead. He also tries to murder Rojack.

The novel has no outer reality, for none of the characters has any substance other than the surface provided by Mailer's still capable descriptive powers. These here take an alienated form: "He was Italian, some stout lump of rejection from the Mafia," or, "He gave his large smile. A sort of fat sweet corruption emanated from him." And the novel has no inner, psychological reality, of the kind one finds for example in a Kafka fantasy. What does come through is that Mailer is a deeply troubled mind, who no longer has any standards to distinguish between sanity and insanity. His art is only one casuality of this.

One of the achievements of contemporary American Negro literature, aside from its artistic values, is its service in liberating the Negro people from the public image in which they have been cast not only by racists but well-meaning friends who shape the image to fit their own drives and frustrations. Jazz, a gift of the Negro to America in which Negro musicians have continued to predominate as creative figures, has notably suffered from such misguided, enthusiastic distortions. Thus the creative blues and jazz of the 1920's and 1930's, with their protesting pathos and subtle humor, their outgoing march and dance spirit, their bravura or meditative improvisations which asserted a people's dignity and right to free self-expression under the most adverse conditions, were "praised" as an aphrodisiac or "sexual" music, or an assertion of the defiant "primitive" in the face of a "decaying" civilization. Henry Miller writes of jazz, in *The Colossus of Maroussi*, "Boil 'em alive, feathers and all—that's how the Dipsy-Doodle works. It's barbarious, Madame, but that's how it is." Norman Mailer praises jazz as "the music of orgasm, good orgasm and bad."

By contrast, this is how the Negro writer, James Baldwin, writes of a jazz performance in the novel, *Another Country*.[13] It happens to be "modern" jazz, which, while still produced collectively, embodies a highly personal and inward sensitivity and loneliness, as if the musician had to put up a barrier against society in order to find his own humanity.

He stood there, humping the air, filling his barrel chest, shivering in the rage of his twenty-odd years, and screaming through the horn, Do *you love me? Do you love me?* And, again, Do *you love me? Do you love me? Do you love* me? This, anyway, was the question Rufus heard, the same phrase, unbearably, endlessly, and variously repeated, with all of the force the boy had. The silence of the listeners became strict with abruptly focused attention, cigarettes were unlit, and drinks stayed on the table; and in all of the faces, even the most ruined and most dull, a curious, wary light appeared. They were being assaulted by a saxophonist who perhaps no longer wanted their love and merely hurled his outrage at them with the same contemptuous, pagan pride with which he humped the air. And yet the question was terrible and real.

Baldwin's first novel, *Go Tell It On the Mountain* (1953) represented a new stage in the literary depiction of the American Negro. Drawn from his own childhood, it is a powerful portrayal of a Negro family in New York's Harlem, centered around the church. The book is written with a poetry reminiscent of James Joyce's *Portrait of the Artist as a Young*

Man. It achieved rich and profound psychological insights into the fourteen-year-old boy, his brother, his father, his mother and his aunt. In a way the book was an answer to Faulkner's implication that the Negroes were "primitives," and only the cultured white gentry had tragic conflicts and complex minds. Balwin's memorable characters are a permanent addition to the stock of real and significant personages with which American literature has enriched the knowledge of the land, its history and people.

Baldwin's subsequent creative writing, however, shows a diminution in breadth of characterization, along with a turn to existentialism. Yet in all of his writings—with the exception of the novel *Giovanni's Room*, a study in homosexuality —he expresses powerfully the temper of the struggle for equal rights and Negro liberation in the 1960's. There is now no tone of pleading for civil rights or for an end to discrimination, no meek request for understanding, no asking for favors. It is now a demand. As a writer, Baldwin spurns any restriction on subject matter because he is a Negro. He will write on whatever he pleases, give a searching analysis of "white civilization" and people, and take the whole realm of world culture for his own. He knows that he will be read mostly by the white world and he openly expresses his scorn for that world, his contempt for the moral depravity and hypocrisy in which it is entangled.

The truth upon which Baldwin firmly rests is that the liberation of the Negro people, their achievement of full civil, social, political and human rights, and full opportunity for their own development, is a necessity not alone for the Negroes. It is equally necessary in order to save the white people from their own degradation, the destruction of whatever democracy they live by, the loss of whatever freedom they possess. But what is typically existentialist is Baldwin's dissociation of this truth from the class forces in society that are an integral part of it, the lack of faith that the masses of people, as history presents them with its inexorable questions, will find the right answers, the tendency to seek a solution from the enlightened "few." And so a conflict arises in his writing, as in his mind, between the "man alone" and the man of social engagement, the cry for freedom as an impotent act in a meaningless and inhuman world and the cry for freedom as an expression of one of the great and real historical movements of the time.

In the tradition of Camus and Sartre, Baldwin is a brilliant essayist as well as writer of fiction. His essay, "Letter from a Religion in My Mind," first published in the *New Yorker* magazine, November 17, 1962, and then reprinted in the book *The Fire Next Time* (1963),[14] is an embodiment of the above conflict. There is the existentialist death-hauntedness, with the need to act posited not as a demand of one's social relationships and awareness of historical forces, but as an answer to death:

Behind what we think of as the Russian menace lies what we do not wish to face, and what white Americans do not face when they regard a Negro reality—the fact that life is tragic. It seems to me that one ought to rejoice in the *fact* of death—ought to decide, indeed, to *earn* one's death by confronting with passion the conundrum of life.

The United States, he says, far from being in the forefront of world progress, is doomed to "sterility and decay," along with the other colonialist nations that see themselves as "white," as racially superior, but it can also bring "new life" to Western achievements and "transform" them, through "the unconditional freedom of the Negro."

In one passage Baldwin leaps from the existentialist denial of "necessity" and of the reality of historical forces to a recognition of these forces, namely that the masses of people have again and again fought shoulder to shoulder for freedom, and achieved one stage after another. He makes this connection by calling these achievements of history, miracles, the achievement of the "impossible."

I know that what I am asking is impossible. But in our time, as in every time, the impossible is the least that one can demand—and one is, after all, emboldened by the spectacle of human history in general, and American Negro history in particular, for it testifies to nothing less than the perpetual achievement of the impossible.

Having made this allusion to the historical fact that in real life the most oppressed and exploited people have, in struggle for their own freedom, overcome ignorance, backwardness, racist divisions, and raised society to a higher level, he returns to the existentialist emphasis on the "few," in what is nevertheless a moving appeal:

If we—and now I mean the relatively conscious whites and the relatively conscious blacks, who must, like lovers, insist on, or create, the consciousness of the others—do not falter in our duty now, we may be able, handful that we are to end the racial nightmare, and achieve our country, and change the history of the world.

Why does Baldwin speak of historic achievements—and not by the learned few but the great, unlettered many—as the achievement of the "impossible"? Does not the fact that they happened—and repeatedly—show them to be "possible"? The reason is that he lacks a real grasp of the movement and "laws" of history, and the role of the working people, the exploited, who do not always move when they are expected to, but when they do move raise all society to a higher level. During the American Civil War, despite the fact that racism poisoned the North as well as the South, the great mass of working people from factory, shop and farm who formed the Union armies welcomed the fact that it was a war to end slavery. It was the textile workers of England, though un-

employed because of the shortage of raw cotton, who nevertheless fought against the attempt of the English industrial
middle class and aristocracy to bring England into the war
on the side of the South. To these workers, slavery had to
be eradicated. Again, in the middle 1930's, it was the working
people, in the great union-organizing drives, North and South,
who delivered powerful blows against racism.

But Baldwin must see the end of racism as the achievement of the "impossible" precisely because, overlooking the
working people and their history, he appeals mainly to the
"few," who are least likely to grasp the problem and most
impotent to do anything about it. This limitation shows
itself also in his latest novel.

Another Country (1962), is full of partially unresolved
conflicts and unanswered questions. There is beautiful writing. The evocation quoted above, of the protest and frustration expressed in a jazz improvisation, is a humanization of
reality, making something that might have been strange to
the reader, moving, understandable, and a part of him; a
contrast to "alienated" writing.

The locale is New York City. Rufus Scott is a Negro jazz
drummer, a forceful, talented musical personality. He is aflame
with resentment of and anger at the white man's world in
which he must make his way. It is to him as discriminatory
and offensive in its pinpricks as in its frontal assaults, in its
gestures of good-fellowship without understanding as in its
open racist discrimination. He has an affair with a young white
woman, Leona, who has left her husband. It is an unhappy
affair, for he cannot contain his anguish and anger. He treats
her so brutally that she lands in a mental institution. He quits
his music, breaks from his family and friends, roams the
streets, but can find no relief. Driven mad by remorse for what
he has done to Leona, though he knows that the forces which
impelled him were uncontrollable, he makes one last desperate

attempt to reestablish his life, getting in touch with his closest friend, a young and serious writer, Vivaldo Moore, Irish and Italian in ancestry, who has been brought up in the tough life of the Brooklyn slums. But Rufus feels too blocked from the old life, or any life, and jumps off the George Washington Bridge.

The remaining four-fifths of the novel deal with the memory of his life and manner of death, as it effects the lives of those who knew and were close to him.

The chief characters are now Vivaldo and Rufus Scott's sister, Ida, a beautiful young woman with potentialities as a singer. They had known each other slightly, but after the funeral they find themselves closely tied in their mutual sense of loss, fall in love and live together. The other characters are all white people. Richard Silenski is a writer, who after many trials scores a success, but at the price of commercializing his gifts. His wife, Cass, finds herself, while still in love with Richard, estranged because of his self-centredness and lack of real concern for her. There is Steve Ellis, an opportunist theatre producer, who makes pretenses of patronage toward Negro artists. There is also an actor, Eric Jones, who has had a brief homosexual affair with Rufus. He gets an offer to play an important role in a Broadway play and comes to New York shortly after he hears of Rufus's death.

It is mainly through sexual attachments and antagonisms that the novel works itself out. The affair between Vivaldo and Ida is central, and the deep attachment between the two is so broken by flares of antagonism that it seems they can never really be at peace with one another. Cass has an affair with Eric Jones. Ida, in a flare-up of rebellion against Vivaldo, briefly becomes Steve Ellis's mistress, although she despises him. Vivaldo, in turn, has a brief homosexual affair with Eric Jones. At the close, Vivaldo and Ida are together again. They both loved Rufus, and they love one another. But there is no promise of a smooth and happy road before them; rather an intimation of the opposite.

If the novel is sharp and direct in raising the question of Negro-White relations, this is weakened by the special intensity of and emphasis on physical love relations, both heterosexual and homosexual. It is as if the truth of life were centered in the sheer momentary act of sexual assertion. While there is no question about the reality of the moment itself and the vividness with which we see the characters, the people themselves are insufficiently filled out. We are not told enough about them to make them real and understandable, like the great characters of fiction of whom we can think as more real to us than people whom we actually know. For the truth is that, despite the importance of love relations, it is only through knowing people in their diverse interplay in society that we can grasp what they are. Because of the narrowness of Baldwin's focus, even the central characters, Rufus, Vivaldo, Ida, remain somewhat insubstantial. Vivaldo, for example, is a dedicated writer. But we get no inkling of what kind of writer he is, or what he wants to say or embrace in his writing.

And because of this, the profound theme of Negro-White relations is reduced here to personal and sexual ties. We again are faced with the flaw at the heart of so many existentialist novels; namely the impossibility of doing justice to social themes from a viewpoint that leaves society itself out of the picture. Baldwin's thesis, as it emerges from the novel, is the impossibility of white people ever understanding the Negro, or of Negro and white ever attaining complete kinship. This conclusion comes not from a grasp of the full sweep of life, but as a special case of the existentialist approach which accepts alienation as a law of life. It is impossible, the belief is, for any person really to know another. Each person is alone in an alien world.

The theme of the constant abrasion between Negro and

white, even when intimate friends or living as man and wife, is insisted upon, as for example with Vivaldo and Rufus:

"Well," said Vivaldo, "I'm different."

"Yeah," said Rufus, "I bet you are."

"I just want to be your friend," said Vivaldo. "That's all. But you don't want any friends, do you?"

"Yes, I do," said Rufus quietly. "Yes, I do." He paused; then slowly, and with difficulty, "Don't mind me, I know you're the only friend I've got in the world, Vivaldo."

And that's why you hate me, Vivaldo thought, feeling still and helpless and sad.

Ida says to Cass, "You don't know, and there's no way in the world for you to find out, what it's like to be a black girl in this world, and the way white men, and black men too, baby, treat you. You've never decided that the whole world was just one big whorehouse. . . ." Or, Ida is talking to Vivaldo:

"This all began because I said that you people—"

"Listen to yourself. You people—"

"—didn't know anything about Rufus—"

"Because we're white."

"No. Because he was black."

This is not a statement of how deep are the roots of racism, and how painful and difficult it is to trace them and destroy them. It is a thesis of alienation. People must claw at each other precisely because they are so inexorably attached to one another.

Faulkner, in *Light in August*, expressed this about Negro and white in reverse terms. One of his characters ruminates that the white man is "crucified" by the Negro, that the white man must always suffer the Negro as a tragic and inescapable burden. So to Baldwin, the white man is a crucifixion of the Negro, and this is what their pattern of life will continue to be, unless the "impossible" happens.

Connected to this is the other main theme of the novel;

namely the exalted, rhapsodically described plane on which
it puts homosexual love. Baldwin is keen enough to see it as
a flight from conflict. He has a homosexual say, "Maybe I'm
crying because I wanted to believe that somewhere, for some
people, life and love are easier—than they are for me, than
they are." And again, of homosexual love: "This was as far
removed as anything could be from the necessary war one
underwent with women." However, the self-destructiveness
of such a homosexual flight is minimized. Contrasted to its
"peace" is the "war" that heterosexual love entails, whether
with Rufus and Leona, Cass and Richard Silenski, or Ida
and Vivaldo. Here, as in the picture of Negro-White relations, there is always the unresolvable conflict, always the
impossibility of one ever knowing the other.

The result is an inconclusive novel and it leaves one with
a deep concern, less for Baldwin's characters than for Baldwin
himself. For the social theme is integrally bound up with his
mind and thought. The great virtues of the book, aside from
the writing, are the honesty with which Baldwin puts the
questions in his mind, and the sharp, revelation of the spiritual poison of racism, not only for those who openly avow
it but also for all who are part of a system infected by it.
If he consigns human society to the realm of the unknowable,
fixes it in unresolvable conflict and the perpetual torment of
alienation, this means relinquishing this world as a subject
for his own artistic investigation, and blocks the path to his
growth as a writer.

14

THE MORALITY OF HUMAN PROGRESS

This study of the existentialist influence and the spread of alienation in American literature has tried to show how American literature reveals the deep spiritual wounds that the country has inflicted on itself. It has also tried to show that these wounds are not incurable.

It is not true that each person is an isolated world of his own. Certainly every individual differs from another, and absolute understanding of one person by another, in the sense of total identification, is impossible. By the same argument, no man can ever know wholly what it is to be a woman, no person living as a white in a racist society can ever know completely what it is to live as a Negro, no person who has always lived in comfortable circumstances can ever know wholly what it means to live in poverty, no person brought up as a Christian can ever know completely what it is to be brought up as a Jew, and no person raised in one set of national traditions can ever understand wholly what it is to be raised in a different nationality. But along with differences among people is their identity with others. They live in the same world, are subject to the same laws and conflicts, find their growth and freedom along similar paths, and learn from one another.

The proof lies in real life and its reflection in literature. The great anti-feudal revolutions, spreading through Europe and the Americas, then to Asia and Africa, showed conclusively that ideas and paths to freedom were the common property of all peoples, however different the national forms and traditions in which they worked themselves out. A triumph of humanism in the arts was its revelation of the common humanity of people whatever their caste or class, even as it showed the distortion and alienation of this humanity through caste and class. And a particular achievement, even a revolutionary one, of the 20th century, has been the creation of a world literature, with one country after another making its contribution while absorbing the cultural creations of others.

We are still in an early stage of this formation through culture of a world consciousness, but out of it one incontrovertible truth has appeared. It is that the more profoundly true the expression a nation gives to its own problems, struggles and historical experiences, the more it finds not incomprehensibility but kinship and understanding elsewhere. Along with this broadening scope of what can be called the "world treasurehouse" of literature, there has been a growing revolution in its content. The exploited, the working people, the colonial people, the peons and peasantry of "undeveloped" countries whose resources are plundered by outside interests, are no longer the forgotten men of literature, or noticed only with condescension and pity. A literature now voices their own humanity, and their consciousness of their power to shape history. In it a critical eye is turned, sometimes caustic, sometimes contemptuous, sometimes pitying, on the rich and "mighty" of the world who regard themselves as their natural superiors.

In the Soviet Union and other socialist countries, a literature centered about the working class and asserting its social morality is termed "socialist realism," for it adds a conscious aim to participate in the building of socialism. This is part of a much broader stream of literature in which the working people stand at the center. It appears in every land in the world that has a literature free of fascist or proto-fascist dictatorship over culture. Its roots go well back in the 19th century. It has produced giants like Maxim Gorky of old Russia, Mikhail Sholokhov of the Soviet Union, Sean O'Casey of Ireland, Martin Anderson Nexo of Denmark, Arnold Zweig of Germany, Pablo Neruda of Chile, Haldor Laxness of Iceland, Jorge Amado of Brazil.

It has also been a continuous current in American literature. One of its historic achievements is Mark Twain's *Huckleberry Finn*, in which, in the guise of comedy, a white southern boy who is the poorest of the poor, when he breaks down his racist prejudices and discovers his common humanity with a Negro, rises to a far higher moral level than his "betters."

This current has flowed unbroken. The literature of the "proletarian 'thirties," so often described as a kind of temporary aberration, was only an especially strong and notable manifestation of it. It reappeared in the best writing of the Second World War, at the center of which stood the common soldier. And it has continued throughout the "cold war," and the McCarthyite and witch-hunt era, despite the prohibitive difficulties of securing publication.

Examples that can be cited are Philip Stevenson's novel cycle, *The Seed* [*Morning, Noon and Night* (1954), *Out of the Dust* (1956), *Old Father Antic* (1961) and *The Hoax* (1961)], published under the pen name of Lars Lawrence; Albert Maltz's *A Long Day in a Short Life* (1956); and Phillip Bonosky's *The Magic Fern* (1961). Far from their social approach causing any loss in individual personality—a charge often levelled against the social realistic novel—their individuality is enhanced. In style, mood, manner and construction, the three differ from one another more than any three American novels in the "alienation" trend. Although only in Maltz's book is an exposure of racism the central theme, all three show that a white man can understand what it means to be a Negro, the sense of kinship coming from overlapping experience. In a period when American writing is commonly termed a literature of "no heroes," they restore the heroic to American literature, projecting characters whose lives embody the historical forces that affect the people of the land.

Stevenson's novel is set in a mining town near the New Mexico-Colorado border, during the 1930's, and deals with Mexican, Indian, Spanish-speaking American, Negro, Polish, Slovak, Greek and Italian workers who have formed a union which the coal and copper corporation, operating a "company town," is determined to break. Maltz's novel is set in a jail in Washington, D.C., at about 1950. One of its main characters is a young Negro student who has been picketing against school segregation and has been attacked by a white racist. Bonosky's novel is set in a Pennsylvania steelmill city at about 1950. It deals, among other things, with the repercussions in the lives of the steel workers—Lithuanian, Irish, Negro—and in the unions, of the automation "revolution."

The significance to the American people of these novels, over and above the fellow human beings we learn to know from them, is that they address themselves to a central problem of American life. This is the conflict between the democratic principles on which the nation was founded and the forces of violence against the working people, "lawless" yet wrapped in the sanctity of the law, which have been a continuous thread in its history. On the one hand there is the tradition of the Declaration of Independence, the Bill of Rights, the Abolition Movement and the Underground Railroad, the Emancipation Proclamation, the New Deal. On the other, there is vigilante tradition, the Ku Klux Klan, the "company towns" in which corporations own the political apparatus, press, police and courts, the armies of thugs and detectives hired to break strikes, destroy unions, and shoot down organizers, the lynch mobs, chain gangs and White Citizens' Councils. And the bitter truth is told how quick are the courts, police, legislators, F.B.I. and the government bureaucracy to defend property rights against human rights, and how slow to operate, if they can be gotten to operate at all, to protect the working people.

The aim of novelists like Stevenson, Maltz and Bonosky is to foster the humanization of human relations in America. If their books are boycotted by the channels of literary information and discussion, this too is part of a pattern. That pattern is observable in every attempt to make democracy work in America, and extend it to the dispossessed. Those who make the attempt are persecuted in behalf of those who would willingly scrap every democratic institution if it interfered with their property and profit. Part of this pattern is the treatment of Marxism as the "forbidden tree of knowledge" in American life. There is no intention here to suggest that Marxism offers "all the answers," but it is a consistent and documented theory which holds out a future for the American people. Ironically, this is boycotted, while every theory which denies progress, which holds out only the bleakest of futures for America and all humanity, is lauded.

In the deep freeze imposed on Marxist thought or on any searching critique of the operations of monopoly capitalism, the discussion of ideas offered to the public tends to descend to the level of using traditional intellectual methods to destroy the intellectual heritage. One fashion follows another, and the latest mode is to assure the public that science is futile, reason is suspect, and the origins of their problems are unknowable. An example of this obscurantism is William Barrett's introduction, "Zen for the West," to a selection of writings on Zen Buddhism by D. T. Suzuki.

Barrett starts by recommending that the West examine

its own prejudices by the "wisdom" of the non-Western peoples. Now, by this "wisdom," he does not mean their progress, as in China, India and other countries, to discard the intellectual fog which overlay their feudal-type societies and their victimization by the West. He means precisely the "fog" which they are discarding and which he now offers to the West. "When we turn," he says, "to Indian thought, we are at first staggered by the vision of vast spaces, endless aeons of time, universe upon universe, against which man looks very small and meaningless; then we realize these are the spaces and times of modern astronomy, and the Indian idea is therefore closer to us."[1]

To join the mystical universes of Indian theosophy to modern astronomy is like calling modern chemistry and physics, which can change one element into another, a return to alchemy, which tried to change lead into gold by magic spells. Modern astronomy, like physics and chemistry, far from assuring man of his "meaninglessness"—how glibly this term is thrown about in this atmosphere of intellectual chicanery—show what mighty powers man can now exert over nature. When telescopes now penetrate incredibly vast spaces, and visits to other planets are on the order of realistic possibility, Barrett must turn these very strides into disillusion with science and a "proof" that man is small and impotent. And his adulation of Eastern "wisdom," which the East in its real wisdom is now viewing much more critically than Barrett does, is not accompanied by any move on his part to exchange his comfortable Western life for the squalor, disease and starvation that were the lot of the masses of Asia and the base over which this feudal "wisdom" arose.

Barrett continues to distort the very achievements of science into a skepticism of science:

In science itself, modern developments have combined to make our inherited rationalism more shaky. . . . Mathematics is like a ship in mid-ocean that has sprung leaks (paradoxes) which have been temporarily plugged, but our reason can never guarantee that the ship will not spring other leaks. That this human insecurity should manifest itself in what had hitherto been the very citadel of reason, mathematics, marks a new turn in Western thinking.[2]

The truth which Barrett transforms into nonsense is that with the penetration of the atom and the exploration of interstellar spaces, the concepts and methods of viewing reality inherited from the old mechanical materialism no longer apply. Science has always discarded old concepts for new. This did not engender "insecurity" because it was the real, if limited, serviceability of the old concepts which enabled scientists to finally move into areas for which new concepts had to be fashioned. Thus Einstein's theory of gravitation is different from Newton's, but without the achievement and use of Newton's, Einstein's could never have arisen. And there was no "insecurity" for the added reason that each forward step was accompanied by new and real powers to transform environment.

There are aspects of modern science which do make people feel "insecure." For when the direction of science and its applications are controlled by private property and its military adjuncts, people are faced with the dread of nuclear bombs and the anxiety over being automated. But this misuse of science is not what Barrett is pointing out. It is this aspect of reality, which is certainly open to scientific understanding, that he tries to obscure. His thesis is that science is suspect, reason is suspect, insecurity is permanent and man is impotent. One must abandon reason.

To glamorize Zen, Barrett refers to the interest in it of Heidegger, whom he describes as "the most original and influential philosopher now alive on the European continent," and Jung. A knowledge of the fascist connections of both of these men might suggest a critical examination of both their eminence and thought, but Barrett neglects to inform the reader of this.

An obscurantism which goes so far as to shelter from criticism views that helped foster fascism is bound to arise in an intellectual milieu where Marxism is dismissed as a "devil-theory" because it presents a rational, materialist and scientific view of human progress. For in the Marxist view of progress, no institutions are sacred and eternal, not those of capitalism, not those of socialism. Marxism says that as people change their conditions of life, they change their thinking and the products of their thinking. In the ascent to ever new vistas of human freedom, or the power to turn the surrounding world into an arena for human growth, every institution erected in society, no matter what position it once held in the advance to freedom, eventually becomes outmoded. And no matter what the terms of nightmarish horror in which Marxist views are now depicted, the fact remains that any other view, unless it embraces basic concepts of Marxism, must eventually be one of "no progress."

The concept of progress was instrumental in the birth of capitalism. But now every outmoded, pre-capitalist and pre-scientific ideology is dusted off and offered as a new thought, a refuge for the modern mind presumably lost in an inscrutable universe. So Barrett finds the ancient "wisdom" that the East is happily discarding, the only salvation for "us Westerners," since "the march of our own history, as the great world of medieval religious images recedes even further from our grasp and an increasingly secularized society engulfs us, has stripped Western man naked and left no rocklike security anywheres to lean on."[3] Alas for the West, which because of attention to "secular" or real life, no longer has the rocklike security of the Middle Ages, when millions lived in misery, a few parasites lived on their backs, life was cheap, heretics were burned, and justice was promised when the trumpets blew on the Day of Judgment!

We could dismiss this kind of nonsense as a pastime or highbrow commercialism, a pseudo-intellectual blurb-writing, were it not that this turn to the past has brought many minds to the acceptance of fascism. And it is one of the characteristics of the "deep freeze" that those who moved near the orbit of fascist ideology, like T. S. Eliot, or adjusted themselves to it, like C. G. Jung, or lauded it, like Heidegger, or propagandized for it, like Ezra Pound, are taken up by influential cliques entrenched in university and editorial circles and made by them into cultural heroes of our time. An old accusation against the influence of Marxism on the arts was that it sought to put art at the service of politics. But it is the anti-Marxist "intellectual" who is now making art serve devious political ends.

The existentialist is the modern counterpart of the ancient rebel against a world he saw as corrupt, who withdrew to a cave or monastery. What is modern is the fact that the withdrawal now takes place in the mind. The existentialist announces that the one question, primary to all others, is that of what is "existence," or "being." To this lone question he devotes himself, even while declaring that it is unanswerable. And so he lives in a multi-faceted world while renouncing the knowledge of it. Furthermore he cannot cut his real ties to the society he renounces in theory. And so the existentialist can be described as one who lives in society but as an "outsider." He is ignorant of the fact that the very intensity with which the question rises before him shows that he is enslaved by history.

The existentialist movement, as this study has tried to show, actually rose in revulsion against the corruption of values in capitalist society. Its basic conviction was that the evils it perceived were to be ascribed to the very concept and existence of society. It rejected any view of the human being as a social animal, growing, enriching himself, and realizing his freedom in his social relations to others. Therefore evil was ascribed to science, the accumulation of knowledge, the exploration of reality, the study of economics and history, the expansion of democracy and the devotion to reason, all the tools of progress that had been collectively forged by society. Man had to renounce them in order to concentrate on the "essential question" of "existence." Seeking the "truth" of man outside of society, it carried its psychological alienation from society into three different directions, each with its own theory and "morality."

One is the religious. This existentialist religiousness is as characteristic of the crisis of capitalism as Catholicism may be considered characteristic of European feudalism and Protestantism of the rise of capitalist nations. It has no church or systematized dogma. It projects no image of God, the after-life, heaven or hell. It calls for a personal relation to God which abandons as irrelevant all attempts to improve the human lot. Its morality is "faith," or "love of God."

A second can be called the "primitivist." It appears to welcome life but it concentrates on the immediacy of "being," or "existence," and spurns all higher and deeper generalizations and scientific discoveries of life, nature, human relations, society, the actual world. It exalts ignorance. Its morality calls for the acknowledgement and liberation of the instincts and "primal" forces of nature, the forces of "life," freeing them from the corruption of reason, logic, science, civilization and concern for the plight of others. It is the branch that moves closest to fascism.

The third may be called "anarchistic" in that, while asserting the individual's responsibility for the world and demanding that he make his "decision" about it, that he "act," it

sees the individual's freedom as resting on his ability to renounce all social ties, all outer compulsion of necessity. His
capacity to act with freedom is posited on his scorn for the
world in which he lives and must act. He asks no rights for
himself that he will deny to others. However, his action is
not for others but for himself, to preserve his own integrity.
Its morality rests on the view that all conventional moral
precepts are hypocrisy, asserted by a society which violates all
precepts when its self-interest demands it. Any act is per-
missible, if carried out as an assertion of scorn for society and
a search for individual integrity, the integrity of the eternal
"rebel."

Existentialist-minded artists have produced, as we have
seen, significant works of art, distinguished by their hard-
won integrity. Yet to the great writers of the humanist tradition, from a Shakespeare and Cervantes to a Whitman and
Dreiser, integrity never seemed to be a problem. It was taken
for granted that truth was the artist's road, that honesty
was a means integral with the end; that his function was
the humanization of reality, breaking down the isolation of
people by giving them a consciousness of the world they were
collectively shaping, creating a kinship between the writer
and his readers through an illumination of the forces affecting all of them. It was from looking at the lives of others
that the artist discovered, step by step, what he himself was
and could be.

But now integrity has become a fetish. The means replaces
the end, becoming an end in itself. The writer (or painter
or composer) decides that he cannot be true to himself unless
he discovers what he himself is. As he fixes his gaze inward,
he turns away from the broad vistas of human life that might
help him to self-understanding and develop him into a real
"self" capable of change and growth. What he presents as
"life" or "truth" becomes a narrow, one-sided or distorted

view, reflecting only his struggle to be "himself" in a world
that seems to be populated by enemies and whose ground is
sown with buried mines.

It is not hard to see why many who embrace such sweeping "revolutionary" doctrines, consigning all of society and
its hard-won heritage of knowledge and practice to the ash-
can, should scorn Marxism as "conservative." This attitude
is often expressed in the arts, where the apostles of each new
"revolution" that appears every few years in the capitalist
world disdain the arts of the Soviet Union or of any artists
guided by a Marxist outlook as "backward." This does not
mean that every work advanced in the socialist countries as
"realism" is realism in the true sense, uniting outer and inner
worlds, subject and object, a changing world and a changing
psychology. But what is shocking to those who embrace
an alienated expression as the "new" is not the lapse from
genuine realism but the general trend of this "backward" art
to the restoration in art of humanized reality.

It is also not hard to see why in these circles which now
fear change the most, these "revolutions" are welcomed while
Marxism is excoriated and banned. It offends no defender of
the status quo to be told that his world is corrupt, meaningless, inhuman, irrational and absurd, but securely eternal. On
the other hand, Marxism rests on the tradition of continual
change, the raising of problems, solving them, and finding
new challenges rising out of the very employment of what
it has learned. It stands as a unifier of, clarifier of and en-
courager in the study of the accumulated knowledge of what
the world is like; knowledge that has risen out of the struggles
and achievements of human beings to raise themselves above
the animal kingdom and reshape the world to fit their
awakening needs. It has contributed to this knowledge. It
rests its confidence in human progress on the main lesson of

history itself; that human society has consistently carried through these transformations, swept away the obstacles to its growth, and opened up fresh paths for its development. So it is with morality. The basic tenets of morality, renewed from era to era, are not dictated from "on high" or called for by the "human heart," but rise out of the needs of society. Through his conscious relations to others, treating them as kin, a human being can grow. For this reason a story like that of Cain and Abel, with the horror aroused not only by Cain's act of murder but also by his question, "Am I my brother's keeper?" is so affecting today. These principles have always, however, operated within historic limitations. When society divided into opposing classes, rulers and ruled, those who commanded the means of production and those who did the labor, these principles remained in day-to-day life, for society had to hold together. But always there were two "higher imperatives." One was: "Thou shalt not question or rebel against the ruling class, for that is the most terrible sin of all." The other was: "When the ruling class tells you out of its wisdom to suspend everything you have been told in the name of morality, to lie, kill, murder, rob and cheat, that thou shalt do." It was this way in the ancient slave-holding civilizations, and in the Middle Ages. It is not hard to see these "higher imperatives" operating in bourgeois society today.

But this does not mean that all morality is hypocrisy; it means only that there is a conflict, a contradiction, in the realm of morality, reflecting the contradictions in exploitive society. The task on the order of history today is to bring a society into being in which the basic principles of social morality, of each man being his brother's keeper, can work without suspension or limitation. Means and ends unite. The only way to create a society in which all men are brothers is to begin to act like brothers. And the "higher imperative" which now appears is organically bound to the process itself: "Thou shalt remove exploitation from the face of the earth."

It is a truism to say that if there is no future for human society, there is no future for art. In subscribing to the theory that humanity has no future, some talented artists are committing premature artistic suicide, wasting their future by detaching themselves from the present. An artist must express himself. But this "self" is not only an eye, ear and hand, it is also a mind. An artist may believe that he is arbitrarily deciding how to construct his work, but a work of art is a net thrown into life, and it is real life, as he sees it and grasps it, that constructs his work for him. The more the impoverishment of outer life, as he sees it, drives him inward, the more his inner life contracts.

Art is not a substitute for philosophy, sociology or politics, but neither is it an activity isolated from them.

Without talent, and integrity in using it, there is no art at all. But the significance, power and greatness of art depend also upon the artist's stature as a person, in which integrity is but the first step. Next comes his philosophy, sociology and politics. An artist's philosophy—not the one he may pay lip-service to but the one he lives by—generalizes how he sees his own needs, yearnings and conflicts in relation to the movement of life and people about him. His sociology summarizes what he has learned from people; the extent to which his relation to them has enabled them to educate him. His politics summarizes the extent to which he has enriched his mind with what society has made it possible for him to know, and the extent to which he is willing to engage himself with the forces, in the country and the world, that control his destinies along with those of his fellow men. "The senses of social men are different from those of unsocial men."

Reference Notes

REFERENCE NOTES

CHAPTER II
1. Tillich, Paul, "Existentialism and Psychotherapy," in Ruiten-beck, H. M., Ed., Psychoanalysis and Existential Philosophy (Dutton, N.Y., 1962), p. 5.
2. Marcel, Gabriel, The Philosophy of Existentialism (Citadel, N.Y., 1961), pp. 120–24.
3. Kant, Immanuel, The Critique of Pure Reason, Preface to the Second Edition, 1787.
4. Hegel, G. W. F., Science of Logic (Allen & Unwin, London, 1951), Vol. I, p. 185.
5. Hegel, G. W. F., The Philosophy of Fine Art (Bell, London, 1920), Vol. I, pp. 327–28.
6. Engels, Frederick, Feuerbach (International Publishers, N.Y., 1941), pp. 10, 11.

CHAPTER III
1. Kierkegaard, Søren, Either/Or (Doubleday, Garden City, N.Y., 1959), Vol. I, p. 134.
2. Ibid., Vol. II, p. 232.
3. Ibid., p. 233.
4. Ibid., p. 356.
5. Kierkegaard, Fear and Trembling and The Sickness Unto Death (Doubleday, Garden City, N.Y., 1954), p. 44.
6. Kierkegaard, Concluding Unscientific Postscript (Princeton University Press, Princeton, N.J., 1941), p. xv.
7. Kierkegaard, Fear and Trembling and The Sickness Unto Death, p. 22.
8. Ibid., p. 24.
9. Ibid., p. 31.
10. Ibid., pp. 51–61.
11. Ibid., pp. 64, 77, 131.
12. Kierkegaard, Concluding Unscientific Postscript, p. 350.

13. Reinhardt, K. F., *The Existentialist Revolt* (Ungar, N.Y., 1960), p. 27.
14. Kierkegaard, *Fear and Trembling and The Sickness Unto Death*, p. 168.
15. *Ibid.*, pp. 155, 159.
16. Kierkegaard, *Concluding Unscientific Postscript*, p. 178.
17. *Ibid.*, pp. 182–83.
18. Kaufmann, Walter, *Existentialism, from Dostoievsky to Sartre* (World, Cleveland, 1962), p. 92.
19. Marx and Engels, *Manifesto of the Communist Party* (International Publishers, N.Y., 1932), pp. 11, 12.
20. Engels, *Herr Eugen Dühring's Revolution in Science* (International Publishers, N.Y., 1939), pp. 125–26.

CHAPTER IV
1. Everyman Library, E. P. Dutton, New York, 1913.
2. Modern Library, New York, 1929.

CHAPTER V
1. Jaspers, Karl, *Reason and Existenz* (Farrar, Straus & Cudahy, N.Y., 1955), p. 46.
2. Nietzsche, Friedrich, *Beyond Good and Evil* (Modern Library, N.Y.), pp. 178–79.
3. Nietzsche, *The Birth of Tragedy from the Spirit of Music* (Modern Library, N.Y.), p. 203.
4. *Ibid.*, p. 181.
5. *Ibid.*, pp. 318–19.
6. *Ibid.*, p. 237.
7. *Ibid.*, p. 263.
8. Jung, C. G., *Modern Man in Search of a Soul* (Harcourt, Brace, N.Y., 1953), p. 163.
9. *Ibid.*, p. 240.
10. Nietzsche, *The Birth of Tragedy*, pp. 328–29.
11. Marx, *The Economic and Philosophic Manuscripts of 1844* (International Publishers, N.Y., 1964), p. 107.
12. Nietzsche, *Beyond Good and Evil*, pp. 14, 43.
13. *Ibid.*, p. 186.
14. *Ibid.*, p. 189.
15. Nietzsche, *Ecce Homo* (Modern Library, N.Y.), p. 71.
16. Nietzsche, *Beyond Good and Evil*, pp. 36, 53, 67–68, 116.

17. *Ibid.*, p. 200.
18. Nietzsche, *The Birth of Tragedy*, p. 331.
19. Nietzsche, *The Genealogy of Morals* (Modern Library, N.Y.), p. 13.
20. *Ibid.*, pp. 15, 79.
21. Wilde, J. T., and Kimmel, W., Ed., *The Search for Being* (Twayne, N.Y., 1962), p. 98.
22. Kaufmann, Walter, *From Shakespeare to Existentialism* (Beacon, Boston, 1959), pp. 12–13.
23. Kaufmann, Walter, *Nietzsche* (World, Cleveland, 1962), pp. 49, 71.
24. Nietzsche, *The Birth of Tragedy*, p. 267.
25. Nietzsche, *Ecce Homo*, p. 66.
26. Nietzsche, *Beyond Good and Evil*, pp. 184–85.
27. Kaufmann, *From Shakespeare to Existentialism*, p. 199.
28. Nietzsche, *The Birth of Tragedy*, pp. 328–29.
29. Mann, Thomas, *The Coming Victory of Democracy* (Knopf, N.Y., 1938), p. 12.

CHAPTER VI

1. Husserl, Edmund, *Ideas: General Introduction to Pure Phenomenology* (Collier Books, N.Y., 1962), pp. 37, 39.
2. *Ibid.*, p. 100.
3. *Ibid.*, p. 348.
4. *Ibid.*, p. 7.
5. Bernal, J. D., *Science in History* (Watts, London, 1954), pp. 81–82.
6. *Ibid.*, pp. 138–39.
7. Engels, Frederick, *Anti-Dühring* (Foreign Languages Publishing House, Moscow, 1954), p. 458.
8. Husserl, *op. cit.*, p. 358.
9. *Ibid.*, pp. 7, 21.
10. Kaufmann, *From Shakespeare to Existentialism*, p. 303.
11. Heidegger, Martin, *An Introduction to Metaphysics* (Doubleday, Garden City, N.Y., 1961), pp. 1–2, 5, 6–7, 8, 21.
12. *Ibid.*, pp. 118, 172.
13. *Ibid.*, p. 47.
14. *Ibid.*, p. 12.
15. *Ibid.*, p. 102.
16. *Ibid.*, p. 31.

17. *Ibid.*, p. 32.
18. *Ibid.*, pp. 35, 37.
19. *Ibid.*, p. 166.
20. Kaufmann, *Existentialism from Dostoievsky to Sartre*, p. 133.
21. Shirer, W., *The Rise and Fall of the Third Reich* (Fawcett, Greenwich, Conn., 1962), p. 93.
22. Jaspers, Karl, *Man in the Modern Age* (Doubleday, Garden City, N.Y., 1957), p. v.
23. *Ibid.*, p. 116.
24. *Ibid.*, p. 40.
25. *Ibid.*, p. 63.
26. *Ibid.*, pp. 164, 175, 176, 189, 208, 209.
27. Jaspers, Karl, *Reason and Existenz*, pp. 23, 25, 47.
28. *Ibid.*, pp. 139, 141.
29. Jaspers, Karl, *Way to Wisdom* (Yale University Press, New Haven, Conn., 1954), pp. 155–56, 162.
30. Engels, *Feuerbach*, pp. 14, 15.
31. Engels: "A Critique of Political Economy," in Marx, *Economic and Philosophical Manuscripts of 1844*, pp. 212–13.
32. Engels, *Socialism: Utopian and Scientific* (International Publishers, N.Y., 1935), pp. 72, 73.
33. Reinhardt, *op. cit.*, pp. 10–14.
34. *Ibid.*, p. 130.

CHAPTER VII

1. Camus, Albert, *The Myth of Sisyphus and other essays* (Knopf, N.Y., 1959), pp. 3, 17.
2. *Ibid.*, p. 90.
3. Camus, Albert, *The Stranger* (Knopf Vintage Books, New York, 1960).
4. Sartre, Jean-Paul, *Being and Nothingness* (Philosophical Library, New York, 1956), p. 547.
5. *Ibid.*, p. 445.
6. Marx, *The Economic and Philosophic Manuscripts of 1844*, p. 138.
7. Sartre, *op. cit.*, p. 543.
8. Camus, *The Rebel* (Knopf Vintage Books, New York, 1958), p. 192.
9. *Ibid.*, pp. 284, 301.
10. Camus, *The Myth of Sisyphus*, pp. 149–50.

11. Thody, Philip, *Albert Camus* (Grove, N.Y., 1957), p. 124.
12. Camus, *The Plague* (Knopf, N.Y., 1958).
13. White, M., *The Age of Analysis* (New American Library, N.Y., 1961), p. 125.
14. *Ibid.*, p. 133.
15. Sartre, *Nausea* (New Directions, N.Y., 1949).
16. Sartre, *Paths to Freedom—The Age of Reason The Reprieve, Troubled Sleep* (Knopf, N.Y., 1947, 1950).
17. Sartre, *Search for a Method* (Knopf, N.Y., 1963), pp. 7, 8.
18. *Ibid.*, p. 65.

CHAPTER VIII
1. Marx, *Economic and Philosophic Manuscripts of 1844*, p. 100.
2. *Ibid.*, p. 108.
3. Marx, *Capital* (International Publishers, N.Y., 1947), Vol. 1, p. 603.
4. Marx, *Economic and Philosophic Manuscripts of 1844*, pp. 147, 150.
5. Marx, *Capital*, Vol. 1, p. 605.
6. Marx, *Economic and Philosophic Manuscripts of 1844*, p. 156.
7. *Ibid.*, p. 139.
8. Engels, *Origin of the Family, Private Property and the State* (International Publishers, N.Y., 1964), pp. 63–5.
9. Marx, *Economic and Philosophic Manuscripts of 1844*, pp. 111, 134.
10. Dreiser, Theodore, *The Color of a Great City* (Boni and Liveright, N.Y., 1923), p. 241.
11. *Ibid.*, pp. 137, 141.
12. *Ibid.*, pp. 154–55.
13. Adams, Henry, *The Education of Henry Adams* (Modern Library, N.Y., 1931), pp. 225, 344.

CHAPTER IX
1. Thoreau, Henry, *Walden, and Other Writings* (Modern Library, N.Y., 1950), pp. 433–34.
2. Stein, Gertrude, *Four Saints in Three Acts* (transition, June 1929).
3. Frost, Robert, *Collected Poems* (Holt, N.Y., 1930).

4. Lowell, Robert, *Lord Weary's Castle* (Harcourt, Brace, N.Y., 1946).
5. Eliot, T. S., *The Complete Poems and Plays* (Harcourt, Brace, N.Y., 1952).
6. Steinbeck, John, *The Grapes of Wrath* (Viking Press, N.Y., 1939).
7. Fitzgerald, F. Scott, *Selected Stories* (Scribner's, N.Y., 1951).
8. Fitzgerald, *The Great Gatsby* (Scribners, N.Y., 1925).
9. Fitzgerald, *This Side of Paradise* (Scribners, N.Y., 1920).
10. Fitzgerald, *The Crack-Up* (New Directions, N.Y., 1925).
11. Eliot, T. S., *Selected Prose*, ed. J. Heyward (Penguin Books, Harmondsworth, 1955), pp. 41, 42.
12. Eliot, "The Waste Land," in *The Complete Poems and Plays* (Harcourt, Brace, N.Y., 1946).
13. Eliot, "East Coker," *ibid*.
14. Eliot, "Murder in the Cathedral," *ibid*.
15. Hulme, T. E., *Speculations* (Harcourt, Brace, N.Y., 1924), p. 116.
16. Eliot, *Selected Essays* (Harcourt, Brace, N.Y., 1950), p. 438.
17. *Ibid*., pp. 116–18.
18. Eliot, *Selected Prose* (Penguin Books, Harmondsworth, 1955), pp. 217–18.

CHAPTER X

1. Aptheker, Herbert, *Towards Negro Freedom* (New Century, N.Y., 1956), p. 67.
2. Wolfe, Thomas, *The Hills Beyond* (Harper, N.Y., 1941).
3. Faulkner, William, *The Rievers* (Random House, N.Y., 1962).
4. Faulkner, *Light in August* (Random House, N.Y., 1950).
5. Faulkner, *Intruder in the Dust* (Random House, N.Y., 1948).
6. Faulkner, *Absalom, Absalom!* (Random House, N.Y., 1951).
7. Faulkner, "That Evening Sun," in *Collected Stories* (Random House, N.Y., 1948).
8. Faulkner, *The Hamlet* (Random House, N.Y., 1940).

CHAPTER XI

1. Dos Passos, John, *Manhattan Transfer* (Harper, N.Y., 1925).
2. Dos Passos, *U.S.A.* (Harcourt, Brace, N.Y., 1937).
3. Miller, Henry, *Tropic of Cancer* (Grove, N.Y., 1961).
4. Miller, *Tropic of Capricorn* (Grove, N.Y., 1961).

5. Miller, *The Colossus of Maroussi* (New Directions, N.Y., 1941).
6. Burroughs, William, *Naked Lunch* (Grove, N.Y., 1959).

CHAPTER XII
1. Riesman, David, *The Lonely Crowd* (Yale University Press, New Haven, 1961), pp. xxxiv, xxxv.
2. Williams, Tennessee, *Cat on a Hot Tin Roof* (New Directions, N.Y., 1955).
3. Styron, William, *Lie Down in Darkness* (Bobbs-Merrill, N.Y., 1951).
4. Styron, *The Long March* (Random House, N.Y., 1952).
5. Aptheker, Herbert, *American Foreign Policy and the Cold War* (New Century, N.Y., 1962), pp. 147–48.
6. Burroughs, William, *Naked Lunch* (Grove, N.Y., 1959).
7. Salinger, J. D., *The Catcher in the Rye* (Little, Brown, Boston, 1951).
8. Salinger, *Franny and Zooey* (Little, Brown, Boston, 1961).
9. Salinger, *Raise High the Roof Beam, Carpenters and Seymour: An Introduction* (Little, Brown, Boston, 1959).
10. Jung, *Modern Man in Search of a Soul*, p. 240.
11. Tillich, Paul, "Existential Analysis and Religious Symbols," in Herberg, *Ed.*, *Four Existentialist Theologians* (Doubleday, Garden City, N.Y., 1958), p. 291.
12. *Ibid.*, p. 285.
13. Suzuki, *Zen Buddhism* (Doubleday, Garden City, N.Y., 1956), p. 103.
14. *Ibid.*, pp. 263–64.
15. Albee, Edward, *Who's Afraid of Virginia Woolf?* (Atheneum, N.Y., 1963).
16. Steinbeck, John, *Travels with Charlie in Search of America* (Viking, N.Y., 1962).

CHAPTER XIII
1. Lowell, Robert, *Life Studies* (Random House, N.Y., 1959).
2. Updike, John, *Rabbit, Run* (Knopf, N.Y., 1960).
3. Updike, *The Centaur* (Knopf, N.Y., 1963).
4. Purdy, James, *Malcolm* (Farrar, Straus & Cudahy, N.Y., 1959).
5. Purdy, *The Nephew* (Farrar, Straus & Cudahy, N.Y., 1960).

6. Miller, Arthur, *Death of a Salesman* (Viking, N.Y., 1958).
7. Watts, Richard, Foreword to Miller: *The Crucible* (Bantam Books, N.Y., 1959).
8. Bellow, Saul, *Herzog* (Viking, N.Y., 1964).
9. Bellow, *The Adventures of Augie March* (Viking, N.Y., 1953).
10. Bellow, *Henderson the Rain King* (Viking, N.Y., 1959).
11. Mailer, Norman, *The Naked and the Dead* (Rinehart, N.Y., 1948).
12. Mailer, *Advertisements for Myself* (Putnam, N.Y., 1959).
13. Baldwin, James, *Another Country* (Dial, N.Y., 1962).
14. Baldwin, *The Fire Next Time* (Dial, N.Y., 1963).

CHAPTER XIV
1. Barrett, W., "Zen for the West"; in *Zen Buddhism: Selected Writings of D. T. Suzuki* (Doubleday, Garden City, N.Y., 1956), p. x.
2. *Ibid.*, pp. x, xi.
3. *Ibid.*, p. xix.

Index

Index

INDEX

P 13 - Good descr of exs+lsm

15 - For class Decl of Ind